Territorial Policy and Governance

In response to both policy and conceptual debates, alternative narratives have begun to emerge about territorial governance and policymaking. As local and regional policy actors strive to respond to the geographically uneven effects of the economic crises of the early twenty-first century, a crucial question emerges: what are the opportunities and challenges presented by alternative forms of territorially based governance and policy?

The aim of this edited volume, therefore, is critically to explore the opportunities and challenges presented by different forms of territorial policy and governance. Drawing on conceptual debates and empirical research from the United Kingdom and other international contexts, the contributors engage with issues around the politics and governance of territorial development, economic development, planning and regeneration and the environment. *Territorial Policy and Governance* addresses the question of how alternative forms of territorial governance and policy can help to shape patterns of urban and regional development, highlighting the related opportunities, constraints and challenges that confront their operationalisation.

This book will be essential reading for international audiences with an interest in territorial development, governance, politics, human geography and planning and regeneration.

Iain Deas is a Senior Lecturer in Planning and Environmental Management at the University of Manchester, UK.

Stephen Hincks is a Senior Lecturer in Planning and Environmental Management at the University of Manchester, UK.

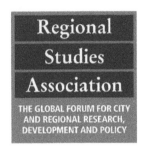

Regions and Cities

Series Editor in Chief
Susan M. Christopherson, *Cornell University, USA*

Editors
Maryann Feldman, *University of Georgia, USA*
Gernot Grabher, *HafenCity University Hamburg, Germany*
Ron Martin, *University of Cambridge, UK*
Kieran P. Donaghy, *Cornell University, USA*

In today's globalised, knowledge-driven and networked world, regions and cities have assumed heightened significance as the interconnected nodes of economic, social and cultural production, and as sites of new modes of economic and territorial governance and policy experimentation. This book series brings together incisive and critically engaged international and interdisciplinary research on this resurgence of regions and cities, and should be of interest to geographers, economists, sociologists, political scientists and cultural scholars, as well as to policy-makers involved in regional and urban development.

For more information on the Regional Studies Association visit www.regionalstudies.org

There is a **30% discount** available to RSA members on books in the *Regions and Cities* series, and other subject related Taylor and Francis books and e-books including Routledge titles. To order just e-mail Georg Wanek, Georg. Wanek@tandf.co.uk, or phone on +44 (0) 207 017 6364 and declare your RSA membership. You can also visit www.routledge.com and use the discount code: **RSA0901**

Territorial Policy and Governance

Alternative Paths

Edited by Iain Deas and Stephen Hincks

LONDON AND NEW YORK

First published 2017 by Routledge

2 Park Square, Milton Park, Abingdon, Oxfordshire OX14 4RN
52 Vanderbilt Avenue, New York, NY 10017

Routledge is an imprint of the Taylor & Francis Group, an informa business

First issued in paperback 2019

British Library Cataloguing in Publication Data
A catalogue record for this book is available from the
British Library

Library of Congress Cataloging in Publication Data
Names: Deas, Iain, editor. | Hincks, Stephen, editor.
Title: Territorial policy and governance: alternative
paths/edited by Iain Deas and Stephen Hincks.
Description: Abingdon, Oxon; New York, NY: Routledge, 2017.
Identifiers: LCCN 2016043155| ISBN 9780415661379 (hardback) |
ISBN 9781315734644 (ebook)
Subjects: LCSH: Regionalism. | Regional planning.
Classification: LCC JF197 .T47 2017 | DDC 338.9–dc23
LC record available at https://lccn.loc.gov/2016043155

ISBN: 978-0-415-66137-9 (hbk)
ISBN: 978-0-367-86773-7 (pbk)

Typeset in Times New Roman
by Deanta Global Publishing Services, Chennai, India

This book is dedicated to the memory of the late Professor Francesc Morata Tierra, who co-authored Chapter 6 of this volume.

Contents

Illustrations

Figures

Maps

Tables

Box

Contributors

Philip Allmendinger is Fellow of Clare College and Head of Department/ Professor of Land Economy at the University of Cambridge. He has published extensively in the areas of property and planning, planning theory, policy and practice, land and property regulation, housing and local government.

Claire Colomb is Reader (Associate Professor) in Planning and Urban Sociology at the Bartlett School of Planning, University College London. Her research interests cover urban and regional governance, planning and urban regeneration in European cities, urban social movements, European spatial planning and territorial cooperation and comparative planning systems and cultures. She is the co-author of *European Spatial Planning and Territorial Cooperation* (Routledge, 2010, with S. Dühr and V. Nadin) and author of *Staging the New Berlin: Place Marketing and the Politics of Urban Reinvention Post-1989* (Routledge, 2012).

Ian Cook is a Senior Lecturer in Social Sciences at Northumbria University. His primary research interest is in urban-policy mobilities. He has published in numerous journals including the *Annals of the Association of American Geographers*, *Planning Theory and Practice* and *Urban Studies*.

Iain Deas is a Senior Lecturer in Planning and Environmental Management at the University of Manchester. He has published on the politics of urban regeneration and the governance of territorial policy, including recent articles on post-politics and city-regions, policy actor networks and economic development agencies in England and 'agglomeration boosterism' and regional policy.

David Gibbs is Professor of Human Geography at the University of Hull. His research interests focus on the political economy of the environment and on economy-environment inter-relationships. He has directed projects on green entrepreneurs, eco-industrial parks, environmental governance, urban carbon flows, low-carbon shipping and resource recovery. He has also contributed to policy-related research for the European Community, OECD, Local Government Association and the Centre for Local Economic Strategies.

Xavier Oliveras González is Assistant Professor in the Department of Urban Studies and Environment at the Colegio de la Frontera Norte in Matamoros, Mexico. He was formerly a post-doctoral researcher in Geography at the Universitat Autònoma de Barcelona. His research interests centre on the creation of cross-border regions and trans-national spaces through meta-geography, regional construction, debordering and rebordering processes and cross-border cooperation.

Antoni Durà Guimerà is Associate Professor in the Department of Geography, Universitat Autònoma de Barcelona. His research in Europe and North America focuses on territorial cooperation, cross-border governance and urban networks. His work has included research on Euroregions, macro-regions and inter-city networks in the Western Mediterranean and Euro-Mediterranean region. He is currently one of the leading members of the research network RECOT (Red Europea de Cooperación Territorial – European Network on Territorial Cooperation).

John Harrison is Reader in Human Geography at Loughborough University and an Associate Director of the Globalization and World Cities (GaWC) research network. His research focuses on how regions are conceptualised and how regional concepts are mobilised in policy. He is an editor of the journal *Regional Studies* and co-editor of *Planning and Governance of Cities in Globalization* (Routledge, 2013) and *Megaregions – Globalization's New Urban Form?* (Edward Elgar, 2015).

Graham Haughton is a human geographer and planner. Since 2010, he has been Professor of Urban and Environmental Planning at the University of Manchester. From 2000–10 he was a Professor of Human Geography at the University of Hull. His recent research has focused on urban, environmental and regional planning, flood risk, the uneven impacts of austerity and environmental controversies.

Stephen Hincks is a Senior Lecturer in Planning at the University of Manchester. His research focuses on the dynamics of spatial development. He has recently published articles on the recession and uneven spatial development (in *Regional Studies*, 2014), neighbourhood change in Greater Manchester (in *Environment and Planning A* and *Urban Studies*, 2015,) and the governance and politics of spatial economic rebalancing with a specific focus on the Greater Manchester city-region (in *Cambridge Journal of Regions, Economy and Society*, 2016).

Andrew E.G. Jonas is Professor of Human Geography at the University of Hull. His research interests address the politics of urban and regional sustainability, focussing on the USA and Europe. He has written over 100 journal articles, book chapters, reviews and encyclopaedia entries. He is author of *Urban Geography: A Critical Introduction* (Wiley-Blackwell, 2015) and co-editor of *The Urban Growth Machine: Critical Perspectives Two Decades*

Later (SUNY Press, 1999); *Interrogating Alterity: Alternative Economic and Political Spaces* (Routledge, 2010) and *Territory, the State and Urban Politics* (Routledge, 2012).

Martin Jones is Professor of Human Geography and Deputy Vice-Chancellor at Staffordshire University, working in the broad area of society and space and specifically on the interface between economic and political geography. Author and editor of eight books, he is interested in the geographies of state intervention through economic and social policy in cities and regions, and sub-national political economies therein. His current research, funded by the ESRC as part of WISERD Civil Society, is examining city-region building in England and Wales.

Andrew Karvonen is Assistant Professor in Urban and Regional Studies at the KTH Royal Institute of Technology in Stockholm. He conducts research on the politics and practice of sustainable urban development, with a specific emphasis on the role of infrastructure networks.

Alex Lord is Reader in the Department of Geography and Planning at the University of Liverpool. His research interests cover the economics and politics of cities, particularly the economic effects of urban and environmental planning. His work has included ESRC-funded research on the behavioural economics of planning decisions as well as a project funded by the Royal Town Planning Institute on the potential value of planning in facilitating development.

Philip O'Brien is Lecturer in Urban Planning at the University of Liverpool in London. He has researched extensively on evolving models of regional economic policy in Europe and their influence on spatial strategies and programmes. He has been a regular contributor to conferences on regional studies and has been invited to present his work events hosted by the European institutions.

David Shaw is Professor in Geography and Planning at the University of Liverpool, where he was formerly the Head of the Department of Civic Design. His research interests centre on European spatial planning. He was centrally involved in the European Commission's original Compendium of European Spatial Planning Systems and Policies (1997). He has subsequently worked on several ESPON projects and is currently a member of the Liverpool city-region's European Structural and Investment Fund Committee (ESiF).

Olivier Sykes is Lecturer in European Spatial Planning and Policy Impact Fellow in the Heseltine Institute for Public Policy and Practice at the University of Liverpool. He has published extensively on European territorial policy and international comparative planning and urban policy. He is Chair of the Association of European Schools of Planning (AESOP) Excellence in Teaching Prize Committee and a convenor of the French and British Planning Study Group. His research focuses primarily on the Europeanisation of planning systems and aspects of comparative planning and urban policy. He is currently a member of the editorial boards of *Town Planning Review* and *Urban, Planning and Transport Research*.

Francesc Morata Tierra (1949–2014) was Professor of Political Science and Jean Monnet Chair *ad personam* in EU Political Integration Studies at the Universitat Autònoma de Barcelona. He was one of the leading Spanish scholars on EU integration studies, EU multi-level governance, EU policies and European territorial cooperation. His published work included *La Unión Europea: Procesos, Actores y Políticas* (Ariel, 1998). He founded the research network RECOT (Red Europea de Cooperación Territorial – European Network on Territorial Cooperation) to investigate the role of Spanish and other local and regional actors in cross-border, trans-national and inter-regional cooperation.

Kevin Ward is Professor of Human Geography and Director of the Manchester Urban Institute, University of Manchester. He has edited and written numerous books and journal articles on the politics of economic development, policy mobilities, state restructuring and urban policy and politics.

Brian Webb is Lecturer in Spatial Planning in the School of Geography and Planning at Cardiff University. His research focuses on understanding the multi-scalar impact of government policies on the built environment and how conceptions of space are lived and constructed depending on the scale of analysis, from the neighbourhood to the national level and beyond.

Aidan While is Senior Lecturer in the Department of Urban Studies and Planning at the University of Sheffield in the United Kingdom. His research interests include the relationship between decarbonisation and economic development at urban, regional and national scales. He has published widely on issues of urban and regional sustainability.

Acknowledgements

John Harrison's research for Chapter 4 was in part funded by a Regional Studies Association Early Career Grant. The chapter also draws upon ongoing collaboration with Jesse Heley.

Claire Colomb, Antoni Durà Guimerà and Xavier Oliveras González would like to thank Juan Manuel Trillo-Santamaria for his helpful feedback on an earlier draft of Chapter 6 of this volume.

Brian Webb acknowledges the support of the Economic and Social Research Council in respect of Chapter 11, through funding for the project 'Climate Science and Urban Design – a Historical and Comparative Study' undertaken at the University of Manchester in collaboration with Professor Michael Hebbert and Dr Vladamir Jankovic.

1 Introduction

Iain Deas and Stephen Hincks

Regionalism, its rise and exaggerated demise

The roots of this book lie in a conference organised by the Regional Studies Association in 2011 in Manchester. The trigger for the conference was the British general election of the previous year, the outcome of which was a Conservative-led coalition government that quickly set about dismantling and rebuilding the framework for spatial policy and governance inherited from the previous Labour administration. The prevailing mood amongst academics and policymakers at the conference was one partly of pessimism about the prospects for regional governance and policy, but it was also one of curiosity about the likely shape of what at the time was assumed to be an emerging post-regional era.

The conference came after a period of some two decades in which interest in regionalism in the United Kingdom, as elsewhere in Europe, had grown in some important respects. Paralleling the increasing significance of regionally based policy over much of the preceding 20 or so years had been lively scholarly debate about the dynamics of regional governance and the wider implications for the geographical reorganisation of the state (Rhodes, 1994; Jessop, 2002; Brenner, 2004). The new economic geography that rose to prominence in the late 1980s and early 1990s found particular resonance amongst policymakers (see Krugman, 1991a, 1991b; Martin and Sunley, 2011). Academic writing about ideas like new industrial spaces, neo-Marshallian nodes and clusters of production captured the wider sense not only that geographies of economic activity were undergoing significant change but also that greater policy attention needed to be devoted to understanding and managing the processes that helped create and sustain them (Amin and Thrift, 1992; Scott, 1988, 1996; Porter, 1996, 1998). Research on some of the underlying political and economic processes – concepts such as institutional thickness, untraded interdependencies and a range of other ideas that would normally be dismissed as merely of esoteric scholarly interest – began to inform policy innovation in a tangible way (Amin and Thrift, 1994; Storper, 1995). So, too, did academic interest in what was perceived as the growing importance of globally significant city-regions, prompting concerted (and continuing) efforts by government to bolster the competitiveness of urban areas and their regions in the face of what, for a time, was seen as the diminishing capacity of nation states to manage sub-national economic change (Sassen, 1991).

Inevitably, some of the intellectual energy that had amassed around these topics began to dissolve as both policy and research agendas moved on (see Pike, 2007). Much of the impetus sustaining the notion of a regional world dissipated, reflecting doubts about the capacity of regionally based institutions to deliver policy solutions that were effective, equitable or – in a context of austerity politics and public-sector retrenchment – efficient (Allmendinger, 2015). The advent of this more sceptical perspective regarding the capacity, significance and potential of regionally based governance and policy over the first part of the twenty-first century has had impacts across multiple spatial scales. At a continental scale, the European Commission has begun to invest more interest in developing an agenda for cities, paralleling the much longer standing interest in regional policy and governance (for example, European Union, 2011). The effect has been that the once prominent normative notion of an ordered, hierarchical system of formal and permanent sub-national government across Europe – a Europe of the Regions – has for some time looked implausible, as nation states have proved very obviously able to reassert their primacy. At the same time, the European Union (EU) itself has endured what might be seen as the beginnings of its own existential crisis, with the as yet unrealised possibility of Grexit in the wake of Greece's financial difficulties compounded by the looming prospect of Brexit following the British referendum vote in 2016 to secede (Lapavitsas *et al.*, 2012; Nicholls, 2015). Against this challenging backdrop, predictions of a radical recasting of the state and its geography, with regions beginning to supplant nations and supranational institutions becoming ever more important, have proved to have limited empirical basis.

Within some countries, meanwhile, uncertainty about regional governance and policy making has resulted in efforts to dismantle existing regional institutions and replace them with territorial bodies defined in different ways (see, for instance, Pike *et al.*, 2015; Saurugger and Terpan, 2016). In some cases, this has involved the establishment of an array of alternative, sometimes experimental, policies and governance structures for territories that cross-cut, and sometimes challenge, conventional regional configurations (Allmendinger *et al.*, 2015). Disruption to the established pattern of regional institutions has also resulted from the increased emphasis on developing governance structures for more narrowly defined city-regions, representing a further alternative geography for economic-development policy (Harrison, 2012).

These incipient forms of territorial governance and policy have aroused uncertainty about what shape regional institutions and policies might take – or even whether they could continue to exist. The election in the United Kingdom in 2010 of a new government that from the outset very explicitly set out its rejection of regionally based governance embodied these *fin-de-siècle* concerns. The first government of former Prime Minister David Cameron had as its defining characteristic a commitment to austerity, as a means not only of 'rebalancing the books' in the short term but also, more fundamentally, of shrinking the state and accelerating the established process of liberating markets and freeing citizens from the supposedly suffocating influence of big government (see Kisby, 2010; Grimshaw and Rubery, 2012; Rogers, 2015). Attempting to realise this goal apparently left little room for regional governance and policy. A new guiding philosophy for spatial policy and governance – localism – signalled the Government's commitment to shift the geographical locus of sub-national policy from the region to more disaggregated units (see Allmendinger, 2015; Pike *et al.*, 2015). It also signalled the Government's rejection of the supposed *dirigisme* of the previous administration: a view that although some sub-national intervention continued to be warranted, the shape and extent of policy ought to be dictated by empowered local citizens and businesses rather than imposed by a remote central government (Kisby, 2010).

The upshot of these various intellectual and political upheavals has been renewed research interest in the shape, form and geographies of emergent institutions and policies and their impacts (Kitson *et al.*, 2011; Clarke and Cochrane, 2013; Haughton *et al.*, 2013; Pike *et al.*, 2015). Research interest has converged on what to some appears to be a new era in which state actors often play a less overt role, with national coordination of sub-national spatial policy deliberately loosened in an attempt to allow a range of new bottom-up entities to emerge (Clarke and Cochrane, 2013; Deas, 2013). As Allmendinger (2015) argues, systematic nation-wide coverage of centrally funded regional bodies appears likely to be a casualty, abandoned and replaced by a disparate array of participants from the local voluntary sector, business and a residual of local political and policy elites (Lowndes and Pratchett, 2012). The era of conventional, ordered and systematic forms of regional governance and policy, it appears, has very decisively ended, and research attention is turning increasingly to identifying the lineaments of new forms of sub-national policy and governance. What shape might these take and how might they be interpreted? In what ways might the policy initiatives and institutional structures emerging from the latest series of territorial governance reforms differ from their predecessors? And along what routes or pathways might the transition to new forms begin to take shape?

Towards new modes of regional policy and governance? Constructing, deconstructing and reconstructing regions

The period around the turn of the century was, therefore, one in which in some respects support for regional governance and policy peaked. The logic that had for some years underlain regional thinking was potent and multi-faceted (see Harrison, 2008, for a review). Policy actor perspectives in many countries alighted on the potential economic benefits of regional governance, by linking policy geographies to functional market areas, creating institutional infrastructures tailored more closely to local economic circumstances, or developing policies that were outward looking and would operate with the explicit goal of competing against other territories (Jones and Paasi, 2013). Renewed interest in developing regional policy and governance as a means of stimulating economic development also provided a fillip for political and administrative aspects of regionalism. Advocates of regionalism drew on well-established arguments that developing institutions at a regional scale could help to enhance the scope for strategic thinking about policy, create scale economies for more efficient service delivery and provide a more stable fiscal basis on which to deliver services (Storper, 1995, 1997; Scott, 1998). In some cases, they also drew upon identity politics, linking regional institution building to wider centrifugal forces – and resulting in a potential challenge to the territorial integrity of nation states such as the United Kingdom and Spain.

Efforts by the European Commission to implant the notion of an EU based on regions as the basic building block provided a background against which institutional structures in some countries were reformed. The notion of multi-level governance raised the prospect that the standing of regions could continue to grow (Marks, 1993; Hooghe, 1996; Benz and Eberlein, 1999). In more concrete terms, it also provided part of the discursive justification for efforts to empower regional institutions, even if only for the pragmatic reason of procuring a larger share of resources devoted to equalising economic circumstances across the EU's nascent single market (see Hooghe and Keating, 1994, for an early overview).

Some of the arguments in support of regionalism have subsequently waned. The suggestion, for example, that the growth of regional government could ultimately provoke the decline of the nation state (e.g. Ohmae, 1995) now looks to have been wildly overstated, notwithstanding the reinvigoration of secessionist nationalism in Scotland, Catalonia and elsewhere. And yet regions, and regional thinking, have in some respects proved remarkably resilient. Pessimistic prognoses about the future of regionalism may have underestimated the degree to which sub-national initiatives have been able not merely to withstand austerity-driven efforts to rationalise government but also to reform and transform as new forms of territorial governance and policy have emerged and grown (Harrison, 2012). While the vision of a permanent, formalised system of recognisable regional governments operating within a multi-level hierarchy has proved to be illusory, there is abundant evidence that regionalism continues to exist – prosper, even – albeit expressed in multiple, perhaps less conventional, ways. This is reflected in the now-burgeoning literature, for instance, on soft spaces of governance, cataloguing the emergence of a series of often relational, transient and flexibly configured spaces which sometimes sit uneasily alongside the more familiar geography of formal regional territories (see, for example, Allmendinger *et al.*, 2015).

Over the last decade or so, attempts to reconceptualise regional spaces along relational lines have led to a productive dialogue between those advocating the 'boundlessness' of space (Allen *et al.*, 1998; Amin, 2004) and those who point to the everyday reality of 'performing' local and regional development (Paasi, 2002; 2009a; Jones, 2009). Rather than viewing the constitution of regions in binary terms – absolute or relational, for instance – there is now much more recognition of the polymorphic nature of regions and their associated geographies and underlying socio-spatial relations (Jones, 2016). The contemporary challenge is to rethink existing attempts to theorise regional governance and policy in light of both the experiences of established regions subject to increased challenge – as a result of austerity, for example – and the array of soft or informal spaces of governance that have emerged alongside or in succession to them.

In other words, the research challenge that provides the rationale for this book is to extend the literature on how regional governance territories are constructed but also to add to the as yet imperfectly understood process of regional *deconstruction* and *reconstruction*. While there is an extensive literature on the formation of regions and the ways they become institutionalised (see, for example, Paasi, 2009b), comparatively less attention has been paid to the ways in which regional spaces adapt and change in response to a variety of intra- and extra-regional exigencies. These might include moments when existing initiatives and institutions are abolished and/or when alternative policy initiatives or governance structures emerge. They might also include challenges to established modes of practice, bringing pressures to innovate. The research emphasis on regional births is perhaps understandable given the obvious appeal of the new. But the limited attention devoted to the evolution of existing regions, or to the experience of superficially 'post-regional' spaces in which formal structures have been removed or their powers and resources curtailed, is more surprising in light of the stress on conceiving regions as relational entities, defined by their social, political and cultural dynamics as much as their political or administrative boundaries.

Aims and objectives of the book

The book draws on conceptual debates and empirical research from the United Kingdom and other international contexts to engage with issues around regional policy and the governance of economic development, planning and regeneration and the environment. A first aim is to document experience of the construction, deconstruction and reconstruction of regional policies and institutional structures and the ideas and practices that underpin them, and to think about how empirical change can be interpreted in conceptual terms. Subsequent chapters explore experiences in respect of regional institutional births as well as deaths: of new sub-national governance and policy structures, including those where the label 'regional' is less consistently appended; and of established regional territories and institutions confronted with pressures to change, whether in response to the scarcity of public resources, the changing emphasis of national policy or shifts in the relationship with both sub- and supra-regional bodies.

Accompanying these issues have been wider debates and dilemmas about territorial governance and policy, which provide a second area of investigation for the remainder of the book. As local and regional policy actors strive to respond to the geographically uneven effects of the economic crises of the early twenty-first century, what are the opportunities and challenges presented by different forms of territorially based governance? A recurring theme in chapters throughout the book concerns the implications posed by retrenchment in public finances, the abolition of some key regionally based institutions of governance and the curtailment of powers and resources available to regional policy actors. And yet regional policy and governance, against a backdrop of austerity politics, has on occasion demonstrated a capacity to absorb deleterious reforms and adapt accordingly. While our starting point for this book is that prophesies of a post-regional future are difficult to sustain in light of the continuing presence of regional institutions, the precise implications of austerity need to be explored in more detail.

Linking together both of these aims are a number of objectives. The first is to explore recent experience of change in territorial governance in a holistic way, recognising that regions as socio-political constructs take multiple, sometimes contested and increasingly disparate form. Yet much of the previous research literature on regional policy and governance has tended to be highly compartmentalised. Debates have often focused narrowly on specific contexts: fiscal consolidation and metropolitan regionalism, and latterly 'social movement regionalism' in North America (Mitchell-Weaver *et al.*, 2000; Pastor *et al.*, 2009); regional economic development and strategic planning in English administrative regions (Baker *et al.*, 1999); or the emergence of a variety of soft spaces of governance, such as cross-border regions in an EU context (Deas and Lord, 2006; Allmendinger *et al.*, 2015). The book seeks to complement this by capturing the increased diversity in territorial governance and policy and attempting to build a more complete picture of change across different types of regional space. In this respect, we are guided by Jones and Paasi's (2013) notion of regional worlds, which captures something of the sense of continuing dynamism and emergent diversity in respect of innovation in territorial governance. The argument here is that a multiplicity of alternative regionalisms has emerged, with different territories coexisting and competing in a complex and dynamic way. There is, therefore, a need to recognise multiple regionalisms and their inter-relationships, while also identifying what unites (and divides) them in conceptual terms.

Alongside the emphasis placed on considering regionalism in a holistic way, a second objective applied throughout the subsequent chapters is to emphasise time as well as space in reviewing how regions evolve. It is important to note that the evolution of regional governance and policy is not a unidirectional one. A history of short-lived and largely experimental regionally based initiatives rebuts any suggestion of a clear or linear trajectory in which regional structures and initiatives emerge, flourish and mature. Reflecting this, subsequent chapters of the book draw on case-study evidence to explore why policy innovation is effective in some spatial and temporal contexts, but not in others. Why are some new territories and initiatives able to emerge and subsequently prosper while others perish? What factors explain why some experiments in regional policy are able to secure a greater degree of permanence, whether by procuring resources, accumulating popular credibility, securing buy-in from the private sector or accruing legitimacy in the eyes of policy actors?

As well as exploring different types of regionalism and considering the intersection between temporal and spatial processes in helping to make and remake regions, a third objective of the book is to capture non-corporeal forms of regionalism. There is a need to 'accentuate the regional' when thinking about ostensibly non-regional spaces of governance (Jonas, 2013; Soja, 2015). This applies even to those spaces in which explicit regionally based organisations are absent or in decline, but which nevertheless exist as containers for social, economic and political processes that are intrinsically spatial (even if they are not badged as regional). We try to extend ideas about 'regional imaginaries' that connect the real existing regionalism discussed by Addie and Keil (2015) to the processes of regional thinking and identity that help create, sustain and change everything from formal, tangible regional institutions to subtly expressed spatial emphases in public policy. The idea here is that regionalism is a contested product of discourse, territorial relationships and technology (material and political). Chapters in the remainder of the book, therefore, review the narratives constructed to support particular forms of region, the technologies used to help realise them and their interactions as elements of wider constellations of regional space.

Structure of the book

The book is organised around four parts. The first, *Part I: Multi-scalar concepts and practices of regionalism*, provides an overview of how we might think about regions as polymorphic entities, underpinned by synergistic and at times conflictual conceptual viewpoints, scalar perspectives and logics. Martin Jones (Chapter 2) makes the case for a 'return to locality', discussing a concept deployed during the 1980s to explain the shifting intellectual landscape of regional studies but which Jones argues was prematurely discarded. The utility of returning to locality is considered in the context of a policy framework – localism – which advocates see as offering a more flexible and tailored approach to sub-national development than the more rigidly formalised administrative regional framework that preceded it. Through his analysis, Jones makes the case that the most recent model of localism adopted in England represents an attempt by central government to combine anti-state and connected society rhetoric. The localities concept, applied to localism in England, is shown to be sufficiently pliable to reveal the processes occurring within, beyond and between localities by uniting theoretical perspectives of territories as bounded units with recognisable political and administrative significance, and as geographically manifested relational entities.

Two subsequent chapters build on the theoretical debates explored by Jones via case studies of different forms of regional policy and governance. In the first, Philip O'Brien, Olivier Sykes and David Shaw (Chapter 3) reflect on conflict and uncertainty about the right geometry for regional policy. In the context of ongoing debates about the EU's Cohesion Policy, the authors explore competing conceptions and models of regional policy and their evolution over time. Their account of 'place-based' thinking at the level of the EU leads to the argument that the role of the state has transitioned from one based on promoting convergence between member states to one focused more narrowly on economic growth. This has been aided by ongoing reforms to institutions of governance organised at different spatial scales and related shifts in their inter-relationships. The argument here is that the ongoing search by EU policymakers for the optimal territories around which to organise regional policy has led to a complex and sometimes unstable assortment of overlapping and often competing spatial strategies, policies and institutional geographies.

In Chapter 4, John Harrison considers the case of city-regions as an evolving but contested form of regional policy. Reviewing recent experience in the United Kingdom, the chapter details how city-regions have been presented in policy narratives as an alternative to more expansive, polycentric regions as the building block for the sub-national governance of local economic development. Drawing on research in North West England and Wales, Harrison develops a critique of city-regional governance and policy. To understand the advent and evolution of city-regions, he argues, future research needs to be more attuned to substantive issues concerning the distributive socio-spatial consequences of city-regional approaches to local economic-development policy.

The second part of the book, *Part II: Flexible regionalism: soft spaces in theory and practice*, reflects on the adaptable nature of regionalism in the context of soft and cross-border regions. Graham Haughton and Philip Allmendinger (Chapter 5) provide a critical commentary on the proliferation of soft sub-national governance spaces in planning. These have evolved over the past 30 years alongside formal bounded spaces of government. The authors reflect on how the mechanisms through which development is regulated have at various times been 'rolled back', leaving alternative governance arrangements to emerge to occupy the resultant vacuum. Although it is tempting to view the emergence of these soft spaces of governance as a threat to more formal instances of spatial governance, the authors contend that hard and soft spaces can exist symbiotically, but this is characterised by a complex set of interactions – and on occasion by conflict. The implication here is that the inter-relationships between these spaces, through their synergies and conflicts, have far-reaching implications for planning policy and practice, not least in terms of public engagement and democratic accountability.

Claire Colomb, Francesc Morata Tierra, Antoni Durà Guimerà and Xavier Oliveras González build on accounts of the evolution of EU regional policy via a case study of the experience of trans-boundary cooperation in Catalonia, Spain (Chapter 6). The authors examine the extent to which practices of trans-boundary cooperation have helped foster new and alternative types of planning space that straddle national borders. The analysis reveals the emergence of variably institutionalised, multi-scalar planning spaces in which new territorial development strategies and accompanying governance architectures have evolved. The existence of these trans-boundary spaces reflects the pragmatic recognition that relational processes transcend the borders of individual member states. Echoing the argument of Haughton and Allmendinger, the analysis demonstrates how trans-boundary ambitions have, at times, conflicted with the political, symbolic and cultural imperatives of specific institutions and regulatory functions within individual member states. Yet, policy initiatives and planning projects linked to soft spaces, it is argued, have not always destabilised established hard territorial spaces or their accompanying governance structures, but have instead played an important discursive role in fostering new types of regional thinking: what the authors term 'cross-border regionalist engagement'.

In the third part of the book, *Part III: Mobility and circularity in urban–regional policy*, Kevin Ward and Ian Cook (Chapter 7) discuss a particular form of innovation in sub-national economic development, the establishment and evolution of Business Improvement Districts (BIDs) in the United Kingdom. In doing so, they trace the roots of the model to Canada in the early 1970s, and its adoption in the United States in the mid-1970s. Drawing on the policy mobilities literature, the authors explain the import of the model to the United Kingdom in the early 1990s. They reveal the instrumental role played by BIDs in eroding existing strategies for managing town and city centres by promising a more coherent mechanism through which to abate and reverse the longstanding decline of urban commercial cores. Ward and Cook are critical of assessments of the BIDs model that emphasise its international transferability and portability, highlighting the difficulties encountered in transplanting it across divergent urban and regional contexts.

Continuing this emphasis on how polices migrate temporally and spatially, Alex Lord argues in Chapter 8 that sub-national forms of economic-development policy in Britain have long been subject to moments of experimentation, as policymakers seek 'innovations' in the way policy is formulated, moulded and delivered. The extent to which these experiments represent genuinely pioneering solutions to policy problems is contested on the grounds that purported innovation when viewed in historical terms is often of only fleeting importance and impact, and more commonly represents continuity rather than change. Arguing that the neoliberalisation of sub-national economic-development policy is a long-term trend, Lord contends that supposed moments of innovation in urban and regional policy actually constitute a recycling and re-packaging that serves to reinforce the hegemonic logic underpinning reforms of sub-national development at the expense of alternatives.

The fourth part of the book, *Part IV: Embedding environmental concerns in regional governance and policy*, explores the role of environmental issues in shaping conversations about regional development. In Chapter 9, Andrew Karvonen develops a conceptual backdrop to debates about environmental dimensions of regional governance and policy by exploring the multiple ways in which the environment is territorialised. He does so through a 'pathways approach', which recognises the variable ways in which territories of the environment emerge, are envisioned, designed and implemented (or not) in policy and practice. Karvonen focuses on three specific examples of pathways and uses them to illustrate the ways in which knowledge is produced, mobilised and applied by different actors. The challenge this presents is that no one pathway on its own is sufficient to address environmental problems or help society to transition towards low-carbon, sustainable futures. The implication, he argues, is that different pathways will need to coalesce to generate a multi-pronged approach.

David Gibbs, Andrew Jonas and Aidan While (Chapter 10) continue this emphasis on environmental futures, examining the political, economic and social implications posed by promoting forms of development that can be more readily reconciled with reduced carbon emissions. The 'alternative future' of a low-carbon economy, they argue, can be conceived in ways that move beyond seeing the environment as a barrier to economic prosperity. The chapter documents how efforts to regulate carbon emissions are being used by cities and regions as a way of demonstrating competitive advantage. The crux of the argument here is that the emergence of carbon control has introduced to policy discourses a new set of principles centred on environmental regulation and that these in turn may come to challenge mainstream development models. However, the authors are sceptical about how far this will happen, in part because a low-carbon future could be seen as intensifying existing urban and regional disparities.

Extending Andrew Karvonen's analysis, Brian Webb examines the production and consumption of knowledge and its influence on city-regional policy (Chapter 11). Using a case study of PlaNYC, New York City's metropolitan regional plan, Webb explores inter-professional relationships, illustrating how co-produced knowledge is generated 'upstream' by urban climatologists and consumed 'downstream' by policy specialists. Policy outcomes, he argues, reflect complex negotiation between professional groups at different junctures in the plan-making process. The eventual shape of PlaNYC embodied these discussions, as competing policy approaches were adopted, rejected, emphasised or marginalised on the basis of alternative readings of climate science, against a backdrop of political manoeuvring by stakeholders interpreting scientific evidence in different ways. What emerged from this was a series of narratives linked to competing policy prescriptions, only some of which were successfully integrated into PlaNYC.

In combination, the insights posed by subsequent chapters of the book can help us to begin to answer a series of key questions about regions: about their shape and structure, their substantive focus, their effectiveness and the challenges confronting them. To what extent are we witnessing a process of restructuring, as the ordered and relatively stable pattern of regions that has existed in recent decades, in Europe at least, is challenged by a series of new territories that have emerged in the context of the financial crises of the early twenty-first century and the associated economic, political, social and environmental ructions? It is to these questions that we now turn in the following chapters.

References

Addie, J. and Keil, R. (2015) Real existing regionalism: the region between talk, territory and technology, *International Journal of Urban and Regional Research*, 39, 407–417.
Allen J., Massey, D. and Cochrane, A. (1998) *Rethinking the Region*, London: Routledge.
Allmendinger, P. (2015) *Neoliberal Spatial Governance*, London: Routledge.
Allmendinger, P., Haughton, G., Knieling, J. and Othengrafen, F. (eds.) (2015) *Soft Spaces: Re-negotiating Governance, Boundaries and Borders*, London: Routledge.

Amin, A. (2004) Regions unbound: towards a new politics of place, *Geografiska Annaler B*, 86, 33–44.

Amin, A. and Thrift, N. (1992) Neo-Marshallian nodes in global networks, *International Journal of Urban and Regional Research*, 16, 571–587.

Amin, A. and Thrift, N. (eds.) (1994) *Globalization, Institutions and Regional Development in Europe*, Oxford: Oxford University Press.

Baker, M., Deas, I. and Wong, C. (1999) Obscure ritual or administrative luxury? Integrating strategic planning and regional development, *Environment and Planning B*, 26, 763–782.

Benz, A. and Eberlein, B. (1999) The Europeanization of regional policies: patterns of multi-level governance, *Journal of European Public Policy*, 6, 329–348.

Brenner, N. (2004) *New State Spaces*, Oxford: Oxford University Press.

Clarke, N. and Cochrane, A. (2013) Geographies and politics of localism: the localism of the United Kingdom's coalition government, *Political Geography*, 34, 10–23.

Deas, I. (2013) Towards post-political consensus in urban policy? Localism and the emerging agenda for regeneration under the Cameron government, *Planning Practice and Research*, 28, 65–82.

Deas, I. and Lord, A. (2006) From a new regionalism to an unusual regionalism? The emergence of non-standard regional spaces and lessons for the territorial reorganisation of the state, *Urban Studies*, 43, 1847–1877.

European Union (2011) *Cities of Tomorrow: Challenges, visions, ways forward*, Brussels: Commission of the European Union.

Grimshaw, D. and Rubery, J. (2012) Reinforcing neoliberalism: crisis and austerity in the UK, in: Lehndorff, S. (ed.) *A Triumph of Failed Ideas: European Models of Capitalism in Crisis*, pp. 41–57, Brussels: ETUI.

Harrison, J. (2008) The region in political economy, *Geography Compass*, 2, 814–830.

Harrison, J. (2012) Life after regions? The evolution of city-regionalism in England, *Regional Studies*, 46, 1243–1259.

Haughton, G., Allmendinger, P. and Oosterlynck, S. (2013) Spaces of neoliberal experimentation: soft spaces, postpolitics, and neoliberal governmentality, *Environment and Planning A*, 45, 217–234.

Hooghe, L. (ed.) (1996) *Cohesion Policy and European Integration: Building Multi-Level Governance*, Oxford: Clarendon Press.

Hooghe, L. and Keating, L. (1994) The politics of European Union regional policy, *Journal of European Public Policy*, 1, 367–393.

Jessop, B. (2002) *The Future of the Capitalist State*, Cambridge: Polity.

Jonas, A. (2013) Alternative regionalisms, *Progress in Human Geography*, 37, 822–828.

Jones, M. (2009) Phase space: geography, relational thinking, and beyond, *Progress in Human Geography*, 33, 487–506.

Jones, M. (2016) Editorial: polymorphic political geographies, *Territory, Politics, Governance*, 4, 1–7.

Jones, M. and Paasi, A. (2013) Guest editorial: regional world(s): advancing the geography of regions, *Regional Studies*, 47, 1–5.

Kisby, B. (2010) The Big Society: power to the people?, *The Political Quarterly*, 81, 484–491.

Kitson, M., Martin, R. and Tyler, P. (2011) The geographies of austerity, *Cambridge Journal of Regions, Economy and Society*, 4, 289–302.

Krugman, P. (1991a) Increasing returns and economic geography, *Journal of Political Economy*, 99, 483–499.

Krugman, P. (1991b) *Geography and Trade*, Cambridge, MA: MIT Press.

Lapavitsas, C., Kaltenbrunner, A., Labrinidis, D., Lindo, D., Meadway, J., Michell, J., Painceira, J., Pires, E., Powell, J., Stenfors, A., Teles, N. and Vatikiotis, L. (2012) *Crisis in the Eurozone*, London and New York: Verso.

Lowndes, V. and Pratchett, L. (2012) Local governance under the coalition government: austerity, localism and the 'Big Society', *Local Government Studies*, 38, 21–40.

Marks, G. (1993) Structural policy and multilevel governance in the EC, *The State of the European Community*, 2, 391–410.

Martin, R. and Sunley, P. (2011) The new economic geography and policy relevance, *Journal of Economic Geography*, 11, 357–369.

Mitchell-Weaver, C., Miller, D. and Deal, R. (2000) Multilevel governance and metropolitan regionalism in the USA, *Urban Studies*, 37, 851.

Nicholls, W. (2015) Editorial: the politics of regional development, *Territory, Politics, Governance*, 3, 227–234.

Ohmae, K. (1995) *The End of the Nation State: The Rise of Regional Economies*, New York: The Free Press.

Paasi, A. (2002) Bounded spaces in the mobile world: deconstructing 'regional identity', *Tijdschrift voor Economische en Sociale Geografie*, 93, 137–148.

Paasi, A. (2009a) Bounded spaces in a 'borderless world': border studies, power and the anatomy of territory, *Journal of Power*, 2, 213–234.

Paasi, A. (2009b) The resurgence of the 'region' and 'regional identity': theoretical perspectives and empirical observations on the regional dynamics in Europe, *Review of International Studies*, 35, 121–146.

Pastor, M., Benner, C. and Matsuoka, M. (2009) *This Could be the Start of Something Big: How Social Movements for Regional Equity are Reshaping Metropolitan America*, Ithaca, NY: Cornell University Press.

Pike, A. (2007) Editorial: whither regional studies? *Regional Studies*, 41, 1143–1148.

Pike, A., Marlow, D., McCarthy, A., O'Brien, P. and Tomaney, J. (2015) Local institutions and local economic development: the Local Enterprise Partnerships in England, 2010–, *Cambridge Journal of Regions, Economy and Society*, 8, 185–204.

Porter, M. (1996) Competitive advantage, agglomeration economies, and regional policy, *International Regional Science Review*, 19, 85–94.

Porter, M. (1998) Clusters and the new economics or competition, *Harvard Business Review*, 76, 77–90.

Rhodes, R. (1994) The hollowing out of the state: the changing nature of the public service in Britain, *The Political Quarterly*, 65, 138–151.

Rogers, C. (2015) Localism and the (re)creation of capitalist space in the United Kingdom, *British Politics*, 10, 391–412.

Sassen, S. (1991) *The Global City: New York, London, Tokyo*, New Jersey: Princeton University Press.

Saurugger, S. and Terpan, F. (eds.) (2016) *Crisis and Institutional Change in Regional Integration*, London: Routledge.

Scott, A. (1988) Flexible production systems and regional development: the rise of new industrial spaces in North America and Western Europe, *International Journal of Urban and Regional Research*, 12, 171–186.

Scott, A. (1996) Regional motors of the global economy, *Futures*, 28, 391–411.

Scott, A. (1998) *Regions and the World Economy: The Coming Shape of Global Production, Competition, and Political Order*, Oxford: Oxford University Press.

Soja, E. (2015) Accentuate the regional, *International Journal of Urban and Regional Research*, 39, 372–381.

Storper, M. (1995) The resurgence of regional economies, ten years later: the region as a nexus of untraded interdependencies, *European Urban and Regional Studies*, 2, 191–221.

Storper, M. (1997) *The Regional World: Territorial Development in a Global Economy*, London: The Guilford Press.

Part I

Multi-scalar concepts and practices of regionalism

2 New localism, new localities …

Martin Jones

Introduction

> Our approach recognises that places have specific geographic, historic, environmental and economic circumstances that help to determine the prospects for growth and the most suitable approach to support the private sector and residents' opportunities … Policy should therefore recognise that the situation will be different for each place and is likely to be particularly affected by factors such as the inherent skills mix or entrepreneurial tradition of the population; business confidence; quality of infrastructure provision; and proximity of trading markets. There has in recent years been a strong focus on the role that agglomeration effects – the contribution of people and businesses within a defined area – can have on economic performance.
>
> (HM Government, 2010, p. 7)

This quotation from Nick Clegg is taken from the *Local Growth* White Paper, launched in November 2010 in the wake of the United Kingdom's election of a new Conservative-led coalition government. Underpinning the White Paper was the argument that previous attempts at promoting 'economic and social development' (a term used to capture economic development and growth, skills and welfare-state restructuring) had been too centralised and there was a need to curtail top-down initiatives that had ignored the varying needs of different areas. In England, institutions such as the 'bureaucratic' and 'rigid' Regional Development Agencies (RDAs) were to be swept aside and replaced by 'flexible' and 'tailored' Local Enterprise Partnerships (LEPs) and Enterprise Zones (EZs). As the then Deputy Prime Minister continued, this was to mark an end to the 'culture of Whitehall knows best' and create the conditions for 'meaningful decentralisation' (Clegg, 2010: cited in HM Government, 2010, p. 3). The coalition government of 2010–15, and the conservative government from May 2015–, has purported to offer a radically different approach to spatially based economic and social development policy, but did it deliver?

Other chapters of this book deal with the relative successes and failures of the new localist approach to economic and social development, planning and infrastructure development. This chapter offers a contextual framework to explore some of the somewhat *silent geographies* of what I have previously called the 'new new localism' (Jones and Jessop, 2010; Jones, 2013). In doing so, the chapter seeks to offer theoretical insights into the rhetoric of decentralist discourses and the geographical complexities and contradictions of local state remaking on the ground (see Clarke, 2014; Clarke and Cochrane, 2013; Mohan, 2012). The new localism is an old concept (see Peck, 1995) – and it is one that will doubtless recur (see Ward and Hardy, 2013). The latest variant of localist thinking draws extensively on some key antecedents. According to the 'Big Society' guru, Jesse Norman MP, localism 'is a coherent and logistical expression of a conservative tradition which goes back to the 18th century' (Norman, 2011, p. 201). Edmund Burke's 'little platoons' pepper this literature and are presented as progressive enablers for a democratic form of civil society-centred economic and social policy (Willetts, 1994). The reanimation of civil society is in turn viewed as a means of stimulating localist economic development. As one LEP leader has argued, 'growth programmes and policies seem focused more on social re-engineering than growth' (Alex Pratt, Chair of Buckingham Thames Valley LEP, quoted in HoC and BIS, 2013, p. 56). The chapter argues that by attempting to link economic and social policy in local contexts, the Government's new localism is profound and needs to be more fully theorised in undertaking geographical political economy research. In the words of Jesse Norman (2011, p. 197) again, the Conservative's new localism stresses a 'three way relationship between individuals, institutions and the state. It is when this relationship is functioning well that societies flourish. This requires each element in the triad to be active and energised in its own right … Societies should be thought of as ecosystems'. The chapter explores the conceptual significance of this notion of 'ecosystems' for geography and beyond.

This chapter suggests that there is considerable mileage in the notion of 'locality' to advance critical policy analysis and build political economy theory, shedding particular light on the 'agglomeration booster' (Haughton *et al.*, 2014) discourses offered by the Conservatives since 2010. During the mid- to late 1980s, 'locality' was *the* spatial metaphor deployed to describe and explain the shifting world of regional studies (Cooke, 2006). Building on previous research (Jones and Woods, 2013; Jones, 2011), the chapter argues that the resulting 'localities debate' saw a potentially important concept prematurely abandoned. The chapter urges a 'return to locality' to enlighten studies of economic and social development. I offer three new readings of locality, which, when taken together, constitute the basis for thinking about geography through the lens of *new localities*. The chapter suggests that, first, locality can be seen as bounded territorial space, recognised politically and administratively for the discharge and conduct of public services, and for the collection and analysis of statistical data. Second, locality represents a way of undertaking comparative research analysis, linked to processes occurring within and outside localities and also connecting them. Third, locality can be used to read spaces of flows for numerous policy fields, which in turn exhibit spatial variations due to interaction effects. Additionally, the chapter suggests that for locality to have analytical value it must also have both an imagined and a material coherence. Last, the chapter draws on these constructs to argue that uneven development ought not be neglected when thinking about the new localism.

What is locality? The rise and fall of spatial metaphors

'What is locality?' asked Simon Duncan (1989) when commenting on the locality debates of the previous five years. 'Locality' was that buzzword of the mid-1980s, even described as a 'new geography' (Cochrane, 1987), used to frame research on economic geography. It filled the pages of human geography journals and, I would argue, contributed to the intellectual development of regional studies. Reflecting on this, Cooke has gone as far as to argue that debates around localism were 'the most heated yet illuminating wrangles in human geography since those over "environmental determinism" in the 1950s and the "quantitative revolution" in the 1960s. The soul of the discipline seemed to be at stake ...' (Cooke, 2006, p. 1). For Duncan, 'locality' was being used as a misleading catch-all term, an 'infuriating idea' used imprecisely to describe the local autonomy of areas, case-study areas, spatially affected process (social, political, economic, cultural), spaces of production and consumption, the local state and so on.

Massey's (1984) text *Spatial Divisions of Labour* was pivotal to starting what became the locality debate. This was written during an era of intense economic restructuring and challenged how geographers thought about 'the local' in an increasingly internationalising and globalising world in which Fordist and Keynesian certitudes were perceptibly unravelling. The tangible impact of all this was an acceleration of uneven development, with acute job loss in some areas juxtaposed with accelerating growth in others, as distinctive localities began to emerge in the context of globalisation and economic restructuring (see also Lovering, 1989).

The intellectual goal in this was to tease out the dialectic between space and place by looking at how localities were being positioned within, and could themselves help to reposition, the changing national and international division of labour. For Massey (1991), 'the local in the global' was not simply an area around which a line can be drawn; instead, localities were defined in terms of sets of social relations or processes under consideration. This highly influential 'new regional concept of localities' (Jonas, 1988) influenced two government-sponsored research initiatives in the United Kingdom, delivered through the Economic and Social Research Council – the Social Change and Economic Life programme and the Changing Urban and Regional Systems (CURS) programme. Both were given substantial funding and remits to uncover the effects of international and global economic restructuring on local areas, exploring why different responses and impacts were reported in different places. Locality research, independent of these programmes, was already taking place in Lancaster University (Murgatroyd *et al.*, 1985) and Sussex University (Duncan, 1989), which fuelled an interest in this important topic (although as Barnes (1996) notes, notions of 'locality' differ across all these interventions and focusing on the CURS programme is most helpful to get behind the meaning of locality).

In seeking to put 'the local' into 'the global', the CURS initiative set out to undertake theoretically informed empirical research in seven localities between 1985 and 1987. The goal was to examine the extent to which localities themselves could shape their own transformation and destiny as agents and not be passive containers for processes passed down from above. Two edited books documented the fortunes of a series of mainly metropolitan de-industrialising towns/regions and rural areas, tracking the impacts of globalisation and economic restructuring on 'the local' and considering the complex and variable local-global interplay that conditioned locality experiences (Cooke, 1989a; Harloe *et al.*, 1990).

Particularly worthy of note here was the work of Hudson and Beynon (see Beynon *et al.*, 1989), whose research closely followed Massey's theoretical and interpretative framework. Their account of economic change in Teesside seemed to demonstrate a 'locality effect' of local particularities in global times: the different ways in which 'rounds of investment' impinged on the local economic landscape, how local politics played a role in international investment decisions and, in turn, how attempts to cope with de-industrialisation (by either building a service-based economy or using state-sponsored local economic initiatives to create employment opportunities) were expressed on the ground.

As argued by Gregson (1987), Duncan and Savage (1991) and Barnes (1996), there is a fundamental difference between locality research (the CURS findings) and the resulting 'locality debate' across human geography and the social sciences. The latter was fuelled by a desire to rethink the theorisation of socio-spatial relations across disciplines, within the context of a broader transition from Marxist to post-structuralist research enquiry. The localities debate was also informed by shifting research methodologies and practices, such as the rise and fall of critical realism (see Pratt, 2004). In this febrile intellectual context, the journal *Antipode*, between 1987 and 1991, published a series of often-heated exchanges on the conceptual and empirical value of localities (for summaries, compare Cooke, 2006; Pratt, 2004). The initial assault came from North America by Smith (1987), who bemoaned the perceived shift away from (Marxist) theory to a critical realist-inspired regional world of empirics, worthy of nothing more than a 'morass of statistical data'. Smith's memorable dismissal of localities research had it that 'like the blind man with a python in one hand and an elephant's trunk in the other, the researchers are treating all seven localities as the same animal'. This was supported, to a differing degree, by Harvey (1987), who saw these projects as refusing to engage in any theoretical or conceptual adventures. The consequences, for Scott (1991, pp. 256–257), were to encourage 'a form of story-telling that focuses on dense historical and geographical sequences of events, but where in the absence of a strong interpretative apparatus, the overall meaning of these events for those who live and work in other places is obscure'.

Duncan (1989) offered a more sympathetic critique, which saw locality – in the wrong hands – as a form of reified uniqueness and 'spatial fetishism': in what sense can localities act, or is it the social forces within these spaces that have this capacity? In two influential papers with Savage, Duncan made the first serious intervention on the relationships between spatial scales (Duncan and Savage, 1991; Savage and Duncan, 1990). Duncan concluded with some thoughts on three ways forward for research on locality: considerations of spatially contingent effects (processes contained in places), propositions on local causal process (locally derived forces of change) and the notion of locality effects (the combination of the previous two, affording a capacity to localities to act). Warde (1989) recognised the value of locality for empirical research but also argued that the scale of locality changes according to the object of analysis under question. Cooke (1987, 1989b), the Director of CURS, took a more defensive and, ultimately, pragmatic line, arguing that CURS was about seeking to make some general claims from multi-site case-study research, even if this was about nothing more than local labour markets and its boundaries. The CURS findings were, therefore, empirical and not empiricist (see Cooke, 2006).

A special issue of *Environment and Planning A* offered further critique and extension, and contended that locality was still a valuable concept with which to grapple. For Jackson (1991), the danger was that cultural change and political change were overly attributed to economic factors, at odds with a reality in which each was embedded in the other. Pratt (1991) took a similar line and suggested a need to look at the discursive construction of localities and their material effects. Paasi (1991), much inspired by the 'new regional geography' material that the locality debate uncovered and which helped rekindle interest in regions, encouraged scholars to take 'geohistory' more seriously and offered the idea of 'generation' to distinguish between the concepts of locality, place and region. Duncan and Savage (1991, 1989) pushed what they saw as the missing agenda of place formation and class formation and the interconnections of these within and between localities. Cox and Mair (1991; see also Cox, 1993) offered an agenda-setting account of localities in the United States as arenas for economic-development coalitions and as ways of fixing and scaling socio-spatial relations. Their research took debate forward and brought agency and scale to the fore through notions of 'local dependency', the 'scale division of labour' and the 'scale division of the state' – concepts that highlighted the location and mobility of actors at different times. Cox and Mair claimed this avoided 'spatial fetishism' (a criticism levelled by Sayer, 1991) as locality is seen not in physical terms but as a 'localised social structure'. Finally, Massey's (1991, 1994) interventions offered some sensible qualifiers on what CURS had initially set out to achieve, shifting the scale of debate from locality to 'senses of place'.

As Cooke's (2006) subsequent retrospective commentary noted, because CURS and the locality debate became so quickly mired in these debates, the potentially useful notion of locality was jettisoned somewhat prematurely. Debates moved on, and during the mid-1990s economic geographers became preoccupied not so much with localities *per se* but with the links between space and place as a way of looking at the 'local in the global'. Massey (1994) argued that globalisation is happening but that the extent of time-space compression is socially and spatially uneven due to the variable mobility potential of people in place. 'Power geometries', a metaphor for capturing geographies of power, exist and, therefore, constrain some and enable others. This makes generalisations about the powerlessness of 'the local' in a globalising world unwise (see Harvey, 1989). The argument here was that localities need to be understood in terms of 'global senses of place' – as inter-connected nodes in spaces of flows, stretching back and forth, ebbing and flowing according to how they are positioned by, and positioning, socio-spatial relations. Two distinctions are then made to get a handle on 'the local in the global'. The first is a 'regressive sense of place', based on the rejection of the potentials of globalisation and the embrace, instead, of heritage and other forms of 'romanticized escapism'. The second is a more 'progressive sense of place', based on harnessing and making the most of difference and diversity through those stretched-out connections. Massey discusses this through her own experiences of living in Kilburn (a cosmopolitan area of North London) and her approach has no truck with locality perspectives that stick to administrative boundaries or tightly drawn labour market areas. Localities as 'global senses of place' are *relational* in the sense of seeing the local as an unbounded mosaic of different elements always in a process of interaction and being made. In short, one cannot explain locality or place by only looking inside it, or outside it; the 'out there' and 'in here' matter *together* and are dialectically intertwined (see Massey, 2005, 2007).

Bringing the metaphor back: towards 'new localities'

In the early 1990s, 'region' replaced locality as the spatial descriptor around which economic and political geography cohered. Academic trends tend to closely mirror political and policy events (see Cooke and Morgan, 1998) and economic geographers began increasingly to focus on the perceived re-emergence of regional economies and new spaces of economic governance across the globe. These spaces had been initially flagged by writers talking about post-Fordism and the geographies of flexible accumulation. From these initial efforts came wider attempts to delimit the contours of a 'regional world' (Storper, 1997). Scott, for instance, in the text *New Industrial Spaces* (1988), offered a new way of looking at agglomeration and the development of distinct local territorial production complexes or industrial districts. Whereas Fordist accumulation was favoured by and grew in accordance with economies of scale and vertical integration, economic development after Fordism was seen to be linked to spatially specific economies of scope resulting from the vertical disintegration of production and the development, amongst other things, of flexible working practices and shared support mechanisms. The geographical extent of this phenomenon and its reproducibility and sustainability were discussed at length in various edited collections (see Storper and Scott, 1992). Inspired by this, debates gradually shifted throughout the 1990s to examine the governance of local economies in global contexts through a 'new regionalist' perspective – as part of a broader 'institutional-turn' in economic geography. A parallel set of debates, also drawing on 'new regionalist' thinking, took place in political science on 'multilevel governance', driven by the so-called 'hollowing out' of the national state and the 'Europe of the Regions' thesis (Keating, 1998; Scott, 2001). For Cooke, this was important for locality studies:

> Probably the longest-lasting legacy of locality studies has been the rise of so-called 'new regionalism'. Already spotted around the time of his return from Australia by Nigel Thrift (1983) this theorised regional political econ-omy analysis was gaining ground rapidly as we have seen, in the new times of 'global localisation'. The locality studies themselves and the comparative methodology that allowed spatial variety to be explained within a coherent and satisfying theoretical framework furthered this impulse."
>
> (Cooke, 2006, p. 10)

This orthodoxy and alleged theoretical coherence referred to by Cooke, has, of course, been subjected to piercing academic critique. In a similar manner to some of the critiques of locality, philosophically (via critical realism), the new regional-ism is deemed guilty of 'bad abstraction' in that it ignores the role of multiple and contingent factors (both economic and non-economic) that produce regions. For this reason, Lovering argues that the region is becoming a 'chaotic conception'; generalised claims are being made based on selective empirical evidence to sup-port the centrality of this scale for stimulating economic growth. Consequently, he argues, this approach is a theory led by selective empirical developments and recent public policy initiatives. It is 'a set of stories about how *parts* of a regional economy *might* work, placed next to a set of policy ideas which *might* just be use-ful in *some* cases' (Lovering, 1999, p. 384, emphasis original). These arguments have been developed and extended by others (see MacLeod, 2001; Hadjimichalis, 2006; Painter, 2008; Harrison, 2010).

New regionalist thinking has been, in turn, challenged by relational approaches to space, where – building on the work of Massey (1994) above – geographies are made through unbounded relations influenced by global flows and local nodal interactions. Space, here, is a reflection of networked, nodal and open place-based relationships, rather than merely a container or an independent backdrop for exist-ence. This argument, of course, has been clearly articulated by those advocating that space is a relational concept (Amin, 2004, 2007; see also Marston *et al.*, 2005). 'Unbounded' or 'relational' regions need not be territorially coherent or contiguous. 'Alternative regional geographies' involve spatial configurations and boundaries that are no longer necessarily or purposively territorial or scalar, since social, economic, political and cultural processes are constituted through actor networks which are becoming increasingly dynamic and varied in spatial constitu-tion (Massey, 2007, p. 89; Massey, 2011; Amin, 2004).

Radical open-ended politics and economics of *place* are proposed, in opposi-tion to frameworks of so-called 'bounded territorial economic development', to create spaces of opportunity for localities under globalisation. This perspective is evidenced in the text *Cities: Reimagining the Urban*, where Amin and Thrift (2002) view localities as unbounded, fuzzy, fluid, complex and mixed entities, formed through recurring practices, movements and experiences. They claim this has implications for developing successful economies in a context of economic globalisation, building institutional and policy frameworks for economic governance, nurturing civic participation and delivering radical democracy (see Massey, 2007). Putting 'the local into the global' has 'far less to do with territorial properties (such as localized linkage, local identity and identification, scalar politics and governance) than with *the effects of spatial and temporal exposure and connectivity* (such as continual and open-ended change, juxtaposition of difference, overlap of networks of different global connections)' (Amin, 2002, p. 391; emphasis added).

This is a perspective that stretches the imagination of economic geography, but those working within state theoretic frameworks and more grounded approaches to economic geography have taken issue with the *realpolitik* of 'the local' grappling with the challenges of globalisation. For example, it is important to consider the ways in which cities and regions can be categorised as problematic by the state and those seeking to direct resources to different geographical areas. It is also important not to lose sight of the ways in which contentious politics are being played out across the globe. One instance of this in recent years has seen campaigns for devolved government and cultural rights linked to territorially articulated spaces (see Jones and MacLeod, 2004; Keating, 2013). For Tomaney (2007), localities, then, are more than the local articulation of global flows, and concerns with territorialised culture need not necessarily be atavistic, archaic or regressive.

Commentators on the territorial-relational debate suggest several ways forward. Jonas (2012) suggests that the distinction between territorial and relational can be 'registered obsolete' if critical attention is paid to matters of territory and the nature of territorial politics, both of which are products of bounded and unbounded forces. Moreover, he argues, the form this takes is contingent and requires empirical investigation. The way forward, then, is 'further examples of both relational thinking about territorial politics and of territorial thinking about relational processes' (Jonas, 2012, p. 270; see also Allen and Cochrane, 2014).

'New localities' research agendas

Some 25 years on, in the wake of long-running debates about the new regionalism and glocalisation and about relational and bounded territoriality, how useful is the concept of locality? Can it be energised by these debates and developed to begin to answer the challenges thrown up by Jonas (2012)? In this respect, it is worth revisiting Duncan's (1989) claim:

Localities in the sense of autonomous subnational social units rarely exist, and in any case their existence needs to be demonstrated. But it is also misleading to use locality as a synonym for place or spatial variation. This is because the term locality inevitably smuggles in notions of social autonomy and spatial determinism, and this smuggling in excludes examination of these assumptions. *It is surely better to use terms like town, village, local authority area, local labour market or, for more general uses, place, area or spatial variation.* These very useable terms do not rely so heavily on conceptual assumptions about space vis-à-vis society.

(Duncan, 1989, p. 247 [emphasis added])

Counter to this analysis, I would suggest that locality has the capacity to capture those spatial categories deemed by Duncan (1989) to be more useful units of analysis. It is exactly those 'conceptual assumptions' which render locality free of charges of 'spatial determinism'. *Locality is a meaningful term.* This stance, however, requires some hard thinking and the introduction of a new conception of locality: that of 'new locality'. Savage *et al.* (1987, p. 30) argue that '[g]reater clarification of the concept "locality" should start with an analysis of the signifi-cance of space in general'. In response, three readings of 'new locality' can be formulated from the three commonly understood notions of space used in the physical and social sciences – absolute, relative and relational – which, as Harvey (1969) has highlighted, can coexist.

This coexistence can be illustrated in relation to the conceptual treatment of local areas in a global context. In the *absolute* understanding of space, the local is treated independently; locality is a discrete space around which a line can be drawn and where a loose spatial determinism has some purchase. Concerns with *relative space,* by contrast, lead us to consider the relationship between localities in an increasingly internationalising world of processes and patterns. The notion of *relational space*, by way of further contrast, is a truly radical attempt to col-lapse analysis into networked concerns such that there is no global and local to talk about, only unbounded and networked geographies of 'jostling' (Massey, 2007), 'throwntogetherness' (Massey, 2005) and becoming (Woods, 2007). Sites become the sources of analysis, but how they relate to each other is not clear, such that research needs to pay attention to power and policy relations flowing through localities. These three notions of space, therefore, inform different ways of iden-tifying localities as objects of research, each of which can be found employed in the social science literature, viz:

From the perspective of *absolute space*, localities can be presented as bounded territories, such as local authority areas, which are recognised politically and administratively for reasons of electoral accountability, for the discharge and con-duct of public services and for the collection and analysis of statistical data. They are not naturally occurring entities (though some may be contiguous with natural features such as islands), but they do have a stable and precisely delimited mate-riality that can form the focus for traditional, single place-based or comparative case-study research (Bennett and McCoshan, 1993).

From the perspective of *relative space*, localities can be seen as connected con-tainers for spatial analysis. Here, localities are identified by their cores, not their edges, and are not necessarily consistent with formal administrative geographies. In this perspective, the boundaries of localities are relative, fuzzy and sometimes indeterminate, contingent on the processes and phenomena being observed, and shaped by dynamics within, outside and between localities. Such a notion of locality forms the basis for research sensitive to connective forms of enquiry, including, for example, work on city-regions and nested hierarchies (Etherington and Jones, 2009).

From the perspective of *relational space*, localities are nodes or entanglements within networks of interaction and spaces of flow. They are not 'bounded' in any conventional understanding of the term, but have a topography that is described by lines of connectivity and convergence. Localities transgress inscribed territories and are not necessarily discrete, sharing points of coexistence. Such a conceptualisation of locality lends itself to counter-topographical research (Katz, 2001; see also Heley and Jones, 2012) or the practice of a 'global ethnography' (Burawoy, 2000).

Unlike earlier locality debates, the 'new localities' approach does not seek to adjudicate between these different representations of locality, but, rather, recognises that all are valid ways of 'talking about locality', and each captures a different expression of locality. New localities are, therefore, multi-faceted and multi-dimensional. They are 'shape-shifters' whose form changes with the angle from which they are observed. As such, the identification of localities for research can be freed from the constraints of the rigid territoriality of administrative geography and should move beyond the reification of the local-authority scale that was implicit in many previous locality studies. Warde's comments of 20-plus years ago on this remain critical:

> Deciding on an appropriate spatial scale depends initially on the research problem. If we want to know about foreign policy we might choose states; if voting behavior, constituencies; if material life, perhaps the labour market; if everyday experience, maybe the neighbourhood. Greater difficulty arises if we want to know about the intersection of several of these, the burden of the restructuring thesis. Concepts with substantive spatial properties ought to be theoretical predicates. Conscripting the concepts of locality requires that a theoretical decision be made.
>
> (Warde, 1989, p. 277)

In recognising the contingency and impermanence of localities, and acknowledging Warde's (1989) plea for notions of 'intersection', the new localities approach also focuses attention on processes of 'locality-making', or the ways in which stable and popularly recognised representations of locality are brought into being through the moulding, manipulation and sedimentation of space within ongoing social, economic and political struggles (see Jonas, 2012; Pierce *et al.*, 2011). Indeed, it is in these acts of locality making that localities are transformed from mere points of location (a description of where research was conducted) to socio-economic-political creations that provide an analytical framework for research. For the concept of locality to have analytical value, it must be possible to attribute observed processes and outcomes to social, economic and political formations that are configured in a given locality, and this, it can be argued, requires a locality to possess both material and imagined coherence.

Material coherence refers to the particular social, economic and political structures and practices that are configured around a place. Thus, material coherence may be provided by the territorial ambit of a local authority, by the geographical coverage of an economic-development initiative, by the catchment area of a school or hospital, by a travel-to-work area, by the reach of a supermarket or shopping centre, or by any combination of these and other similar structures and practices. Material coherence, hence, alludes to the institutional structures that hold a locality together and provide vehicles for collective action.

Imagined coherence relates to the collective resident consciousness and the sense of shared identity and affinity with a place, resulting in a perceived community with shared patterns of behaviour and common geographical reference points. Imagined coherence, therefore, makes a locality meaningful as a space of collective action. There are territorial units that exhibit material coherence but lack a strong imagined coherence (such as artificially amalgamated local authority areas), and there are territories with an imagined coherence but only a weak material coherence (for example, where institutional boundaries bisect contiguous urban areas or where areas with strongly developed popular consciousness exist within much larger institutional units). Areas falling into either of these categories could not be considered coherent functioning localities.

Both material coherence and imagined coherence are also important in fixing (through multiple intersections) the scale at which localities can be identified (Jones and Woods, 2013). The imagined coherence of a locality is framed around perceived shared forms of behaviour, whether linked to common patterns of collective consumption, shared affinity with sporting or cultural institutions, or common geographical/historical reference points. However, this imagined coherence is not founded on direct inter-personal connection between residents (see Anderson, 1991). In this sense, it differs from the social coherence of a neighbourhood – which may share some of the previously named attributes, but is framed around the probability of direct interaction between members. It also differs from the imagined coherence of a region – which is a looser affiliation that draws more on perceived cultural and political identities and economic interests.

Similarly, the material coherence of a locality should be denser and more complex than that found at a neighbourhood or regional scale. The material coherence of a neighbourhood will be restricted by its situation within a larger geographical area for employment, administrative and many service-provision functions, while the material coherence of a region could be fragmented by the inclusion of several different labour markets, local authority areas, sub-regional shopping centres and so on. Savage's (2009) work on 'granular space' is illustrative of these concerns:

People do not usually see places in terms of their nested or relational qualities: town against country: region against nation, etc. but compare different places with each other without a strong sense of any hierarchical ordering. I further argue that the culturally privileged groups are highly 'vested' in place, able to articulate intense feelings of belonging to specific fixed locations, in ways where abstract and specific renderings of place co-mingle. Less powerful groups, by contrast, have a different cultural geography, which hives off fantasy spaces from mundane spaces.

(Savage, 2009, p. 3)

The outlined attributes of localities do not easily translate into discrete territorial units with fixed boundaries. Labour-market areas overlap, as do shopping catchment areas; residents may consider themselves to be part of multiple localities for different purposes and at different times; the reach of a town as an education centre may be different to its reach as an employment centre and so on. The boundaries that might be ascribed to a locality will vary depending on the issue in question (Warde, 1989).

All this has a bearing on how localities are identified, defined and constructed for case-study research. The argument of Beauregard (1988) on the 'absence of practice' in locality research is important here, in calling for both methodological and political interventions. The application of the approach discussed logically leads us to start by identifying localities by their cores – whether these be towns or cities or geographical areas – rather than as bounded territories, and working outwards to establish an understanding of their material and imagined coherence. This process will necessarily require mixed methods, combining cartographic and quantitative data on material geographies with qualitative evidence of imagined coherence and performed patterns and relations. This is more than just an exercise in boundary drawing. Whilst it may be possible to identify fixed territorial limits for the reach of a locality with respect to certain governmental competences or policy fields, when applying proxy boundaries to imagined localities one must necessarily assume a degree of permeability and consider that localities may be configured differently depending on the object of inquiry.

Coda: don't forget uneven development

This chapter has proposed a new approach to thinking about localities in the context of the new localism in the United Kingdom. This approach recognises that localities do not only exist in absolute space as bounded territories but also have expression in relative and relational space where boundaries are at best 'fuzzy' and permeable. Whilst each representation may be legitimately employed to frame localities in particular contexts, taken together they point to a new understanding of localities as multi-faceted, dynamic and contingent entities that change shape depending on the viewpoint adopted. Constructing localities as frames for the analysis of social, economic or political phenomena, therefore, requires investigation of both their imagined and material coherence, which in combination make a locality meaningful and create a capacity for action.

This chapter has proposed that the 'new localities' approach has at least three implications for case-study oriented geographical research. First, it provides a revised model for understanding locality effects that does not take localities as a given bounded spatial unit, but instead emphasises the contingency and relationality of localities. Second, the new localities approach therefore requires identification and description of the locality to be incorporated as an intrinsic part of the research process, rather than treating locality as a taken for granted backdrop. This approach further recognises that the shape, reach and orientation of a locality might differ according to the research questions being examined. Third, the new localities notion consequently demands a new body of research concerned with establishing the material and imagined coherences of localities, employing mixed-method strategies. Through these mechanisms, 'locality' can be reclaimed as a meaningful and useful concept in social and economic research. In its resurrected guise, 'locality' can be freed from the shackles of fixed boundaries. As such, whilst locality research can be spatially focused, it should not be spatially constrained, and it needs to be prepared to follow networks and relations across scales and spaces to reveal the full panoply of forces and actors engaged in the constitution of a locality (Jones and Woods, 2013).

All of this raises the issue of relationships within and between localities, constituted in and as the landscapes of combined and uneven development. On the one hand, there are statements from the UK government such as

> We think that the best means of strengthening society is not for central government to try and seize all the power and responsibility for itself. It is to help people and their locally elected representatives to achieve their own ambitions. This is the essence of the Big Society ... The Localism Act sets out a series of measures with the potential to achieve a substantial and lasting shift in power away from central government and towards local people.
>
> (Greg Clark MP, Minister of State for Decentralisation, Foreword, *A Plain English Guide to the Localism Act*, DCLG, November 2011)

> *The policy implications of theories of agglomeration is that enabling people and firms to benefit from proximity to centres of activity, bring beneficial economic outcomes ...* This implies empowering and incentivising local government, firms and people across economic centres and natural economic geographies [Cities] to promote growth and correct the market and government failures which are acting as barriers to economic development.
>
> (BIS, 2010, p. 25 [emphasis added])

These 'atomist' localist ideologies are being echoed in turn by the actors involved in institutional developments, such as LEPs:

> As a City Region, *collaboration* is our trump card. The networks, the relationships and our strong history of partnership working are the *envy* of other LEPs and will be a *comparative advantage* as we close the gap on rival LEP areas. Collaboration has been a driving principle of our LEP and will be key to transforming our local economy.
>
> (James Newman, Chair Sheffield City Region LEP, quoted in Sheffield City Region LEP 2013 [emphasis added])

Such sentiments, though, explicitly ignore the complex and contradictory relationships within and between places and regions. Expressed simply, everywhere cannot win; everywhere cannot raise performance above the average (because it is the average); and everywhere cannot mobilise the so-called 'local agglomeration forces' into temporary permanent fixes for economic success, social cohesion and democratic renewal (see Bond, 2010; Cheshire *et al.*, 2014). The landscape of England's localities is a story of competition hotspots and not-spots; a tapestry of some places developing out-of-control, boom-to-bust tendencies; and other places stagnating and witnessing little in the way of sustained economic development (see Ward and Hardy, 2013). Drawing parallels with literature in development studies, it remains the case that 'by focusing so heavily on "the local" … mani-festations tend to underplay both local inequalities and power relations as well as national and transnational economic and political forces' (Mohan and Stokke, 2000, p. 247). This is due not just to the historical long-run dynamics of British capitalism and a macro-economic policy environment that favours finance-led accumulation in London and the South East. The institutions of economic govern-ance simply lack the *regulatory capacity* to correct market or governance failure. Actors involved in the new localism acknowledge some of this and also highlight serious issues of blurred accountability and outright confusion:

> The LEP boundaries and sizes seemed sometimes to be politically driven under the camouflage of functional economies – insufficient strategic con-sideration was given to the LEP coverage of the Country; and little serious consideration seemed given to the confusing impact of allowing overlapping LEP areas. This has resulted in an overcomplicated network of massively different LEPs based more on political geographies, rather than sub-regional economic areas. *Localism is an interesting concept but if applied to my car, if all four wheels were allowed to be different sizes, shapes and positions, it wouldn't aid the car much in its progress.*
>
> (Alex Pratt, Chair of Buckingham Thames Valley LEP,
> quoted in HoC and BIS, 2013, p. 15 [emphasis added])

> Chair (Adrian Bailey MP): I need to conclude fairly quickly but I have a couple of questions to finish with on accountability. Very briefly, who do you feel you are accountable to as a LEP?
>
> Linda Edworthy (Tees Valley Unlimited): local business and local residents.
>
> Mark Reeve (Chair Grt Cambs & Grt Peterb LEP): both public and private sector within the LEP.
>
> James Newman (Chair Sheffield City Region LEP): to a certain extent to the Ministers who appoint us as well, in terms of their expectations of us – very much so.
>
> Adrian Shooter (Chair Oxford LEP): I would add to that to the people who we are supposed to be finding jobs for, which is why we are there.
>
> David Frost (Chair LEP Network): There is a wide range, but of course we are also accountable, where there are funding streams, to those Departments that are providing it."
>
> (HoC and BIS, 2013, p. 12)

Where next for the new localism, or even the new new localism? With 'English votes for English laws' presented at the heart of the Conservative Party campaign for the 2015 General Election (see Redwood, 2014), following the rejection of Scottish independence and the subsequent 'devo-max' settlement to consolidate devolution to Scotland, issues of 'locality-making' (Jones and Woods, 2013) are of increasing importance to state spatiality and state territoriality.

References

Allen, J. and Cochrane, A. (2014) The urban unbound: London's politics and the 2012 Olympic games, *International Journal of Urban and Regional Research*, 38, 1609–1624.

Amin, A. (2002) Spatialities of globalisation, *Environment and Planning A*, 34, 385–399.

Amin, A. (2004) Regions unbound: towards a new politics of place, *Geografiska Annaler*, 86B, 33–44.

Amin, A. (2007) Rethinking the urban social, *City*, 11, 100–114.

Amin, A. and Thrift, N. (2002) *Cities: Reimagining the Urban*, Cambridge: Polity.

Anderson, B. (1991) *Imagined Communities: Reflections on the Origin and Spread of Nationalism*, London: Verso.

Barnes, T. (1996) *Logics of Dislocation: Models, Metaphors, and Meanings of Economic Space*, New York: Guilford.

Beauregard, R. (1988) In the absence of practice: the locality research debate, *Antipode*, 20, 52–59.

Bennett, R. and McCoshan, A. (1993) *Enterprise and Human Resource Development: Local Capacity Building*, London: Paul Chapman.

Beynon, H., Hudson, R., Lewis, J., Sadler, D. and Townsend, A. (1989) 'It's all falling apart here': coming to terms with the future in Teesside, in: Cooke, P. (ed.) *Localities: The Changing Face of Urban Britain*, London: Unwin Hyman.

BIS (Department for Business, Innovation and Skills) (2010) Understanding Local Growth, *BIS Economics Paper 7*, London: BIS.

Bond, P. (2010) *Red Tory: How Left and Right Have Broken Britain and How We Can Fix It*, London: Faber and Faber.

Burawoy, M. (2000) *Global Ethnography*, Berkeley, CA: University of California Press.

Cheshire, P., Nathan, M. and Overman, H. (2014) *Urban Economics and Urban Policy: Challenging Conventional Policy Wisdom*, Cheltenham: Elgar.

Clarke, N. (2014) Locality and localism: a view from British human geography, *Policy Studies*, 34, 492–507.

Clarke, N. and Cochrane, A. (2013) Geographies and politics of localism: the localism of the United Kingdom's coalition government, *Political Geography*, 34, 10–23.

Cochrane, A. (1987) What a difference the place makes: the new structuralism of locality, *Antipode*, 19, 354–363.

Cooke, P. (1987) Clinical inference and geographical theory, *Antipode*, 19, 69–78.

Cooke, P. (ed.) (1989a) *Localities: The Changing Face of Urban Britain*, London: Unwin Hyman.

Cooke, P. (1989b) Locality-theory and the poverty of 'spatial variation', *Antipode*, 21, 261–273.

Cooke, P. (2006) Locality debates, Mimeograph, Centre for Advanced Urban Studies, Cardiff, Wales: Cardiff University.

Cooke, P. and Morgan, K. (1998) *The Associational Economy: Firms, Regions, and Innovation*, Oxford: Oxford University Press.

Cox, K. (1993) The local and the global in the new urban politics: a critical view, *Environment and Planning D: Society and Space*, 11, 433–448.

Cox, K. and Mair, A. (1991) From localised social structures to localities as agents, *Environment and Planning A*, 23, 197–213.

DCLG (Department for Communities and Local Government) (2011) *A Plain English Guide to the Localism Act*, London: DCLG.

Duncan, S. (1989) What is locality? in: Peet, R. and Thrift, N. (eds.) *New Models in Geography: Volume Two*, London: Unwin Hyman.

Duncan, S. and Savage, M. (1989) Space, scale and locality, *Antipode*, 21, 179–206.

Duncan, S. and Savage, M. (1991) New perspectives on the locality debate, *Environment and Planning A*, 23, 155–164.

Etherington, D. and Jones, M. (2009) City-regions: new geographies of uneven development and inequality, *Regional Studies*, 43, 247–265.

Gregson, N. (1987) The CURS initiative: some further comments, *Antipode*, 19, 364–370.

Hadjimichalis, C. (2006) Non-economic factors in economic geography and in 'new regionalism': a sympathetic critique, *International Journal of Urban and Regional Research*, 30, 690–704.

Harloe, M., Pickvance, C. and Urry, J. (eds.) (1990) *Place, Policy and Politics: Do Localities Matter?* London: Unwin Hyman.

Harrison, J. (2010) Networks of connectivity, territorial fragmentation, uneven development: the new politics of city-regionalism, *Political Geography*, 29, 17–27.

Harvey, D. (1969) *Explanation in Geography*, London: Arnold.

Harvey, D. (1987) Three myths in search of a reality in urban studies, *Environment and Planning D: Society and Space*, 5, 367–376.

Harvey, D. (1989) *The Condition of Postmodernity: An Enquiry into the Origins of Cultural Change*, Oxford: Blackwell.

Haughton, G., Deas, I. and Hincks, S. (2014) Making an impact: when agglomeration boosterism meets antiplanning rhetoric, *Environment and Planning A*, 46, 265–270.

Heley, J. and Jones, L. (2012) Relational rurals: some thoughts and relating things and theory in rural studies, *Journal of Rural Studies*, 28, 208–217.

HM Government (2010) *Local Growth: Realising Every Place's Potential*, London: HM Government.

HoC and BIS (House of Commons and Department for Business, Innovation and Skills) (2013) *Innovation and Skills Committee, Local Enterprise Partnerships: Ninth Report of Session 2012-13, HC 598*, London: The Stationery Office.

Jackson, P. (1991) Mapping meanings: a cultural critique of locality studies, *Environment and Planning A*, 23, 215–228.

Jonas, A. (1988) A new regional concept of localities, *Area*, 20, 101–110.

Jonas, A. (2012) Region and place: regionalism in question, *Progress in Human Geography*, 36, 263–272.

Jones, M. (2011) The local in the global, in: Leyshon, A., Lee, R., McDowell, L. and Sunley, P. (eds.) *The Sage Handbook of Economic Geography*, London: Sage.

Jones, M. (2013) It's like déjà vu, all over again, in: Ward, M. and Hardy, S. (eds.) *Where Next for Local Enterprise Partnerships*, London: Smith Institute.

Jones, M. and Jessop, B. (2010) Thinking state/space incompossibly, *Antipode*, 42, 1119–1149.

Jones, M. and MacLeod, G. (2004) Regional spaces, spaces of regionalism: territory, insurgent politics and the English question, *Transactions of the Institute of British Geographers*, 29, 433–452.

Jones, M. and MacLeod, G. (2011) Territorial/relational: conceptualizing spatial economic governance, in: Pike, A., Rodrigues-Pose, A. and Tomaney, J. (eds.) *Handbook of Local and Regional Development*, London: Routledge.

Jones, M. and Woods, M. (2013) New localities, *Regional Studies*, 47, 29–42.

Katz, C. (2001) On the grounds of globalization: a topography for feminist political engagement, *Signs*, 26, 1213–1234.

Keating, M. (1998) *The New Regionalism in Western Europe*, Cheltenham: Elgar.

Keating, M. (2013) *Rescaling the European State: The Making of Territory and the Rise of the Meso*, Oxford: Oxford University Press.

Lovering, J. (1989) The restructuring approach, in: Peet, R. and Thrift, N. (eds.) *New Models in Geography: Volume One*, London: Unwin Hyman.

Lovering, J. (1999) Theory led by policy: the inadequacies of the 'new regionalism' (illustrated from the case of Wales), *International Journal of Urban and Regional Research*, 23, 379–395.

MacLeod, G. (2001) New regionalism reconsidered: Globalization, regulation, and the recasting of political economic space, *International Journal of Urban and Regional Research*, 25, 804–829.

Marston, S., Jones, J.P. III and Woodward, K. (2005) Human geography without scale, *Transactions of the Institute of British Geographers*, 30, 416–432.

Massey, D. (1984) *Spatial Divisions of Labour: Social Structures and the Geography of Production*, Basingstoke, UK: Macmillan.

Massey, D. (1991) The political place of locality studies, *Environment and Planning A*, 23, 267–281.

Massey, D. (1994) *Space, Place and Gender*, Cambridge: Polity.

Massey, D. (2005) *For Space*, London: Sage.

Massey, D. (2007) *World City*, Cambridge: Polity.

Massey, D. (2011) A counterhegemonic relationality of place, in: McCann, E. and Ward, K. (eds.) *Mobile Urbanism: Cities and Policy-making in the Global Age*, Minneapolis, MN: University of Minnesota Press.

Mohan, G. and Stokke, K. (2000) Participatory development and empowerment: the dangers of localism, *Third World Quarterly*, 21, 247–268.

Mohan, J. (2012) Geographical foundations of the Big Society, *Environment and Planning A*, 44, 1121–1129.

Murgatroyd, L., Savage, M., Shapiro, D., Urry, J., Walby, S., Warde, A. and Mark-Lawson, J. (1985) *Localities, Class, and Gender*, London: Pion.

Norman, J. (2011) *The Big Society*, Buckingham: The University of Buckingham Press.

Paasi, A. (1991) Deconstructing regions: notes on the scales of spatial life, *Environment and Planning A*, 23, 239–256.

Painter, J. (2008) Cartographic anxiety and the search for regionality, *Environment and Planning A*, 40, 342–361.

Peck, J. (1995) Moving and shaking: business elites, state localism and urban privatism, *Progress in Human Geography*, 19, 16–46.

Pierce, J., Martin, D. and Murphy, J. (2011) Relational place-making: the networked politics of place, *Transactions of the Institute of British Geographers*, 36, 54–70.

Pratt A. (1991) Discourses of locality, *Environment and Planning A*, 23, 257–266.

Pratt, A. (2004) Andrew Sayer, in: Hubbard, P., Kitchin, R. and Valentine, G. (eds.) *Key Thinkers on Space and Place*, London: Sage.

Redwood, J. (2014) We were unanimous at Chequers: England needs a settlement of its own, *The Daily Telegraph*, 23 September, p. 2.

Savage, M. (2009) Townscapes and landscapes, Mimeograph, Department of Sociology, University of York, York, England.

Savage, M., Barlow, J., Duncan, S. and Saunders, P. (1987) Locality research: the Sussex programme on economic restructuring, social change and the locality, *Quarterly Journal of Social Affairs*, 3, 27–51.

Savage, M. and Duncan, S. (1990) Space, scale and locality: a reply to Cooke and Ward, *Antipode*, 22, 67–72.

Sayer, A. (1991) Behind the locality debate: deconstructing geography's dualisms, *Environment and Planning A*, 23, 283–308.

Scott, A. (1988) *New Industrial Spaces: Flexible Production Organisation and Regional Development in North America and Western Europe*, London: Pion.

Scott, A. (1991) Book review: Philip Cooke (ed.) Localities: The Changing Face of Urban Britain, *Antipode*, 23, 256–257.

Scott, A. (2001) Globalization and the rise of city-regions, *European Planning Studies*, 9, 813–826.

Sheffield City Region LEP (2013) *Regional Growth Plan Update*, Sheffield: Sheffield City Region LEP.

Smith, N. (1987) Dangers of the empirical turn: some comments on the CURS initiative, *Antipode*, 19, 59–68.

Storper, M. (1997) *The Regional World: Territorial Development in a Global Economy*, New York: Guilford Press.

Storper, M. and Scott, A. (eds.) (1992) *Pathways to Industrialization and Regional Development*, London: Routledge.

Tomaney, J. (2007) Keep a beat in the dark: narratives of regional identity in Basil Bunting's Briggflatts, *Environment and Planning D*, 25, 355–375.

Ward, M. and Hardy, S. (eds.) (2013) *Where Next for Local Enterprise Partnerships*, London: Smith Institute.

Warde, A. (1989) A recipe for a pudding: a comment on locality, *Antipode*, 21, 274–281.

Willetts, D. (1994) *Civic Conservatism*, London: Social Market Foundation.

Woods, M. (2007) Engaging the global countryside: globalization, hybridity and the reconstitution of rural place, *Progress in Human Geography*, 31, 485–507.

3 Evolving conceptions of regional policy in Europe and their influence across different territorial scales

Philip O'Brien, Olivier Sykes and David Shaw

Introduction

This chapter explores evolving approaches to territorial policy and governance within the context of the European Union's (EU) Cohesion Policy. The chapter traces evolving conceptions and models of regional policy in Europe, paying attention to the emergence of place-based and territorial approaches to promoting development and exploring the ways in which they have been manifested in reforms of the EU's Cohesion Policy and the restructuring of sub-national policy and governance in England. The chapter addresses, in turn, the emergence of a 'place-based' approach to regional policy within the context of debates around whether to tailor public investments to specific places or to use similar investments across the national space; how such a place-based approach has been adopted in recent reforms to the EU Cohesion Policy; and the representation of place-based and territorial approaches to development in the context of state rescaling in England, with reference to the case of the Liverpool City Region.

Contemporary reform of territorial governance and regional policy arrangements relates to a wave of economic restructuring that has taken place in Europe and the USA from the 1980s onwards, as nation states have been forced to adapt an industrial model rendered increasingly ineffective under conditions of rapidly integrating international trade. The closed space of the nation state was intrinsic to Keynesian approaches to economic regulation, where common currency, laws and institutions, together with trade tariffs across international borders, permitted containment of fiscal interventions and the possibility of common dialogue between state, capital and labour (Radice, 1984; Martin and Sunley, 1997). With increasing economic globalisation, the model of achieving a spatially even pattern of development and distribution of the proceeds of national growth, dubbed 'spatial Keynesianism' (Martin and Sunley, 1997), was called into question. This took effect particularly in respect to wages in manufacturing regions, which were rendered uncompetitive by international standards, and to the precept of demand management, which became less effective as demand for goods produced at home was increasingly fulfilled abroad and vice versa.

The (re-)emergence of the region as an economic, social and political unit has been in large part a response to this challenge to the effectiveness of the nation state as the institutional scale of choice for the territorial organisation of social and economic processes. The breakdown of the spatially redistributive model of government that characterised post-war Keynesianism and the dislocation of cities and regions from national systems of state-controlled planning and development has, according to the new regionalist literature, allowed regions to acquire agency beyond their national borders as actors within the global economy, becoming economic, social, political and institutional spaces in their own right (Keating, 1998). The role played by the state in this process has been characterised as a transition from the promotion of spatial convergence within a strongly conceptualised national space to the endorsement of particular places as growth nodes within a global network of capital and labour. The primary task of the state is now the provision of the spatially fixed prerequisites for growth, such as infrastructure and basic scientific research (Brenner, 1999, 2004). The following sections relate the history and practice of regional policy to the wider trends in economic geography just outlined.

Towards a paradigm shift in regional policy? The emergence of the 'place-based' approach

The period since the early 2000s has seen significant reform to territorial policy and governance arrangements across the EU and its member states (see, for example, Bachtler, 2001). Agenda-setting reports by the The Organisation for Economic Co-operation and Development (OECD) (OECD, 2009a, 2009b), the European Commission (Barca, 2009), the Corporación Andina de Fomento (CAF, 2010) and the World Bank (2009) saw debates about regional development policy increasingly revolve around 'space-neutral' or 'place-based' approaches (Barca *et al.*, 2012). The former was advocated by the World Bank (2009), which highlighted the importance of cities and regions in development, following the logic of the New Economic Geography in understanding growth as intrinsically uneven and the result of agglomeration, often underpinned by an active local or regional state (Gill, 2010). As a result, the report advocated improvements in the basic institutions of law and order, regulation of land, labour and property markets, macro-economic stability and the provision of basic services such as education and health. Such improvements were described as being 'spatially-blind' in order to make the point that they were not tailored to particular places and thus were intended to facilitate the movement of capital and labour according to market conditions rather than policy choices (World Bank, 2009). Once these improvements have been achieved, the issue of spreading the efficiency gains made can be addressed using an openly spatial approach, by investing in connective infrastructure in order to encourage market integration by reducing travel times to more prosperous places, while using spatially targeted interventions as an ancillary tool, reserved for where economic and social problems exist within cities and regions. In this way, it is suggested, aggregate growth is promoted in the most efficient way possible, while labour mobility between lagging and leading regions ensures that the proceeds are shared more equitably (World Bank, 2009).

The place-based approach is articulated in reports by the OECD (OECD, 2009a, 2009b), the European Commission (Barca, 2009) and the Corporación Andina de Fomento (CAF, 2010), as part of what Bachtler (2010) terms a 'new paradigm' of regional policy. The use of place-based interventions by policymakers is not new; for instance, Regional Selective Assistance, a business-grant policy used in the United Kingdom since the 1970s, targets areas based on measures of unemployment and per capita Gross Domestic Product (GDP), while similar examples exist across Europe and in the form of the European Union Structural Funds. Theoretical treatment of place-based policies has focused on the tendency for intangible capital to be generated by locally specific factors and combinations of factors (Bolton, 1992), as well as on the case for place-based interventions where market failures exist (Kline and Moretti, 2012). In particular, these may be due to phenomena such as the immobility of capital, labour and land, the monopoly power granted by space, fixed costs as a barrier to market entry and exit, the existence of spatially bound externalities and the distance-decay effect present in knowledge (Kilkenny and Kraybill, 2003). Critics, however, have charged advocates of place-based interventions with failing to come to terms with the inherently unbalanced nature of growth (Gill, 2010), of protectionism carried out by powerful local interests, of misattributing wage differences to areas rather than individuals (Gibbons *et al.*, 2010), of encouraging poor people to remain in poor areas (Glaeser and Gottlieb, 2008) and of increasing economic activity in less productive regions (Glaeser, 2008).

The underlying premise of the place-based approach endorsed by the European Commission (Barca, 2009) is that economic and social behaviours are fundamentally embedded in place and, as such, are subject to local economic, social, cultural and institutional contexts. In the post-Fordist knowledge economy, this is of particular importance because the exchange of untraded interdependencies that is vital for competitive firms is dependent on contextual factors and therefore varies markedly between places (McCann and Rodríguez-Pose, 2011). 'Underdevelopment' – the failure of regions to make productive use of the resources available to them (Farole *et al.*, 2011) – occurs primarily due to a failure to deliver effective investments and institutions, the consequence either of local elites being unable or unwilling to do so or because of flows of capital and labour out of the region following a process of agglomeration (Barca, 2009).

The debate between advocates of place-based and spatially blind approaches to regional development that ensued (Scott, 2009; Gill, 2010; Barca and McCann, 2010; Garcilazo *et al.*, 2010; Rodríguez-Pose, 2010; Murphy, 2011; van Oort, 2011) appears to rest on two differences in assumptions in relation to the causal factors behind the process of agglomeration (Kim, 2011) and the resulting degree of efficiency derived from regional policy measures. Where agglomerations are the result of market forces, public investment in other areas is said to be inefficient and can be justified solely from an equity perspective. Thus, in the name of an optimal distribution of mobile factors, it is argued that regional development should take the form of spatially blind investments that support market-driven agglomerations (World Bank, 2009; Gill, 2010; Glaeser, 2011). However, if the process of agglomeration is strongly affected by non-market forces, the determination that large urban centres are the most productive is problematic. The inference is that spatially blind investments are rarely spatially neutral (McCann and Rodríguez-Pose, 2011) and, moreover, that they frequently encourage the active promotion of particular cities at the expense of others. These debates have been echoed in recent dialogue on spatial policy in the UK context (Haughton *et al.*, 2014; Overman, 2014).

Purportedly spatially blind policies may, in fact, have strong differential effects over space (Barca, 2009), as incentives are granted to industries whose presence is stronger in some regions than in others, or transport investments are made solely where there is shown to be a demand-oriented case, reinforcing existing agglomerations rather than investing in the growth of lagging regions. Additionally, private investments are frequently made in concert with public investments, due to the need for public goods and services to make possible the efficient functioning of the markets in which private actors exist, whether over the medium and long term in education and training or potentially more directly in urban and land-use planning. The result is a process of cumulative causation, in which state and private investment occur iteratively (Barca, 2009).

Research by the OECD (OECD, 2009a, 2009b, 2012) similarly eschews the notion that there is an inevitable trade-off between equity and efficiency as investment aims, noting that, while the contribution to aggregate growth made by individual non-core regions is small, the sum of the contribution of the 'long tail' of regions makes up a significant share (OECD, 2012). As a result, small improvements in productivity across a range of non-core regions make a significant additional contribution to aggregate growth (Garcilazo, 2011). Given that all regions show potential for growth and that different bottlenecks exist in different regions (OECD, 2009a), an effective policy approach that simultaneously addresses equity and efficiency concerns requires the provision of 'integrated bundles of investments', tailored according to local knowledge that is the product of a deliberative process involving a range of actors (Barca, 2011). This approach is thus dependent on open and inclusive stakeholder engagement and improvements in the functioning of local institutions (Barca, 2009).

The justifications for, and the fundamental premise of, the place-based or territorial approach advocated by the OECD and the European Commission, are reflected in the gradual evolution of regional policy. This has progressed from a top-down approach that was primarily concerned with influencing the location of industry via mechanisms such as subsidies and infrastructure investment, with the aim of reducing spatial inequality, to a place-based model that seeks to influence an array of regionally embedded factors considered to influence growth through an approach designed and operated by local institutions. The aim here is not regional convergence but the fulfilment of regional potentials for growth. As Bachtler (2010) explains, this paradigm shift is the culmination of two decades or more of evolution in the design of policy, and it is the combined result of a number of factors, including the perceived failure of the previous model of regional policy and its replacement by new approaches which recognise the place-contingent nature of economic and institutional factors (Bachtler and Yuill, 2001; Garcilazo, 2011; Farole *et al.*, 2011; Barca *et al.*, 2012). The paradigm shift has also been driven by the increasingly restricted ability of the nation state to influence the spatial distribution of growth in an era of rapidly increasing integration of global trade. This has meant that regions have increasingly been seen to have supplanted nation states, as a transition from Fordist to post-Fordist production systems has taken root (Piore and Sabel, 1984; Amin, 1994) and as territorial governance has strengthened in line with 'new regionalist' thinking (Keating, 1997; MacLeod, 2001). This view has, however, come to be seen as an oversimplified reading of economic trends and political power, leading to an oversimplified reading of the decline of the nation state when in fact what is occurring may be more akin to a restructuring (Lovering, 1999; Jessop, 2000).

A number of dimensions of the new paradigm of regional policy in practice can be identified, which can be usefully contrasted with equivalent features of antecedent approaches to regional policy, as detailed in Table 3.1.

These dimensions are observable to a greater or lesser degree across a number of European countries as part of the ongoing paradigm shift, and in the reform of the EU Structural Funds, which have increasingly promoted a place-based approach (Bachtler, 2001; Elias, 2008; Garcilazo, 2011). Indeed, a considerable influence has come from the EU. For instance, this has occurred through EU competition policy, which has limited the extent to which governments are able to

Table 3.1 Old and new paradigms of regional policy

	Old paradigm	*New paradigm*
Instruments	Sectoral interventions and industry incentives	Strategic frameworks and plans are to align diverse policy fields to address a wide range of factors influencing growth
Resources	Exogenous investments	Endogenous assets
Policy goals	Inter-regional convergence; addressing disadvantage	Growth and competitiveness; addressing opportunity and potential
Spatial scales	Bounded administrative units	A range of different spatial scales and an emphasis on networking and connections between places
Spatial focus	Lagging regions	All regions
Institutional basis	Central government, local and/or regional administration	Strengthened sub-national tiers of government, sometimes with devolved powers; multi-level governance; use of multiple stakeholders
Timescale	Open-ended	Programmatic approach using multi-annual programming periods
Evaluation	*Ex post*	*Ex ante*, interim, *ex post*; increased focus on accountability and learning

Sources: Bachtler and Yuill, 2001; OECD, 2009b; Bachtler, 2010.

use subsidies or bid for Foreign Direct Investment. EU influence has also been evident more directly in the shape of its Cohesion Policy on national and regional strategies (Bachtler, 2010), as well as through the engagement of a wider range of actors and the development and strengthening of sub-national levels of government (Leonardi, 2005). EU Cohesion Policy clearly exhibits a number of facets of the new paradigm in advocating horizontal coordination, through the partnership principle, and vertical coordination, through the operational programmes. In the 1988 reforms, the latter established shared goals over multi-fund, multi-annual agreements between national and regional levels of government. The focus on factors such as innovation, productivity and skills, over inter-regional convergence, has also been echoed by the competitiveness agenda of the EU's Lisbon and Europe 2020 strategies (Bachtler, 2010).

The addition of territorial cohesion to the existing objectives of economic and social cohesion in the preamble of the European Union Treaty formalises the focus on place which permeates the reform of the Structural Funds (CEC, 2010). Inter-governmental agreements such as the two Territorial Agenda documents (German Presidency, 2007; Hungarian Presidency, 2011) are also imbued with thinking which resonates with the new paradigm of regional policy. The Territorial Agenda 2020 (Hungarian Presidency, 2011, p. 4), for example, states that 'we believe that territorial cohesion … enables equal opportunities for citizens and enterprises, wherever they are located, to make the most of their territorial potentials' and that 'territorial cohesion complements solidarity mechanisms with a qualitative approach and clarifies that development opportunities are best tailored to the specificities of an area'. Waterhout (2007) has identified a number of key themes underpinning the idea of territorial cohesion which capture both its substantive spatial objectives and a desire to ensure that sectoral and territorial policies are complementary. Again, as illustrated by Table 3.2, these embody assumptions that are consistent with the characteristics of the new paradigm of regional policy.

The place-based approach and the reform of EU Cohesion Policy

The new paradigm and the notion of place-based development advocated in the Barca Report (2009), and already implicitly present in the Cohesion Policy since the 1988 reforms, are aspects of an ongoing concern with space and territory in the EU, manifested in the Cohesion Policy and in the concept of territorial cohesion. The Barca Report (2009) has been characterised as an attempt by the Commission to re-legitimise the Cohesion Policy and to provide a more solid basis from which to defend it during the budget negotiations for the 2014–20 Multi-annual Financial Framework of the EU. Mendez (2013) detects a fluid spreading of the place-based development discourse throughout the Cohesion Policy community, citing the appearance of the term in speeches, European Commission papers and reports, EU Presidency Initiatives, member-state consultation responses, European Observation Network for Territorial Development

Table 3.2 Dimensions of the new regional policy paradigm, EU territorial and development themes and domestic policy and initiatives in England (2014)

Dimensions of the new regional-policy paradigm	EU territorial cohesion 'Storyline' (Waterhout 2007)	EU sustainability/ 'Europe 2020' dimensions	Policies and initiatives in England (post-2010)
Emphasis on regional potential, rather than national convergence, and encouraging opportunity, rather than addressing disadvantage. Growth occurs in different sorts of regions and the contribution to overall growth made by the long tail of regions is noted.	'Europe in Balance' – addressing regional disparities, securing universal access to services of general interest and promoting a 'polycentric' pattern of development in Europe.	Society/inclusive growth.	There is a stated aspiration to 'rebalance' the national economy, reducing reliance on sectors such as financial services and fostering more spatially balanced growth (HM Treasury and BIS, 2011, p. 11). Major infrastructure projects, such as the High Speed 2 (HS2) railway line, are being justified, at least in part, against the goal of promoting more balanced regional competitiveness and growth (Department for Transport, 2013). The links between sectoral rebalancing and spatial rebalancing are, however, not clearly articulated in government documents (Wong et al., 2012).
Integrated spatial approach to be achieved through 'bundles' of interventions drawn from across a range of sectors, tailored to specific places.	'Coherent European Policy' – securing effective horizontal coordination of EU policies so that these do not generate contradictory territorial impacts 'on the ground'.	Integration of sustainability elements/ development of territorial impact assessment.	Planning's wider integrative role in relation to public policy has been downplayed since the arrival in power of the coalition government in 2010. The National Planning Policy Framework (NPPF) does, however, task the planning system with delivering across the dimensions of sustainability.

(Continued)

Table 3.2 (Continued)

Dimensions of the new regional-policy paradigm	EU territorial cohesion 'Storyline' (Waterhout 2007)	EU sustainability/ 'Europe 2020' dimensions	Policies and initiatives in England (post-2010)
Existence of trade-offs between equity and efficiency aims of regional policy, thus acceptance of some degree of uneven growth as necessary and beneficial. Nevertheless, growth occurs in different sorts of regions and the contribution to overall growth made by the long tail of regions is noted.	*'Competitive Europe'* – focusing on competitiveness in the global context by fostering the diverse territorial potential/capital of places in Europe so that they can 'make the most' of their intrinsic attributes.	Economy/ smart growth.	A concern with competitiveness and growth has inspired a range of policies, including improving the United Kingdom's infrastructure, cutting red tape, root and branch reform of the planning system and boosting trade and inward investment' (HM Treasury and BIS, 2013, p. 1). The NPPF sees the planning system as having 'an economic role– contributing to building a strong, responsive and competitive economy' stating that '*development* means growth' (italics in original) and that 'we must accommodate the new ways by which we will earn our living in a competitive world' (DCLG, 2012, p. i). Initiatives aimed at promoting growth and competitiveness at sub-national level (e.g. Local Enterprise Partnerships, or LEPs) have synergies with the place-based approach and EU territorial development thinking, and draw on similar notions of 'tailoring' policy and intervention scales to make the most of the intrinsic attributes of places (Heseltine, 2012, p. 9).
Addresses sustainability as an objective alongside efficiency and equity, seeking to identify trade-offs and exploit complementarities between these, based on analysis of place-specific conditions.	*'Clean and Green' Europe* – relating to sustainable development and management of the natural environment, including climate change, environmental protection and sustainable energy production.	Environment/ sustainable growth.	The NPPF explicitly states that 'the purpose of the planning system is to contribute to the achievement of sustainable development' and makes reference to three forms of EU-related impact assessment: Environmental Impact Assessment, Habitats Regulations Assessment and Flood Risk Assessment') (DCLG, 2012, p. i, 45). There was an initial post-2010 emphasis on 'Green Growth' and there are some examples of initiatives to further this.

and Cohesion (ESPON) research outputs and among researchers more widely. The model of regional development policy discussed by Barca (2009) emphasised the importance of strong regional governance (often on a multi-level basis), with stakeholder participation a part of a network-based approach.

The reforms to the Structural Funds for the 2014–20 programming period can be understood within this context, as the place-based approach has made its influence felt alongside other stimuli for change, such as the need to make more efficient use of the funds in the context of the Europe-wide fiscal crisis and the budget debate, as well as the criticisms of the delivery of the Funds as being too fragmented and administratively too complex. Increased strategic coherence of the funds is to be sought through integration into a Common Strategic Framework of the Cohesion Fund (CF), the European Regional Development Fund (ERDF), the European Social Fund (ESF), the European Agricultural Fund for Rural Development (EAFRD) and the European Maritime and Fisheries Fund (EMFF). Hence, as part of a simplification agenda, these funding streams will be delivered in a more integrated manner and, in theory, will be better targeted at the needs of particular places. Yet, this integration of funds, together with the thematic concentration on a relatively small number of priorities that are consistent with the Europe 2020 agenda of 'smart sustainable and inclusive growth' (CEC, 2010) (see Table 3.3), could also be seen to represent the Commission's desire to formulate developmental policy at higher territorial scales. Trans-national, national and regional bodies who seek European funding need to frame their overarching strategies around the Europe 2020 themes, focusing on no more than four of the 11 sub-priorities shown in Table 3.3.

Table 3.3 European priorities within the community-support framework

Smart growth	1	Strengthening research, technological development and innovation;
	2	Enhancing access to, and use and quality of, information and communication technologies;
	3	Enhancing the competitiveness of small and medium-sized enterprises, the agricultural sector (for the EAFRD) and the fisheries and aquaculture sector (for the EMFF);
Sustainable growth	4	Supporting the shift towards a low-carbon economy in all sectors;
	5	Promoting climate-change adaptation, risk prevention and management;
	6	Protecting the environment and promoting resource efficiency;
	7	Promoting sustainable transport and removing bottlenecks in key network infrastructures;
Inclusive growth	8	Promoting employment and supporting labour mobility;
	9	Promoting social inclusion and combating poverty;
	10	Investing in education, skills and lifelong learning;
	11	Enhancing institutional capacity and an efficient public administration.

These strategic reforms are supplemented by an increased focus on performance, addressed by imposing *ex ante* and *ex post* conditions that will govern the initial disbursal of funds and the issuing of additional, performance-based, funds. The reorientation of the funds from convergence to competitiveness is also redolent of aspects of the place-based approach. It is consistent, too, with the previous Lisbon and Europe 2020 agendas, so it clearly does not originate solely from debates in the late 2000s about the future of Cohesion Policy. Mendez (2013) notes, for example, that the Commission has acknowledged that it has used the discourse of competitiveness as a way of tying the Cohesion Policy to Europe 2020.

The scope for local and regional autonomy, meanwhile, is addressed through what is referred to in the policy guidance as 'territorial development', an aim to be achieved primarily through the territorial instruments, which allow for cross-sectoral and cross- (administrative) border interventions within and across operational programmes. These comprise Community-Led Local Development (CLLD), Integrated Territorial Investments (ITIs) and sustainable urban development. CLLDs adopt the Liaison Entre Actions pour le Développement de l'Economie Rurale (LEADER) approach already used in rural development, facilitating the use of multi-dimensional and cross-sectoral interventions within place-based strategies as a way of addressing needs in particular sub-regions, and undertaken by local partnerships of public and private socio-economic actors. ITIs constitute recognition that the space over which interventions are effective is not necessarily congruent with the boundaries within which an operational programme is implemented. Their implementation is appropriately flexible, with administration to be delegated to intermediate bodies such as Regional Development Agencies (RDAs), local authorities or NGOs. Resources are ring-fenced for interventions that address sustainable urban development, with mechanisms for knowledge transfer in the case of innovative actions.

Partnership Agreements between member states and the Commission should outline how the Funds will be used in an integrated way to address the territorial development needs of different regions and sub-regions. They should also be used, where necessary, to describe the particular characteristics of the territories covered (whether urban, rural, cross-border or with particular needs such as especially low or high population density). The territorial instruments thus introduce geographical and scalar variety into the use of the Funds, allowing interventions to be tailored to specificities of place and scale. 'Smart Specialisation' is a major element of the Europe 2020 strategy, providing an additional tool for place-based policy. It is intended to guide investment in education, research and innovation and development in order that they help achieve a low-carbon economy, promote economic competitiveness and encourage a socially more cohesive society in line with Europe 2020 (CEC, 2010) goals.

The notion of 'Smart Specialisation' as a framework for innovation intervention has, therefore, shifted from a sectoral logic towards a place-based one. Yet, while the thematic consistency with Europe 2020 echoes the emphasis on competitiveness in the place-based approach, the alignment of Cohesion Policy with a limited number of sectoral objectives may come to detract from its territorial aspect. The Commission's position papers, in which the list of priorities for funding offered to each member state was further restricted, also assume a degree of national internal coherence that may not exist. The subordination of territorial logic to thematic or sectoral principles may remove the necessary freedom to tailor interventions to local context (Mendez, 2013).

This European context for Structural Funds is then operationalised within national contexts, and most of the monies (94%) are supposed to be allocated based on the characteristics of the regions. Sixty-eight per cent of the Structural Funds budget is allocated to the so-called 'Less Developed Regions' (previously known as 'Objective 1 areas') where GDP per head is less than 75% of the EU figure. The 'Transition Regions' are those regions where the GDP per capita is between 75% and 90% of the EU average, accounting for a further 11.6% of the Structural Fund budget. The 'More Developed Regions' (which in the United Kingdom account for most of the state territory) receive an allocation of 15.8% of the budget. The remaining budget is to be spent on the Cohesion Fund allocations targeted on those countries where GDP per head is less than 90% of the EU average, the promotion of cross-border and trans-national cooperation between partners in more than one state and support to Europe's outermost regions. The following section considers the context for the administration and delivery of development policy and the EU Structural Funds in the United Kingdom, with a particular focus on England.

Administering the Structural Funds in a rescaling context: the case of England

Adoption of the EU's language of territorial cohesion/development in England has tended to be restricted, but there are some echoes of place-based development and territorial cohesion themes in domestic thinking on planning and economic development/regeneration. For example, some of the arguments pursued in a major report by Michael Heseltine produced for the 2010–15 coalition government – *No Stone Unturned in Pursuit of Growth* (Heseltine, 2012) – echoed the thinking of earlier OECD and EU discussions on place-based approaches and territorial development (see Table 3.1). Heseltine's report refers explicitly to the place-based approach, emphasising the importance of what is termed local 'conditioning qualities' and the 'vital role of government and the public sector in securing essential public services and facilitating the growth of the economy' (Heseltine, 2012, p. 5). The view that development policy is best pursued at the level of economically 'functional' (e.g. city-regional) geographies can also be found justifying domestic initiatives in England such as LEPs City Deals and further devolution of powers and resources through the creation of combined city-regional authorities.

As regards the implementation of the EU Structural Funds, within the United Kingdom this task is subdivided between the four devolved administrations: England, Wales, Scotland and Northern Ireland. A Partnership Agreement between the UK government and the European Commission articulates, in broad strategic terms, how the allocation of European Structural Funds in the United Kingdom will be used. In England, the new EU programmes are being launched in a context where the governance of spatial planning and economic development has become more local and more national in recent years, in the wake of the demise, after 2010, of most of the regional tier of governance, the RDAs. The result is that spatial planning is now focussed more on the neighbourhood scale, linked to government's programme of localism (DCLG, 2014). Furthermore, with the abolition of the RDAs by the 2010–15 coalition government, the prime focus of economic-development policy and activity has now shifted to the sub-regional scale. The responsibility for designing locally specific growth programmes and priorities was given to a network of 39 LEPs: new sub-regional private-public partnerships designed primarily to identify local priorities and facilitate local economic growth.

The Operational Programme for England was finally signed off by the European Commission in late June 2015, and, hence, it is still too early to be clear on how it will operate in practice. But local growth strategies developed by each LEP provide the broader strategic context within which European funding is to be used. EU funds in England are administered centrally, but guided by locally determined priorities which have been articulated by European Structural and Investment Fund Strategies (ESIFs) developed for each LEP area. In developing their ESIFs, the LEPs have gone through a process where the critical assets and transformational opportunities for their sub-region have been identified. From this, locally specific priorities for investment have been prioritised, to develop the local physical infrastructure (mainly through ERDF funding) and improve the human capital (through ESF) to bring about transformational change in the locality. In other words, European funding is intended to become much more focused, either to exploit opportunities for, or overcome bottlenecks or barriers to, growth based on the indigenous strengths and weaknesses of the LEP areas. The local strategies that have been developed, therefore, build on the specificities of different places (see Box 3.1 for an illustrative discussion of the case of one LEP area: the Liverpool City Region).

Box 3.1 Identifying place-based priorities for the use of EU Structural Funds: the case of the Liverpool City Region

In the Liverpool City Region (LCR), a former Objective 1 area and now a 'Transitional Region', the local growth strategies seek to articulate a narrative of opportunity that emphasises the potential of the place, rather than emphasising uneven national development to justify a case for redistribution. Indeed, it is argued in the LCR 'European Structural and Investment Fund Strategy' that 'the scale, growth potential and unique mix of assets and market facing opportunities mean Liverpool City Region can be a driver of national economic growth' (Liverpool City Region Local Enterprise Partnership, 2016, p. 6). The real challenges the area faces are also discussed. In 2011, Gross Value Added (GVA) per capita within the LCR remained at about 75% of the national average (£15,600 compared with a UK average of £20,900). This in turn leaves a £8.2 billion gap in the spending power of its residents. To bring the city-region to the national average, the number of new businesses needs to increase by about 18,500 and some 90,000 new jobs need to be created (Liverpool City Region Local Enterprise Partnership, 2016, p. 16). In responding to this context, the goal over the 2014–20 EU programming period is to concentrate on 'Focused Action Exploiting Key Assets and Opportunities'. An evaluation of the latter in the LCR has led to the development of a strategy that identifies and focuses on five key areas of activity or 'portfolios':

The Blue/Green Economy is based around the Liverpool City Region's maritime location and the potential for the Super PORT to help deliver a rebalancing of Britain as promoted by Heseltine and Leahy (2011). Linked to this are logistic functions associated with trade and the potential for the development of new jobs based around the low-carbon economy.

The Business Economy priority is designed to create the context within which entrepreneurialism can flourish, whether in terms of creating new businesses in the city-region or attracting businesses to locate some of their activity within the city-region.

The Innovation Economy focuses on harnessing the innovation potential of the key economic sectors outlined to drive growth.

The Inclusive Economy is designed to try and address some of the very deep-seated issues of social exclusion amongst, in particular, the young and long-term unemployed and ensure that the skill needs of existing and future businesses can be better met.

Place and Connectivity complements the other four priorities and seeks to improve the infrastructure to support economic growth and limited place marketing (Liverpool City Region Local Enterprise Partnership, 2016, pp. 16–17).

It is recognised that European funding alone will not deliver the transformational change which is sought in the area and there will be a need to work with other agencies and funding streams (including the private sector) to deliver the change.

This section has provided an overview of current policy approaches to promoting territorial development in England. It seems clear that there are shared themes between influential documents, policies and initiatives in England, and the OECD- and EU-promoted models of place-based and territorial development. Table 3.2 provides an indicative illustration of some of the commonalities which exist between the assumptions, goals and policy approaches of the latter, and the policies and initiatives adopted since 2010 in England.

Conclusion

This chapter has considered the shifting underpinnings of explicitly spatial public intervention that seeks to promote territorial development. It has traced how the assumptions and end goals of regional policy have gradually come under the influence of new ways of thinking about the reasons for the relative success of different places in developing themselves. The shift from top-down and redistributive forms of regional policy towards more endogenous models has been discussed. Similarly, the chapter has also discussed the EU Cohesion Policy's increasing emphasis on fostering the development of territories by encouraging them to look to, and build on, their intrinsic attributes and strengths. New approaches to regional and (at the urban scale) regeneration policies have been characterised by a strong emphasis on place and space. The territorial, or place-based, dimension is being put forward as a means of delivering the most effective and efficient forms of investment in local and regional growth. This is often associated with arguments about the importance of developing policy for 'functional territories' and spaces, something which may require a rescaling and/or redrawing of existing spatial boundaries. The development of new spatial strategies at the EU cross-border, inter-regional and macro-scales, or within states at the intermediate city-regional scale between localities and larger regions, has thus typically been grounded in arguments about the need to formulate and pursue development policy at scales, and within boundaries, which reflect functional or 'pertinent' geographies. Such reasoning can be found in EU documents such as the *Fifth Report on Economic, Social and Territorial Cohesion* (CEC, 2010), or in England where it finds a strong echo in the discourse of the 2000s and 2010s on city-regions and initiatives such as the LEPs. It is therefore possible to talk of converging models of regional policy with similarities in thinking between the territorial development approaches advocated by EU-level documents and a number of domestic policies and initiatives.

The chapter went on to consider the situation in England, where the government has stated it wants to see more balance in the national economy. Documents such as the Heseltine Report articulate assumptions on local/sub-regional growth which are redolent of the new place-based regional policy paradigm and the EU territorial cohesion/development debate. Following the abolition of the RDAs in England, LEPs efforts to promote growth have included place-based approaches supported in part by EU Structural Funds targeted at achieving the EU's sustainability and territorial cohesion goals.

At the EU level, the consecration of the new place-based and territorial paradigm of regional policy in the later 2000s has also coincided with a period in which the financial and economic crisis has led to a reduction of the resources available for future disbursement through Cohesion Policy. In England, the coalition government which came to power in 2010 has placed more emphasis on local autonomy, but there is a contrast between the rhetoric about devolving power and resources and the heavy budget cuts which will see local government budgets cut by 28% between 2011 and 2015, with local authorities with the highest levels of need being most badly affected (Hastings *et al.*, 2015). This is particularly important in England as local government funding overwhelmingly originates from central government and has been cut significantly – by 26% in revenue terms and 45% in capital terms from 2010 to 2015 (Clarke and Cochrane, 2013). Such issues point to the need to further unpack and understand the role of, or the 'work' done by, the new paradigm of regional policy in the context of the current political economic settlement in Europe and other areas with advanced liberal economies. The place-based approach was developed in part as a response to arguments that place-blind policy and regulation is a more efficient way for the state to ensure higher growth at the aggregate level. It has been championed by those who have sought to defend place-based policies, such as the EU Cohesion Policy, from the spatially inchoate models and place-blind policy prescriptions of their critics. It is, therefore, somewhat ironic, though perhaps not entirely surprising, that the 'new paradigm' of regional policy is being melded with a discourse of localism to legitimate an austerity-driven approach to territorial development. In the style of the Western Emperor Honorius's rescript to the Romano-British in AD 410, the approach here is one of instructing local and regional spaces to *'look to your own defences'*.

References

Amin, A. (1994) Post-Fordism: models, fantasies and phantoms of transition, in: Amin, A. (ed.) *Post-Fordism: A Reader*, Oxford: Blackwell.

Bachtler, J. (2001) *Where Is Regional Policy Going? Changing Concepts of Regional Policy*, Glasgow: EPRC, University of Strathclyde.

Bachtler, J. (2010) Place-based policy and regional development in Europe, *Horizons*, 10, 54–58.

Bachtler, J. and Yuill, D. (2001) Policies and strategies for regional development: a shift in paradigm? *Regional and Industrial Policy Research Paper Number 46*, Glasgow: EPRC, University of Strathclyde.

Barca, F. (2009) *An Agenda for a Reformed Cohesion Policy: A Place-Based Approach to Meeting European Union Challenges and Expectations*, independent report prepared at the request of the European Commissioner for Regional Policy, Danuta Hübner. Available: http://ec.europa.eu/regional_policy/archive/policy/future/barca_en.htm (accessed 2 July 2015).

Barca, F. (2011) Alternative approaches to development policy: intersections and divergences, in: *OECD, Regional Outlook 2011*, Paris: OECD.

Barca, F. and McCann, P. (2010) The Place-Based Approach: a Response to Mr Gill. Available: http://www.voxeu.org/article/regional-development-policies-place-based-or-people-centred (accessed 2 July 2015).

Barca, F., McCann, P. and Rodríguez-Pose, A. (2012) The case for regional development intervention: place-based versus place-neutral approaches, *Journal of Regional Science*, 52, 134–152.

Bolton, R. (1992) 'Place prosperity vs. people prosperity' revisited: an old issue with a new angle, *Urban Studies*, 29, 185–203.

Brenner, N. (1999) Globalisation as reterritorialisation: the rescaling of urban governance in the European Union, *Urban Studies*, 36, 431–451.

Brenner, N. (2004) *New State Spaces*, Oxford: Oxford University Press.

CAF (Corporación Andina de Fomento) (2010) *Desarrollo local: Hacia un nuevo Protagonismo de las Ciudades y Regiones*, Caracas: CAF.

CEC (Commission of the European Communities) (2010) Fifth Report on Economic, Social and Territorial Cohesion: Investing in Europe's Future, Brussels: CEC. Available: http://ec.europa.eu/regional_policy/sources/docoffic/official/reports/cohesion5/pdf/5cr_en.pdf (accessed 21 October 2016).

Clarke, N. and Cochrane, A. (2013) Geographies and politics of localism: the localism of the United Kingdom's coalition government, *Political Geography*, 34, 10–23.

DCLG (Department for Communities and Local Government) (2012) *National Planning Policy Framework*, London: DCLG.

DCLG (Department for Communities and Local Government) (2014) Technical Consultation on Planning, London: DCLG. Available: www.gov.uk/government/uploads/system/uploads/attachment_data/file/339528/Technical_consultation_on_planning.pdf (accessed 2 July 2015).

Department for Transport (2013) *The Strategic Case for HS2*, London: Department for Transport. Available: www.gov.uk/government/uploads/system/uploads/attachment_data/file/260525/strategic-case.pdf (accessed 23 July 2016).

Elias, A. (2008) Introduction: whatever happened to the Europe of the regions? Revisiting the regional dimension of European politics, *Regional and Federal Studies*, 18, 483–492.

Farole, T., Rodríguez-Pose, A. and Storper, M. (2011) Cohesion policy in the European Union: growth, geography, institutions, *Journal of Common Market Studies*, 49, 1089–1111.

Garcilazo, E. (2011) The evolution of place-based policies and the resurgence of economic geography in the process of economic development, *Local Economy*, 26, 459–466.

Garcilazo, E., Oliveira Martins, J. and Tompson, W. (2010) Why Policies May Need to Be Place-Based in Order to Be People-Centred. Available: www.voxeu.org/article/why-policies-may-need-be-place-based-order-be-people-centred (accessed 2 July 2015).

German Presidency (2007) *Territorial Agenda of the European Union: Towards a more competitive and sustainable Europe of diverse regions*, as agreed 24–25 May 2007. Available: http://ec.europa.eu/regional_policy/sources/policy/what/territorial-cohesion/territorial_agenda_leipzig2007.pdf (accessed 7 November 2016).

Gibbons, S., Overman, H. and Pelkonen, P. (2010) Wage disparities in Britain: people or place? *SERC Discussion Paper 60*, London: London School of Economics.

Gill, I. (2010) *Regional Development Policies: Place-Based or People-Centred?* Available: www.voxeu.org/article/regional-development-policies-place-based-or-people-centred (accessed 2 July 2015).

Glaeser, E.L. (2008) *Cities, Agglomeration and Spatial Equilibrium*, Oxford: Oxford University Press.

Glaeser, E.L. (2011) *Triumph of the City: How Our Greatest Invention Makes Us Richer, Smarter, Greener, Healthier and Happier*, New York: Penguin Press.

Glaeser, E.L. and Gottlieb, J.D. (2008) The economics of place-making policies, Harvard Institute of Economic Research Discussion Paper No. 2166, Cambridge, MA: Harvard University.

Hastings, A., Bailey, N., Bramley, G., Gannon, M. and Watkins, D. (2015) *The Costs of the Cuts: The Impacts on Local Government and Poorer Communities*, York: Joseph Roundtree Foundation. Available: www.jrf.org.uk/sites/files/jrf/CostofCuts-Full.pdf (accessed 6 July 2015).

Haughton, G., Deas, I. and Hincks, S. (2014) Commentary. Making an impact: when agglomeration boosterism meets antiplanning rhetoric. Staking a claim to expertise, *Environment and Planning A*, 46, 265–270.

Heseltine, M. (2012) *No Stone Unturned in Pursuit of Growth*, London: Department for Business, Innovation and Skills (DBIS). Available: www.gov.uk/government/uploads/system/uploads/attachment_data/file/34648/12-1213-no-stone-unturned-in-pursuit-of-growth.pdf (accessed 2 July 2015).

Heseltine, M. and Leahy, T. (2011) *Rebalancing Britain: Policy or Slogan? Liverpool City Region – Building on Its Strengths*, London: Department for Business Innovation and Skills. Available: www.gov.uk/government/uploads/system/uploads/attachment_data/file/32080/11-1338-rebalancing-britain-liverpool-city-region.pdf (accessed 21 October 2016).

HM Treasury and BIS (2011) The Plan for Growth, London: HM Treasury and BIS. Available: www.gov.uk/government/uploads/system/uploads/attachment_data/file/31584/2011budget_growth.pdf (accessed 2 July 2015).

HM Treasury and BIS (2013) Plan for Growth Implementation Update, London: HM Treasury and BIS. Available: www.gov.uk/government/uploads/system/uploads/attachment_data/file/200019/growth_implementation_update_mar2013.pdf (accessed 2 July 2015).

Hungarian Presidency (2011) *Territorial Agenda of the European Union 2020: Towards a more cooperative and sustainable Europe of diverse regions*, as agreed 19 May 2011. Available: www.nweurope.eu/media/1216/territorial_agenda_2020.pdf (accessed 7 November 2016).

Jessop, B. (2000) The crisis of the national spatio-temporal fix and the tendential ecological dominance of globalizing capitalism, *International Journal of Urban and Regional Research*, 24, 323–360.

Keating, M. (1997) The invention of regions: political restructuring and territorial government in Western Europe, *Environment and Planning C*, 15, 383–398.

Keating, M. (1998) *The New Regionalism in Western Europe: Territorial Restructuring and Political Change*, Cheltenham: Edward Elgar.

Kim, J. (2011) Non-market effects on agglomeration and their policy responses: can we overcome the mismatch? in: *OECD, Regional Outlook 2011*, Paris: OECD.

Kline, P. and Moretti, E. (2012) Place-based policies and unemployment, *American Economic Review*, 103, 238–243.

Kraybill, D. and Kilkenny, M. (2003) Economic rationales for and against place-based policy, *Staff General Research Papers No. 11730*, Ames, IA: Iowa State University, Department of Economics.

Leonardi, R. (2005) *Cohesion Policy in the European Union: The Building of Europe*, Basingstoke, UK: Palgrave.

Liverpool City Region Local Enterprise Partnership (2016) *EU Structural and Investment Fund Strategy 2014–2020*, Liverpool: Liverpool City Region Local Enterprise Partnership. Available: www.liverpoollep.org/wp-content/uploads/2015/04/Final-ESIF-Strategy-4-February-2016-to-DCLG.pdf (accessed 21 October 2016).

Lovering, J. (1999) Theory led by policy: the inadequacies of the 'new regionalism' (illustrated from the case of Wales), *International Journal of Urban and Regional Research*, 23, 379–395.

McCann, P. and Rodríguez-Pose, A. (2011) Why and when development policy should be place-based, in: *OECD, Regional Outlook 2011*, Paris: OECD.

MacLeod, G. (2001) Beyond soft institutionalism: accumulation, regulation, and their geographical fixes, *Environment and Planning A*, 33, 1145–1167.

Martin, R. and Sunley, P. (1997) The post-Keynesian state and the space economy, in: Lee, R. and Wills, J. (eds.) *Geographies of Economies*, London: Arnold.

Mendez, C. (2013) The post-2013 reform of EU cohesion policy and the place-based narrative, *Journal of European Public Policy*, 20, 639–659.

Murphy, J.T. (2011) The socio-spatial dynamics of development: geographical insights beyond the 2009 World Development Report, *Cambridge Journal of Regions, Economy and Society*, 4, 175–188.

OECD (The Organisation for Economic Co-operation and Development) (2009a) *Regions Matter*, Paris: OECD.

OECD (The Organisation for Economic Co-operation and Development) (2009b) *How Regions Grow*, Paris: OECD.

OECD (The Organisation for Economic Co-operation and Development) (2012) *Promoting Growth in all Regions*, Paris: OECD.

Overman, H.G. (2014) Commentary. Making an impact: misreading, misunderstanding and misrepresenting research does nothing to improve the quality of public debate and policy making, *Environment and Planning A*, 46, 2276–2282.

Piore, M.J. and Sabel, C.F. (1984) *The Second Industrial Divide: Possibilities for Prosperity*, New York: Basic Books.

Radice, H. (1984) The national economy: a Keynesian myth? *Capital and Class*, 8, 111–140.

Rodríguez-Pose, A. (2010) Economic geographers and the limelight: the reaction to the 2009 World Development Report, *SERC Discussion Paper 48*, London: London School of Economics.

Scott, A.J. (2009) World development report 2009: reshaping economic geography, *Journal of Economic Geography*, 9, 583–586.

van Oort (2011) Of economics and geography: unity in diversity? *Regional Studies*, 45, 707–710.

Waterhout, B. (2007) Territorial Cohesion: the underlying discourses, in: Faludi, A. (ed.) *Territorial Cohesion and the European Model of Society*, Cambridge, MA: Lincoln Institute of Land Policy.

Wong, C., Baker, M., Hincks, S., Schulze Bäing, A. and Webb, B. (2012) *A Map for England: Spatial Expression of Government Policies and Programmes*, London: Royal Town Planning Institute.

World Bank (2009) *World Development Report 2009: Reshaping Economic Geography*, Washington, DC: World Bank.

4 Constructing alternative paths to city-region policy and governance

John Harrison

> …regional economic growth has to some extent become a symbolic area of policy where governments have to look interested without necessarily solving the problems.
>
> (Niklasson, 2007, p. 27)

Introduction: an alternative to what?

Something which is not hard to find in narratives about territorial governance and policymaking is alternatives, with intellectual and practical debates over regional economic development proving to be no exception. Intellectual alternatives have been derived, in the main, from the either/or debate between 'territoriality' and 'relationality' as opposing ontological and epistemological standpoints which characterised regional studies throughout the 1990s and 2000s. As avant-garde relational approaches were championed as superior alternatives to supposedly more antiquated territorial-scalar approaches, the legacy of this territorial/relational divide in regional studies remains evident through a lexicon of spatial grammar distinguishing 'spaces of flows' from 'spaces of places' (Castells, 1996), 'new regional worlds' from 'the regional world' (Harrison, 2013; Jones and Paasi, 2013), 'unusual'/'non-standard' regions from 'usual'/'standard' regions (Deas and Lord, 2006) and 'soft' from 'hard' spaces of planning and governance (Haughton and Allmendinger, Chapter 5, this volume). Directly related to this intellectual debate, many of the practical alternatives result from recent endeavours to design networked, flexible and smart forms of sub-national planning and governance arrangements, which, within policy debates, are often viewed as better able to reflect the realities of regional spatial configurations.

The focus of this chapter is on the scale of the city-region, where these intellectual and practical debates have featured prominently in the search for alternative paths to regional territorial development and governance. At the beginning of the twenty-first century, academic and political discourses of regional economic development have in some cases moved from promoting a 'global mosaic of regional economies' (Scott, 1998, p. 47) towards championing a 'global mosaic of city-regions' (Scott, 2011, p. 862) as the spatial foundations for a globalising world. This shift has seen city-regionalism presented as a more appropriate path to territorial development and governance. While conventional territorial regional spaces provided the cornerstone for the original 'new regionalist' proposition centred on regions as competitive and strategic territories in an emergent multi-level hierarchy extending from the global to the local, the growing policy focus on city-regions has coincided with increased scholarly interest in understanding the form and function of emerging networked regional spaces. The latter has involved important questions about the (in)compatibility of city-regions – as well as other networked spatial imaginaries – with extant state spatial structures which are predominantly territorially bounded (Ward and Jonas, 2004; MacLeod and Jones, 2007; Harrison, 2010, 2013; Jonas, 2013; Harrison and Growe, 2014).

Occupying the minds of academics, politicians and policymakers alike, it is widely accepted that the creation of policies aimed at building institutional capacity at the scale of city-regions is an officially institutionalised task for many countries across the globe (see Herrschel, 2014; Salet *et al.*, 2003; Vogel *et al.*, 2010). The United Kingdom (especially England) has been no exception: the period 'after regionalism' has seen governments of all political persuasions launch a succession of actual and proposed initiatives designed to operate at a variously defined, regional scale. The in vogue spatial scale among policy elites, there can be no doubt that this conveyor belt of new 'city-region' initiatives has been successful in sustaining interest, debate and discussion (Harrison, 2012). But for all the alternative paths to city-region development, policy and governance that abound, the question of 'an alternative to what' has been overlooked. This chapter argues that in some instances this question of 'an alternative to what' is overlooked completely, while at best it seems only to be acknowledged to justify warranting a new 'city-region' initiative before quickly fading into the background. This is despite, I would argue, a real sense of déjà vu present both intellectually (Harrison, 2007) and practically (Jones, 2013), as similar weaknesses present themselves time and again in ideas and initiatives purporting to offer real alternatives to the failings of previous endeavours in sub-national economic governance.

In this chapter, I argue that myopia to the question of 'an alternative to what' has led to a paralysis of city-regionalism, both intellectually and practically. To develop this argument, the next section examines England in the period 'after regionalism'. Paying particular attention to the UK government's flagship policy for sub-national economic development, this section explores the question: if Local Enterprise Partnerships (LEPs) are the solution, what is the regional economic development and governance problem they are purported to solve? Arguing that a series of longstanding institutional weaknesses have once more been rolled forward in the design of LEPs, the following section then presents two options – the first a non-state approach, the second a region-first approach – which might conceivably be considered a more authentically 'alternative' path to city-region development, policy and governance. Finally, the concluding section reflects on what these alternative narratives about territorial governance and policymaking at the scale of city-regions can tell us about the challenges and opportunities for city-regionalism to bring about meaningful territorial development through appropriate governance arrangements.

'After regionalism' and the paralysis of city-region policymaking

City-regions have for many years been presented as an alternative to regional governance in England (Geddes, 1915; Dickinson, 1964), but latent interest in city-regions only resurfaced in the last two decades. In the wake of the 1998 Regional Development Agencies Act, the Blair governments' efforts to develop economic regionalism (via Regional Development Agencies (RDAs)) and political regionalism (through democratically elected Regional Assemblies) proceeded falteringly, leaving a space into which the idea of city-regions was inserted. This led one commentator to suggest the existence of a 'missing middle' in English territorial governance and the need for meso-scale sub-national institutions to occupy the void between the central and local government in respect of economic development (Harding, 2000). While such suggestions ran very much counter to the thrust of the then-government's emphasis on regionally based governance, interest in city-regions began to grow much more markedly after 2004 and North East England's rejection of proposals for a directly elected regional assembly as potentially the first of a series of such bodies nationally. This heralded the eventual demise of the Labour government's territorially embedded project of political regionalism. In the months after the North East referendum, political leaders at all levels, in their search for palatable alternative narratives for territorial governance and policymaking in England, began increasingly to alight on city-regions.

The rise and fall of city-regionalism in England

The focus on city-regions is underpinned by a clearly identifiable intellectual and practical rationale. Intellectually, city-regionalism is rooted in a geoeconomic logic pertaining to globalisation, competition and agglomerative economic development. Owing to the propensity for high-value economic activity to cluster in dense metropolitan-scaled agglomerations, we can find plenty of assertions to the effect that city-regions constitute important building blocks in an increasingly globalised modern world. In fact, the connection to the global economy is deemed so pronounced that some influential proponents of city-regionalism have argued that city-regions operate quasi-independently of the nation state, increasingly escaping its regulatory control through their ability to transcend state territorial boundaries (Scott, 2001).

Captivated by the strong economic growth experienced by so-called 'global city-regions', policy elites became more convinced of the need to coordinate and integrate policy at the scale of city-regions. As part of a wider reorientation away from spatially redistributive models of regional policy, the city-region became the spatial scale of choice among those who favoured more urban-centric, competitiveness-oriented forms of locational policy. In the race to 'get on' and 'get ahead', as cities and regions vied for prestige amongst their international peers, pressure exerted by policy elites centred on the need for the state to create new, or modified, city-regional strategies to bolster their competitive advantage and enhance their attractiveness to trans-national capital.

In England, the Core Cities Group (a representative group of the eight most economically important cities outside London) mobilised in the late 1990s to lobby the UK government on precisely this premise. Their contention was (and remains) that enhanced powers and increased resources would allow the major regional cities to add additional cylinders to the UK economic engine, in turn rebalancing the UK economy and providing a counterweight to England's one truly 'global' city-region – London. Allied to this was a series of more localised practical concerns relating to the under-bounding of English cities, the fragmented nature of metropolitan areas and difficulties encountered by neighbourhood authorities in developing collaborative strategy, and the aforementioned stalling of the incumbent Labour government's planned programme for the further regionalisation of activity in England (Harrison, 2012).

Responding to both intellectual and practical arguments for city-regionalism, much of the focus in England 'after-regionalism' has concentrated on making necessary adjustments to reorient territorial governance and policy initiatives towards the scale of city-regions. A series of government initiatives was launched to this effect, including the Sustainable Communities Plan (2003), the Northern Way city-region growth strategy (2004), City/Economic Development Companies (2006), Multi-Area Agreements (MMAs) (2006), Statutory City-Regions (2009), LEPs (2010), Elected City Mayors (2011), City Deals (2011) and Combined Authorities (2011). All have been designed to operate at a city-wide or city-region scale and to bring forward the promise of new powers, freedoms and flexibilities to metropolitan areas, with an almost exclusive focus on areas outside of London which, uniquely in the UK context, already had what in effect was its own city-regional authority from when the Blair government established the Greater London Authority in 1999 (Travers, 2002).

In England, as elsewhere, city-regionalism was presented as a clear spatial, institutional and discursive alternative to regional and state territoriality. Yet, the singular logic which saw city-regions framed in this way was quickly lost in the period 'after-regionalism'. In public-policy discourse, city-regions remained one among many other competing spatial imaginaries – localisms, city-regionalisms, sub-regionalisms and pan-regionalisms – for intervening in sub-national economic development (Pike and Tomaney, 2009). Despite achieving a position of international orthodoxy in academic and policy circles, as well as garnering considerable enthusiasm among policy elites nationally, city-regionalism never secured political consensus as the *a priori* spatial scale for public-policy intervention in England.

If the period after regionalism signalled the dissolution of regionalism as a single political project, it certainly did not mark the demise or absence of regions, regional institutions and regional power. Neither, in fact, did it signal the demise or absence of regions as a political project. Between 2004 and 2010, the Labour government kept their regional project on life support with a series of new initiatives including Regional Ministers, Regional Grand and Select Committees and a Regional Economic Council, but none of these gained any traction. They also made RDAs responsible for city-regional initiatives developed as part of the wider Northern Way. Going a long way to explaining why city-regionalism has so far failed to deliver a genuinely alternative path to territorial development, governance and policy, one important consequence of this further regionalisation of sub-national activity was that extant regional power saw city-regions spatially reconfigured along less exclusive lines in order that they became more territorially inclusive (Harrison, 2010, 2013). In sum, there was no smooth transition to a post-regional landscape comprising more networked regional spaces, while what marked city-regionalism out as an alternative path to territorial development, governance and policy had effectively been eroded in the latter years of the Labour government. Allied to this, many 'city-region' initiatives were not in fact new, but the result of reworking and rebranding extant institutional arrangements through a process of scalar amplification or contraction (Lord, 2009).

The formation of a Conservative-Liberal Democrat coalition government in 2010 saw further efforts to identify alternative paths to territorial governance and policy. The incoming Minister made explicit a wish to finally eradicate the vestiges of Labour's regional project and embark on an alternative path of territorial policy and governance:

> I've set about abolishing all the 'R's – Regional Spatial Strategies, regional housing targets, Regional Assemblies, Government Offices for the Regions and Regional Development Agencies. We've said our goodbyes. The arbitrary regional tier of government administration and bureaucracy was unpopular, ineffective and inefficient. So it's the end of regional government: we need a new era of localism.
>
> (Eric Pickles, Secretary of State for Communities and
> Local Government, 2010, n.p.)

Replacing Labour's regional structures were LEPs as the institutional centrepiece of the new agenda for sub-national economic development. Joint local authority-business bodies charged with promoting local economic development, LEPs were to operate across functional economic areas. In this way, localism was presented as an alternative political project to regionalism, LEPs an alternative institutional arrangement to RDAs and functional economic areas the 'natural' spatial alternative to 'unnatural' regional blocks (HM Government, 2010, p. 13). Yet, for all the discursive framing of localism, LEPs and functional economic areas as alternative paths to territorial policy and governance, the reality of implementation failed to match the rhetoric of design. On the crucial issue of spatial economic governance, although the LEPs initiative signalled something of an embrace of city-regionalism in England, and some individual LEPs branded themselves as city-regional, their designated areas were 'not credible' and fell 'short of the principles' necessary to be deemed genuinely city-regionalism in form (Coombes, 2014, pp. 2430–2431; see also Pike *et al.*, 2012). The result is that LEPs, in effect, operate as *de facto* regional entities: spatially inclusive, territorially bounded and state sanctioned.

This casts doubt on the claim that localism and the LEPs provide a credible alternative to regionalism in England. But it also places the spotlight back on to the broader question of whether city-regionalism, as a political project, can be successfully implemented and provide the alternative path to territorial policy and governance its proponents argue is necessary to deliver meaningful economic prosperity, to tackle entrenched inequalities and to enable smart sustainable planning. For if we have learnt anything from the past decade it is that city-regional policy and governance have developed in an uneven way spatially, and progress has been incremental in respect of actual structure and policies. In saying this, let me be clear that I do not deny that there are examples of successful interventions being made by actors working in or for English city-regions; rather, I am saying that these localised successes have often been achieved in spite, rather than because, of the overall political-economic framework within which city-regionalism, as a political project, has been forced to operate.

The limitations of city-region policymaking

The limitations of city-region policymaking reflect three facets of state power. First, there remains the continued reluctance of the central state to devolve authority alongside responsibility to sub-national institutions. In fact, if the transition from RDAs to LEPs is anything to go by, we can go so far as to say that the trend is for spatial economic governance becoming even less governmentalised in England. LEPs lacked much in the way of central funding, particularly in their early years (the combined annual budget for RDAs reached £2.2 billion whereas LEPs began with a £5 million Start-up Fund and £4 million Capacity Fund, with a further £1.4 billion available on a competitive basis over a three-year period through the Regional Growth Fund), had no statutory planning role (RDAs were statutory-planning bodies in their final years) and, although nominally private-sector led, were heavily reliant on local authorities for staffing and assistance. Here lies the great paradox of spatial economic governance in England: contemporary sub-national institutions have been given responsibility for rebalancing an increasingly polarised space economy yet have been granted fewer powers and resources than their predecessors.

Second, political discourses sometimes assume a more or less blank conceptual or policy base, but the reality is there is no *tabula rasa* when it comes to establishing new institutional frameworks for spatial-economic governance. To understand this, we need to distinguish between the geoeconomic and geopolitical logics that underpin city-regionalism (Jonas, 2013). Returning to the earlier example, the framing of LEPs provides a classic example of how capital-centric discourses of globalised economic competitiveness are used to justify further erosion of what are presented as archaic state-centric approaches:

> The secret to success is natural local economies – not *artificial* political regions – that better reflect the *natural* economic geography of the areas they

serve. This is an economic problem that needs an economic solution, not a political one.

(Pickles and Cable, 2010, n.p. [emphasis added])

Yet, if the establishment of LEPs reminds us of anything it is that for all this posturing city-regionalism, with all of its relational inflections, is as much about state territorial power as it is discourses of globalised economic competitiveness. The spatial configuration of 39 LEPs reveals that over half serve areas based on the historic geographical counties of England, while only three areas have a core geography which is trans-regional. In part, the conservatism of the LEP geography reflects some of the practical difficulties in securing agreement among local authority and business leaders over the course of a period which extended to only 69 days in 2010. But the LEP geography also reflected a more fundamental shift in thinking. The globalisation-inspired economic logic for adopting more competitive, selective and differential approaches to spatial economic governance was increasingly bypassed to assuage political demands that LEPs be seen to provide an inclusive approach to regional development.

The answer can be found in a third point, which is that the actions of the state cannot be detached from the ballot boxes through which elected officials are ultimately held accountable and which remain territorially defined. State-led city-regionalism is preconditioned to use the geoeconomic logic for city-regions as agglomeration economies to justify initiatives which privilege urban spaces over non-urban spaces. However, to maintain their own legitimacy and maintain regulatory control and management of the economy in the context of a globalising economy, state actors have expanded the ambit of city-regional governance and policy, augmenting geoeconomic logic for more exclusive regional development with a geopolitical logic that emphasises the need to retain inclusive approaches to regional development. One important consequence of politically (re)constructing city-regions in this way is that over the past decade state-led city-regionalism has been caught betwixt and between two opposing rationales, constantly facing up to the challenge of trying to reconcile geoeconomic demands for more exclusive city-regional development with geopolitical concerns for more emphasis on inclusive city-regional development.

On the general issue of city-regionalism as an alternative path to territorial policy and governance, these developments point to it 'becoming increasingly difficult to disentangle the new economic geography of city-regionalism from its geopolitical construction' (Jonas, 2012, pp. 822–823). Nonetheless, this paralysis of state-led city-region policymaking has not gone unnoticed. In fact, it led to damning early assessments of the LEP project:

> LEPs are likely to fail. Their modus operandi involves rolling forward existing centrally-orchestrated policy regimes, deploying limited levers and mechanisms to influence the business community, and ultimately being unable to correct deep-rooted market failures.

(Jones and Jessop, 2010, p. 1144)

Moreover, the All Party Parliamentary Group (APPG) on Local Growth, LEPs and Enterprise Zones (EZs) (2013, p. 7) pointed out that, despite endeavours by the state to furnish LEPs with new powers, competences and resources, this was offset by the Government's 'inconsistent approach to localism; unresolved issues about whether the LEPs are competitors or collaborators; the risk of function creep and bureaucratisation; LEPs' limited resources and the need for a collective LEP voice'. A national survey of LEPs led by the Centre for Urban and Regional Development Studies (CURDS) went even further, arguing that

> given the lack of long-term vision and strategy for their strategic develop-ment, the fundamental tensions yet to be resolved and their institutional defi-cits in authority, capability and resources, at this stage in their evolution the LEPs will struggle to exercise substantive influence upon local economic growth. Continued state austerity, chronic low growth and brittle and uncer-tain economic conditions in the short and medium-term will further trouble this central task.
>
> (Pike *et al.*, 2013, p. 36)

Despite such downbeat assessments, the concern is that there appears to be no alternative to LEPs being considered. The point, here, is that in these and other critiques (notably Heseltine, 2012), the assumption is that LEPs – and state-led approaches more generally – are the answer. But if LEPs are the solution what is the territorial development, governance and/or policy problem they are purporting to solve? We need to ask this question because uncertainty regarding the future direction of city-region governance and policymaking is exacerbated by the con-tradictions inherent in state-centric approaches and by the restrictions the state imposes on city-regionalism as a political project. For this reason, the remain-der of this chapter looks beyond state-centric models to examine two alterna-tive paths for future city-regional governance. The first considers the increased privatisation of urban and regional development, examining how newly emergent capital-centric models of city-region policy and governance are impacting the balance between capital and state interests. The second examines the potential that functionally dominant approaches to constructing city-regions afford in over-coming the tensions between city-first and region-first approaches to sub-national territorial governance.

Constructing alternative paths to city-region policy and governance

Constructing a non-state alternative to city-region policy and governance

Over the past decade, a critical body of work has emerged documenting how state-led privatisation of urban and regional development has increased the potential for capital interests to engage more prominently in territorial policy and governance (Raco, 2013). Nevertheless, Syrett and Bertotti (2012) have recently argued that failures to understand the motives behind why businesses choose (not) to engage, the tactics and strategies businesses employ when they do engage and the impact their involvement has on practice mean that state-centred models for territorial policy and governance 'provide a fundamentally flawed governance model for addressing the practical realities of pursuing sub-national economic development' (Syrett and Bertotti, 2012, p. 2312). Early evaluations of the LEP programme only served to reinforce this view, with business involvement generally seen to be 'thin' (SQW Consulting, 2010, p. 6), and business leaders who *were* engaged were already 'ready to walk away' if the parameters of this state-centred model meant they were unable to effect change (Cominetti *et al.*, 2012).

With business leaders frustrated by the constraints of state-centred models being repeated in new institutional forms, a more recent trend in narratives of territorial development, policy and governance is the rise of non-state spatial strategies operating at a city-wide or city-region scale. International examples range from Siemens (engineering), BASF (chemicals) and Volkswagen (auto-motive) moving beyond their corporate interests to become actively engaged in metropolitan-scaled policymaking activities as they seek influence over spatial development practices in Erlangen, Rhine-Neckar and Wolfsburg, respectively (Knieling *et al.*, 2012), to the corporate-mining sector governing public land-use decisions in Queensland, Australia (Morrison *et al.* 2012). A UK example worthy of further investigation is the case of a private investment company ('The Peel Group': hereafter Peel) who in 2008 launched a private-sector strategy for unlock-ing economic-development potential in the 'Atlantic Gateway', an area linking the city-regions of Liverpool and Manchester (Deas *et al.*, 2015). One of the most striking features of these more capital-centric approaches is the enhanced possi-bilities for business involvement, engagement and leadership in territorial policy and governance at the metropolitan scale. More open questions relate to why (now) these companies are choosing to engage in this way, how they are seeking to shape patterns of urban and regional development and how they can impact on the future evolution of city-region policymaking (Harrison, 2014a, 2014b).

Turning to examine the first of these questions, Peel is a private investment group with assets worth over £6.5 billion, most of which are concentrated along a 50 km urban corridor connecting the Liverpool and Manchester city-regions. From an initial focus on land and property investments in the 1970s and 1980s, Peel has been expanding to a position where it now has a diverse portfolio of activity (e.g. Peel Airports, Peel Energy, Peel Leisure, Peel Media, Peel Ports) and major equity stakes in national and international companies (e.g. Intu Properties, UK Coal, Pinewood Studios, Vantage Airport Group). Looking to capitalise on extensive land and property assets in North West England, Peel launched Atlantic Gateway, an ambitious proposal to invest £50 billion in 50 pro-jects up to 2050. Through Atlantic Gateway Peel signalled its intention to move beyond selective engagement with state actors (notably the former North West Regional Development Agency (NWDA)) and begin increasingly to fulfil a role as a strategic leader in shaping patterns and trajectories of urban and regional development. This shift was rooted partly in Peel's corporate aspirations. Atlantic

Gateway revealed Peel's long-term desire to move beyond delivering individual large-scale developments (e.g. the £650 million MediaCityUK) to develop much larger scale, longer-term and multi-sector schemes to regenerate whole areas (e.g. the proposals valued at in excess of £5 billion for Liverpool Waters and Wirral Waters). Peel's ambitious investment plans are fuelled by the potential corporate benefits they deliver. Nevertheless, the complex nature of these multi-billion pound investment schemes puts them under increased public scrutiny, not least in the planning approval process where delays and/or rejections to any part of the scheme will incur additional costs and reduce potential returns on investment. Indeed, Peel has previous experience of the financial consequences of protracted planning decisions, having been involved in a nine-year dispute (1986–95) over its plan to build the Trafford Centre, a major out-of-town retail centre opposed by most of Greater Manchester's local authorities.

Seizing on opportunities presented by the ongoing privatisation of urban governance, the prolonged post-financial crisis economic downturn and changes in the national political discourse, Peel took the opportunity to construct a case for a special-purpose planning vehicle to – in the words of Peel Chairman, John Whitaker – 'overcome individual local authority objections' in the delivery of Atlantic Gateway (quoted in Barry, 2008). Peel's strategy involved capitalising on its urban economic infrastructure assets to broker a deal with the NWDA for them to assign Atlantic Gateway priority status in the 2010 Integrated Regional Strategy (RS2010). Appearing in RS2010 was critical to Peel's strategy. As a statutory planning document, RS2010 would see the NWDA act as a planning authority for Atlantic Gateway and reinforce Peel's case in planning disputes. Although RS2010 identified the Atlantic Gateway as the North West's key spatial priority (NWDA, 2010), the Cameron-led coalition government subsequently revoked statutory regional planning provisions. Peel moved swiftly, proposing Atlantic Gateway as a 'private-sector led special purpose LEP' (Peel Group, 2010, p. ii). Subsequently withdrawn as a LEP proposal in the face of opposition from some local authorities, Peel nevertheless ensured a special delivery vehicle was agreed, strategically aligned and integral to the three LEPs established across the Atlantic Gateway.

Peel's political manoeuvring is significant because unlike state-centric models, when private-sector involvement is often preceded by state-actor efforts to script a role for business, the Atlantic Gateway shows the example of business leaders using city-regionalism as a mechanism to negotiate better terms of cooperation. Having lost their main regional ally in the form of the NWDA, Peel's new approach is using Atlantic Gateway to exert its influence not just regionally but nationally. The Conservative-led government on its election in 2010 championed private sector-led economic recovery, spatial and sector rebalancing of the economy, better dialogue between capital and state interests in shaping political praxis and post-recession growth and competitiveness through infrastructure-led economic regeneration. Peel could, therefore, lobby central government to provide appropriate resources in support of Atlantic Gateway initiatives which fitted with this wider approach to economic development. This is significant because capital-centric city-regionalism clearly offers something different to the forms of sub-national governance and policymaking that have tended to predominate in Britain to date. The argument that 'we need LEPs with larger areas, proper funding for running costs, experienced staff, and access to capital' (Ward and Hardy, 2013, p. 9) has prompted some to argue that Atlantic Gateway represents a model for LEPs and other institutions of spatial economic governance:

> If anywhere in the UK can develop the critical mass and momentum to become an alternative growth pole to London, it is the Atlantic Gateway ...[for] there has never been a credible proposition of that nature in Britain to achieve something decades of [state-centred] regional policy failed to achieve.
>
> (Heseltine and Leahy, 2011, pp. 56–57)

In contrast to LEPs (and RDAs before them), Atlantic Gateway is genuinely business led. Heseltine and Leahy (2011), among others, have argued that non-state spatial strategies may provide a genuine alternative to existing forms of city-region policy and governance. But with the emergence of new non-state spatial strategies comes some not insignificant concerns. Favouring capital over state interests in city-region policy and governance brings new opportunities, but also risks and threats. While private-sector assets, power and expertise give businesses a significant voice in influencing and shaping patterns of urban and regional development, their lack of democratic legitimacy undermines their ability to govern city-regions in a more expansive way. It can be argued in this respect that companies such as Peel recognise their lack of a democratic mandate but, nevertheless, perceive an acute need for private-sector resources to make viable economic-development strategies: 'fundamentally, the era of predominantly public finance investment in infrastructure is over and thus regeneration programmes will have to adapt to this new environment' (Howell, 2012, p. 5). In the case of Atlantic Gateway, recent announcements suggest the state's tactic is one that involves capturing, co-opting and reworking Peel's non-state vision for city-region development into a state spatial strategy for Northern England (One North, 2014; Osborne, 2014).

Constructing a region-first alternative to city-region policy and governance

One of the difficulties confronting city-region policymaking is the politically thorny issue of spatial selectivity and the extent to which some areas are prioritised at the expense of others. This is an issue that looms large in academic and political debate:

> The city-region approach *reproduces* a rural development problem. It establishes and *reinforces* out-of-date notions of geographical centrality and hierarchies, and it actively marginalises places, consigning them to the periphery, dividing and polarising.
>
> (Ward, 2006, p. 52 [emphasis added])

> City-regions are an innovative way to manage urban-rural interaction, but at
> present the rural component seems to be ignored.
>
> (OECD, 2011, p. 222)

In the first quote, we see an argument pertaining to current city-region approaches, implicitly bemoaning the lack of any clear alternative path to city-region policy and governance which would allow for greater inclusion and spatial equity. The second quote from the OECD points toward the related issue of city-regionalism privileging major agglomerative economies *vis-à-vis* marginalising non-urban spaces, but does offer hope that there is an alternative city-region narrative. But what might this alternative narrative be? This section considers an emerging body of literature which frames city-regionalism through a regions-first as opposed to cities-first approach to defining and conceptualising city-regions (see Harrison and Heley, 2015).

Working from a belief that city-regionalism's 'implicit marginalisation of rural areas is unwelcome', Coombes (2014, pp. 2429–2430) argues that a crucial point when defining city-region boundaries for governance or policy is to recognise that 'there is an alternative conception of city-regions which does not presume such a dominant role for the city'. Pushing beyond Soja's (2013) notion of regionalised urbanisation and Herrschel's (2014) distinction between urban-centric city-regions and regionalised city-regions, Coombes challenges the consensus of a city-first approach to city-regionalism by testing the idea that regions could (or even should) have primacy over cities when defining the boundaries of city-regions for governance or policy. To understand the potential significance of this we need, first, to reflect on some of the difficulties that currently confound city-region policymaking. Over the past decade or more, endeavours to define boundaries for city-region governance or policy have swayed between a spatially selective, city-first, agglomeration approach infused by more capital-centric discourses of globalised economic competitiveness, and the more territorially inclusive, region-first approaches promoted by the state.

In his analysis, Coombes examines migration and commuting flows in England to argue that a regions-first approach to defining city-region boundaries for governance or policy is capable of 'implementing *all* the fundamental features of the concept' (2014, p. 2426; emphasis added). The resultant map is a mosaic of 39 areas which is, in effect, only a slight variation on the current structure of 39 LEPs. Despite a different starting point (the region rather than the city), the outcome is a newly proposed de facto scale for sub-national governance. Moreover, as Coombes (2014, p. 2440) points out, his empirical analysis 'finds no "non-city-region" in England'. Amounting to an important first step in establishing the principle of defining city-region boundaries for governance or policy by adopting a region-first approach, the result is arguably not too dissimilar to previous attempts to delimit functional regions.

One territory of the United Kingdom does, nevertheless, appear to present an approach to constructing city-regions according to functional regionalism, without necessarily falling back into the city-region trap caused by the agglomeration and state-scalar models. In 2004, the first Wales Spatial Plan (WSP) had all the hallmarks of the spatially selective, city-centric, agglomeration model of

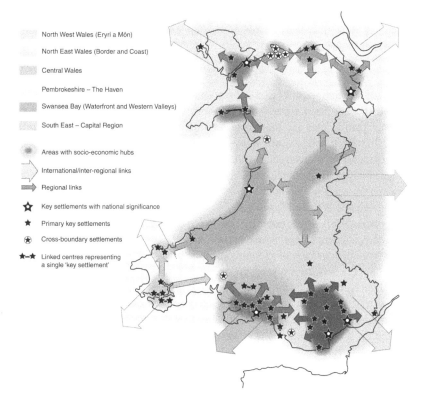

North West Wales (Eryri a Môn)

North East Wales (Border and Coast)

Central Wales

Pembrokeshire – The Haven

Swansea Bay (Waterfront and Western Valleys)

South East – Capital Region

Areas with socio-economic hubs

International/inter-regional links

Regional links

☆ Key settlements with national significance

★ Primary key settlements

✪ Cross-boundary settlements

★—★ Linked centres representing a single 'key settlement'

Figure 4.1 2008 Wales Spatial Plan: the national vision.

Source: WAG (2008, p. 20).

city-regionalism. The spatial vision presented six loosely bounded regional areas, each an urban agglomeration including 33 of the 35 'key centres' and each expanding its reach outwards into non-urban areas (WAG, 2004). Making the Welsh case pertinent is that by the time the second WSP was published in 2008, policy elites had unmistakeably developed a new approach to city-regionalism consistent with the underlying principles of relational regionalism (WAG, 2008; Figure 4.1).

Very much in line with recent intellectual arguments pertaining to the pervasiveness of urban-economic processes across all geographic space (e.g. Scott, 2011, 2012; Brenner, 2013), the urban-rural divide so evident in WSP 2004 has been diluted in WSP 2008 by adopting a functionally dominant regions-first, rather than a form-dominant cities-first, approach to city-regionalism. The result is an opening up of city-regionalism to include 57 'key settlements'.

Including those settlements on the fringes (or even beyond) urban areas is significant for three principal reasons. First, WSP 2008 recognises that

> [Rural] market towns differ from the extensive urban areas …in their relative isolation, their enhanced service function compared to population and their

> interactions with the surrounding rural areas. Because of the Area's rurality, relative peripherality and population sparsity, its most populous settlements need to fulfil roles and functions that would normally be associated with much larger towns.
>
> (WAG, 2008, p. 85)

WSP 2008 is important because it recognises non-city-regions. Functional nodes located in non-urban areas – that is, those that do not easily conform to a city-regional profile and are therefore automatically excluded from form-dominant cities-first approaches – are now included in the discursive framing of Welsh city-regionalism. It recognises that although market towns and tourist hotspots do not easily conform to the stereotypical profile of 'city-region' in their physical appearance, their multi-functional role within the non-urban areas in which they are located needs to be recognised.

Second, WSP 2008 enabled the Welsh Assembly Government simultaneously to recognise and prioritise growth in and beyond metropolitan regions. One important consequence of recognising functional regionalism beyond metropolitan regions is that the framing of WSP 2008 achieves a much greater degree of spatial inclusivity than the cities-first agglomeration approach, and without the explicit territorial division that results from the scalar approach of partitioning and fragmenting space. In short, the typology of key settlements softened the perception that city-regionalism was prioritising growth in a smaller number of more significant urban regions, while also producing the fuzzy boundaries now commonly associated with the emergence of 'soft' (or perhaps more accurately 'softer') spaces for regional planning and governance (Heley, 2013).

Is city-regionalism drinking in the last-chance saloon?

We do not need alternatives for alternatives' sake in intellectual and practical debates over regional economic development. What we do need are solutions to established problems. This requires ideas that are not only alternative in their style but, more importantly, in their substance and implementation. This chapter has sought to unpack the notion of alternative paths to city-region development, policy and governance. Focusing on city-regions is important. Debates surrounding city-regionalism inform broader intellectual discussion in urban and regional studies, particularly in relation to understanding when and where territoriality and relationality appear compatible. Even where the two appear incompatible, it is important to examine how actors have attempted to reconfigure territories in order that they become more complementary (Harrison, 2013; Harrison and Growe, 2014; Paasi and Zimmerbauer, 2016). On a more practical note, city-regions continue to be championed as the 'ideal scale for policy intervention in a globalized world' (Rodriguez-Pose, 2008, p. 1029), but in many cases the path to city-region development, policy and governance has amounted to 'reactionary and incremental adjustments that lack strategic direction, buy-in and focus'(Ayres and Stafford, 2009, p. 619).

Reflecting these tensions, the development of city-region policymaking and governance has been geographically uneven and contingent on a number of factors: (i) city-regional arrangements being less governmentalised than their regional predecessors but tasked with solving a bigger problem (although this now has the potential to change in the United Kingdom following the announcement in November 2014 that the Greater Manchester Combined (City-Region) Authority will, under the auspices of an elected 'metro' mayor, have control over £7 billion of public spending); (ii) there being no blank state, such that city-region policies and initiatives championed as new are generally a reworking of previous institutional structures, territorialities, frameworks and support; and (iii) tension between capital and state interests, manifest in the incompatibility of spatially selective 'agglomeration' and spatially inclusive 'scalar' approaches to city-region development, policy and governance. The main argument of this chapter has, therefore, been that the majority of new – and supposedly alternative – 'city-region' initiatives launched by the UK government over the past decade do not seek to solve the fundamental problems of socio-economic development, thus, constraining the pace and extent of city-region policymaking. Instead, they seek to work within parameters established by the state, resulting in a restricted form of top-down territorial governance that, in some cases, is poorly attuned to local circumstances.

Nevertheless, there are plausible alternatives to the restricted forms of city-region governance and policymaking that are evident in some (but not all) British cities. But while examples such as Peel's Atlantic Gateway Strategy or the WSP represent differing forms of territorial governance, neither ought to be considered exemplary. Both are more symbolic than substantive. Equally, they do stand out from other city-region initiatives because they seek (directly in the case of Peel, indirectly in the case of the Welsh Assembly Government) to provide solutions to the established problems that constrain how city-regionalism is implemented politically. However, and to paraphrase a well-rehearsed refrain in urban and regional studies, what these alternative approaches to city-region policy and governance bring us back to are two fundamental questions which must ultimately be a priority for future research: (i) what kind of city-region development, policy and governance do we want, and need, to shape future patterns of urban and regional development, and (ii) in whose interests should city-regionalism be pursued?

References

All Party Parliamentary Group (APPG) on Local Growth, Local Enterprise Partnerships and Enterprise Zones (2013) *Rising to the Challenge: How LEPs Can Deliver Local Growth Strategies*, London: Westminster City Council.

Ayres, S. and Stafford, I. (2009) Deal-making in Whitehall: competing and complementary motives behind the review of sub-national economic development and regeneration, *International Journal of Public Sector Management*, 22, 605–622.

Barry, C. (2008) Planning supremo seeks planning revolution, Manchester Evening News, 8 September. Available: www.manchestereveningnews.co.uk/business/business-news/peel-supremo-seeks-planning-revolution-966379 (accessed 22 September 2014).

Brenner, N. (2013) *Implosions/Explosions: Towards a Theory of Planetary Urbanization*, Berlin: Jovis Verlag.

Castells, M. (1996) *The Rise of the Network Society*, Oxford: Blackwell.

Cominetti, N., Crowley, L. and Lee, N. (2012) *The Business of Cities: The Private Sector, Local Enterprise Partnerships and Growth*, London: The Work Foundation.

Coombes, M. (2014) From city-region concept to boundaries for governance: the English case, *Urban Studies*, 51, 2426–2443.

Deas, I. and Lord, A. (2006) From a new regionalism to an unusual regionalism? The emergence of non-standard regional spaces and lessons for the territorial reorganisation of the state, *Urban Studies*, 43, 1847–1877.

Deas, I., Haughton, G. and Hincks, S. (2015) 'A good geography is whatever it needs to be': the Atlantic Gateway and evolving spatial imaginaries in North West England, in: Allmendinger, P., Haughton, G., Knieling, J. and Othengrafen, F. (eds.) *Soft Spaces: Re-negotiating Governance, Boundaries and Borders*, pp. 25–44, London: Routledge.

Dickinson, R. (1964) *The City Region in Western Europe*, London: Routledge & Kegan Paul.

Geddes, P. (1915) *Cities in Evolution: An Introduction to the Town Planning Movement and to the Study of Cities*, London: Williams & Norgate.

Harding, A. (2000) *Is There a 'Missing Middle' in English Governance?* London: New Local Government Network.

Harrison, J. (2007) From competitive regions to competitive city-regions: a new orthodoxy, but some old mistakes, *Journal of Economic Geography*, 7, 311–332.

Harrison, J. (2010) Networks of connectivity, territorial fragmentation, uneven development: the new politics of city-regionalism, *Political Geography*, 29, 17–27.

Harrison, J. (2012) Life after regions? The evolution of city-regionalism in England, *Regional Studies*, 46, 1243–1259.

Harrison, J. (2013) Configuring the new 'regional world': on being caught between territory and networks, *Regional Studies*, 47, 55–74.

Harrison, J. (2014a) Rethinking city-regionalism as the production of new non-state spatial strategies: the case of Peel Holdings Atlantic Gateway Strategy, *Urban Studies*, 51, 2315–2335.

Harrison, J. (2014b) The rise of the non-state 'place-based' economic development strategy, *Local Economy*, 29, 453–468.

Harrison, J. and Growe, A. (2014) When regions collide: in what sense a new 'regional problem'? *Environment and Planning A*, 46, 2332–2352.

Harrison, J. and Heley, J. (2015) Governing beyond the metropolis: placing the rural in city-region development, *Urban Studies*, 52, 1113–1133.

Heley, J. (2013) Soft spaces, fuzzy boundaries and spatial governance in post devolution Wales, *International Journal of Urban and Regional Research*, 37, 1325–1348.

Herrschel, T. (2014) *Cities, State and Globalization: City-Regional Governance in Europe and North America*, London: Routledge.

Heseltine, M. (2012) *No Stone Unturned in Pursuit of Growth*, London: BIS.

Heseltine, M. and Leahy, T. (2011) *Rebalancing Britain: Policy or Slogan? Liverpool City Region – Building on Its Strengths: An Independent Report*, London: BIS.

HM Government (2010) *Local Growth: Realising Every Place's Potential*, London: The Stationery Office.

Howell, S. (2012) *Grow Your Own Way: Taking a Localist Approach to Regeneration*, London: Local Government Association/Localis.

Jonas, A. (2012) City-regionalism: questions of distribution and politics, *Progress in Human Geography*, 36, 822–829.

Jonas, A. (2013) City-regionalism as a contingent 'geopolitics of capitalism', *Geopolitics*, 18, 284–298.

Jones, M. (2013) It's like deja vu, all over again, in: Ward, M. and Hardy, S. (eds.) *Where Next for Local Enterprise Partnerships?* pp. 86–95, London: The Smith Institute/ Regional Studies Association.

Jones, M. and Jessop, B. (2010) Thinking state/space incompossibly, *Antipode*, 42, 1119–1149.

Jones, M. and Paasi, A. (2013) Guest editorial: regional world(s): advancing the geography of regions, *Regional Studies*, 47, 1–5.

Knieling, J., Othengrafen, F. and Preising, T. (2012) Privatisierung von stadt-und region-alentwicklung: gesellschaftlicher nutzen oder verwirklichung von unternehmenszielen? 'Corporate spatial responsibility' oder 'corporate spatial strategy'? *Raumforschung und Raumordnung*, 70, 451–464.

Lord, A. (2009) Mind the gap – the theory and practice of state rescaling: institutional morphology and the 'new' city-regionalism, *Space and Polity*, 13, 77–92.

MacLeod, G. and Jones, M. (2007) Territorial, scalar, networked, connected: in what sense a 'regional world'? *Regional Studies*, 41, 1177–1191.

Morrison, T., Wilson, C. and Bell, M. (2012) The role of private corporations in regional planning and development: opportunities and challenges for the governance of housing and land use, *Journal of Rural Studies*, 28, 478–489.

Niklasson, L. (2007) *Joining up for Regional Development*, Stockholm: Statskontoret.

NWDA (2010) *RS2010: Future North West – Our Shared Priorities*, Warrington, UK: NWDA.

OECD (The Organisation for Economic Co-operation and Development) (2011) *OECD Rural Policy Reviews: England, United Kingdom*, Paris: OECD Publishing.

One North (2014) *One North: A Proposition for an Interconnected North*, Manchester: Manchester City Council.

Osborne, G. (2014) We need a Northern powerhouse, 23 June. Available: www.gov.uk/government/speeches/chancellor-we-need-a-northern-powerhouse (accessed 22 September 2014).

Paasi, A. and Zimmerbauer, K. (2016) Penumbral borders and planning paradoxes: relational thinking and the question of borders in spatial planning, *Environment and Planning A*, 48, 75–93.

Peel Group (2010) *A Response by the Private Sector to the Government's Request for Outline Proposals in Relation to Local Enterprise Partnerships (LEPs) in Respect of Atlantic Gateway*, Manchester: The Peel Group.

Pickles, E. (2010) It's the local economy, stupid, *Conservative Home*. Available: http://conservativehome.blogs.com/localgovernment/2010/07/eric-pickles-mp-its-the-local-economy-stupid.html (accessed 22 September 2014).

Pickles, E. and Cable, V. (2010) Economy needs local remedies not regional prescription, 6 September. Available: www.gov.uk/government/speeches/economy-needs-local-remedies-not-regional-prescription (accessed 22 September 2014).

Pike, A. and Tomaney, J. (2009) The state and uneven development: the governance of economic development in England in the post-devolution UK, *Cambridge Journal of Regions, Economy and Society*, 2, 13–34.

Pike, A., Tomaney, J., Coombes, M. and McCarthy, A. (2012) Governing uneven development: the politics of local and regional development in England, in: Bellini, N.,

Danson, M. and Halkier, H. (eds.) *Regional Development Agencies: The Next Generation? Networking, Knowledge and Regional Policies*, pp. 102–121, London: Routledge.

Pike, A., Marlow, D., McCarthy, A., O'Brien, P. and Tomaney, J. (2013) *Local Institutions and Local Economic Growth: The State of the Local Enterprise Partnerships (LEPs) in England – A National Survey*, Newcastle: Centre for Urban and Regional Development Studies.

Raco, M. (2013) *State-led Privatisation and the Demise of the Democratic State: Welfare Reform and Localism in an Era of Regulatory Capitalism*, Aldershot, UK: Ashgate.

Rodríguez-Pose, A. (2008) The rise of the 'city-region' concept and its development policy implications, *European Planning Studies*, 16, 1025–1046.

Salet, W., Thornley, A. and Kreukels, A. (eds.) (2003) *Metropolitan Governance and Spatial Planning: Comparative Case Studies of European City-Regions*, London: Routledge and Spon.

Scott, A. (1998) *Regions and the World Economy: The Coming Shape of Global Production, Competition, and Political Order*, Oxford: Oxford University Press.

Scott, A. (ed.) (2001) *Global City-Regions: Trends, Theory, Policy*, Oxford: Oxford University Press.

Scott, A. (2011) A world in emergence: notes towards a resynthesis of urban-economic geography for the 21st century, *Urban Geography*, 32, 845–870.

Scott, A. (2012) *A World in Emergence: Cities and Regions in the 21st Century*, Cheltenham: Edward Elgar.

Soja, E. (2013) Regional urbanization and third wave cities, *City*, 17, 688–694.

SQW Consulting (2010) Local Enterprise Partnerships: A New Era Begins? London: SQW Ltd. Available: www.lgcplus.com/Journals/3/Files/2010/9/24/SQW-LEPs%20report. pdf (accessed 16 November 2016).

Syrett, S. and Bertotti, M. (2012) Reconsidering private sector engagement in subnational economic development, *Environment and Planning A*, 44, 2310–2326.

Travers, T. (2002) Decentralization London-style: the GLA and London governance, *Regional Studies*, 36, 779–788.

Vogel, R., Savitch, H., Xu, J., Yeh, A., Wu, W., Sancton, A., Kantor, P., Newman, P., Tsukamoto, T., Cheung, P., Shen, J., Wu, F. and Zhang, F. (2010) Governing global city regions in China and the West, *Progress in Planning*, 73, 1–75.

WAG (Welsh Assembly Government) (2004) *People, Places, Futures: The Wales Spatial Plan*, Cardiff: WAG.

WAG (Welsh Assembly Government) (2008) *People, Places, Futures: The Wales Spatial Plan 2008 Update*, Cardiff: WAG.

Ward, K. and Jonas, A. (2004) Competitive city-regionalism as a politics of space: a critical reinterpretation of the new regionalism, *Environment and Planning A*, 36, 2119–2139.

Ward, M. and Hardy, S. (eds.) (2013) *Where Next for Local Enterprise Partnerships?* London: The Smith Institute and Regional Studies Association.

Ward, N. (2006) Rural development and the economies of rural areas, in: Midgeley, J. (ed.) *A New Rural Agenda*, pp. 46–67, London: IPPR.

Part II

Flexible regionalism

Soft spaces in theory and practice

5   Alternative planning spaces

Graham Haughton and Philip Allmendinger

Introduction

There is a divide opening up between different aspects of planning practice, specifically between the 'visible', open and statutory duties and processes of land-use management and public involvement, and the informal, less-visible, facilitative, trans-boundary and multi-disciplinary forms of planning and regeneration. This division transcends the familiar ongoing pattern of deregulation and re-regulation experienced in planning since the mid-1970s under successive governments. What we are witnessing is a more subtle set of changes to planning practice, with an on-off 'rolling back' of its development-controlling governmental forms alongside a continuous 'rolling out' of its growth-pursuing, environment-protecting governance forms. Rather than being contradictory, there is a symbiotic and deliberately fuzzy relationship in these parallel forms of reformulating systems for planning and regeneration.

The key to understanding this is perhaps the 'and regeneration' tag. For planning exists necessarily in close relationship with other aspects of the apparatus of government that seek to develop strategies and policies that, in some way, shape or form, rely on the statutory functions of planning – housing policy, local and regional economic-development policy, urban and rural regeneration initiatives and a wide variety of environmental policies, not least for floods, water supply, energy, pollution, biodiversity and green infrastructure. Few of these other policy fields are quite as constrained to working within the statutory processes and legally defined territorial administrative boundaries of local government as the statutory aspects of planning. There is, of course, nothing new in this – planners have always worked within complex networks of actors and agencies, each working to their own geographies and policy remits. What has changed is that planners can no longer presume to take the lead, nor can they act with their former certainties, powers, resources and misplaced sense of higher moral purpose. Or to put it another way, the planning system can achieve only a small part of what is now expected of it purely through statutory planning. It must work with and through a wide range of other agencies, spaces and timescales, each with its own agenda, constraints and possibilities. It is partly for this reason that the notion of integration became so prominent within planning from the late 1990s onwards, a policy direction given further impetus by the rise of the sustainable development agenda, with its search for approaches that balanced economic, social and environmental priorities, rather than trading off one against another (Haughton and Counsell, 2004; Haughton *et al.*, 2010).

There have been some notable other factors which account for the changing context in which the planning and related systems now operate:

- Changes in global governance, with the deregulatory thrust of competition policy evident in the edicts of the European Union (EU), and in the World Trade Organisation in particular, requiring the dismantling of restrictions on trade, while attempting to tighten up laws to prevent anti-competitive practices. This 'opening up' of national boundaries, combined with the growth in footloose capital, has undermined, if not eliminated, one of the tools of the planning repertoire in helping shift development activity between regions within nation states.
- The evolvement of EU legislation, particularly on environmental issues, which places limits on the ability of national and sub-national governments to deregulate or otherwise reform planning.
- As part of the drift away from the era of the Keynesian welfare state, a growth in the focus on individual rights over collective responsibilities, allied to a growing marketisation of policy, leading to changed public expectations over the standards required of governmental and other service providers. The objectives of planning have subtly evolved to reflect this shift, changing from a focus on the regulation of development in the public interest to one of market supportive, growth facilitation.
- A growth in the media-isation of society and disputes. Where local newspapers were once the main vehicle for expressing differences of opinion on, say, a development project, in an era of vastly improved communications, online petitions, Facebook campaigns and Twitter storms can now be used to give vent to 'outrage' at some aspect or other of policy. It takes a strong politician not to respond to such short-term campaigns, making longer-term, ambitious policies more difficult to orchestrate than ever.
- A growing, educated middle class and the spread of property ownership, which means that more people than ever have a vested interest in protecting their property values and lifestyles when these are threatened by new development proposals. More people also have the financial and intellectual resources with which to take on authority, and fewer people hold deferential attitudes towards those in power.
- An increase in the availability of information and the speed at which issues and campaigns can be circulated, allied to scepticism over the behaviour of big business, big government and big trade unions, in particular, likewise leading to a growing willingness on the part of some to challenge authority, be this technical, scientific or political.
- A growth in demands for accountability and transparency in decision making, alongside rising expectations of improved public consultation in the context

of concerns that elected officials are losing, abusing or, in some cases, failing to use some of their powers while losing touch with their electorates.

- An increased set of objectives for planning, including regeneration, economic growth and development, environmental improvements and climate change, as well as social inclusion, which have challenged the skills and knowledge of planners and pushed planning's scope to and beyond its legal and territorial limits.

To summarise, the policy scope and territorial ambitions of planning have grown, even as its tools and levers have been reinvented and, in some cases, older approaches have disappeared or been dismantled, and new approaches have been developed. In this sense, planning has been subject to similar questions and tensions around the changing nature of society and the role of the state as other areas of public policy.

A particularly important trend for planning has been the growth and more ready accessibility of information in the public domain, plus an increasingly well-informed population. This has generated a new kind of activist, capable of uncovering and using available information or generating their own alternative information with which to challenge the expertise of scientists and technocratic elites, including professional planners and those who advise them. Added to this is a growth of distrust or scepticism about the neutrality of technical experts and about the motives of elected politicians, and a general culture more prone to challenge authority publicly and to stand up to assert individual rights. It is in this context that the planning system in England, and in Europe more widely, has come under sustained pressure to become more transparent, more accountable and more sensitive to the expectations and beliefs of multiple publics. These trends have inevitably created tensions within planning about meeting the differing aspirations for the system's role in controlling and guiding development. This is particularly evident in the context of growing environmental awareness and demands for greater public involvement, on the one hand and, on the other hand, the impacts and demands of 'working with the market' in the context of economic globalisation and the pursuit of national competitiveness.

One consequence is that the traditional debates and crude antagonisms around 'more or less' planning have entered a new equilibrium, in the mind of the public at least. For example, calls for 'more planning' emerge around protecting the countryside, while 'less planning' is the aim if economic development is involved. It would seem that this new settlement or cognitive dissonance amounts to a 'solution' that reconciles the apparently irreconcilable question of 'how can planning please everyone?' This solution is more than simply politicians seeking to appease different audiences by emphasising or playing down aspects of their programme or policies, however. Something more fundamental is occurring as alternative, parallel forms of planning emerge.

In some ways, these tensions are not new and embrace traditional concerns around the appropriate scales, processes and functions of planning: planners have always had to manage tensions between competing and sometimes irreconcilable issues. Yet, there is a contemporary shift in how planning has positioned itself in relation to competing ideas. There has been a move from planning being an arena within which tensions are openly tackled, to one where planners more actively manage the terms upon which debates are framed and undertaken. Yet, the traditional tensions remain. How can planning be, on the one hand, 'top-down', ensuring a consistency of approach across the country and enabling a 'coordinated steer' in pursuit of national objectives while, on the other hand, being 'bottom-up', allowing for differences in public involvement and local circumstances? How can planning provide certainty and quick decisions while also taking time to include communities in deliberations and ensure comprehensiveness and quality? How can planning engage with multiple scales and supra-local, often global, issues within its bounded territorial legitimacy and authority? The contemporary solution to these tensions is to sidestep the binary 'either/or' options that these questions pose.

Rather than having to choose between them, contemporary planning practice seems instead to be able to choose the circumstances in which these very different, though complementary, notions of planning are suitable and appropriate. The coexistence of distinct approaches to planning provides solutions to a range of problems and issues, which is why this 'everything to everyone' form of planning, or spatial planning as it has been labelled in the English context, has garnered support from a wide variety of sources, not least the planning profession. Elsewhere, we have termed this new reality 'neo-liberal spatial governance' (Allmendinger and Haughton, 2013), linking it to flexible forms of neoliberal experimentation (Haughton, *et al.,* 2013) and post-political tactics (Allmendinger and Haughton, 2012). In this chapter, we want to focus on another dimension of neoliberal spatial governance focused on the nature of space and spatial practices.

Planning engages with what we would broadly define as 'territorial space' (e.g. the bounded, jurisdictional space of local authorities) and relational space (e.g. the networked, porous nature of space and scale). In some respects, planners act strategically and relationally, reflecting ideas around the networked, porous nature of space and scale. In other respects, planners act territorially, allocating and defining property rights and policing land-use change. These two roles are linked and are by no means exclusive. In determining a spatial strategy, for example, planners think and act relationally, engaging with multiple audiences and interests on international or global issues such as climate change that go far beyond the locality. Such outward looking and fluid attitudes echo the notion of governance and spatial governance. This relational thinking is necessary to better understand the contexts, issues and options in a locality, drawing on networks and looking beyond territory. Yet, the product of such a process is, by legal necessity, territorial in nature, compressing relational issues and scales into a product or output, whether this is a plan, a strategy or a set of performance targets or indicators. So, while relational thinking is emergent, plural and a process rather than a product, the strategy and decisions on property rights are jurisdictional and territorial in the sense of determining a singularity: time and space are frozen or closed in order to impose one set of rights, claims and visions over others. Such strategies only have meaning if they influence decisions and actions 'on the ground', usually of private actors in developing land and property. This role of defining legal rights to develop also has to be policed and such enforcement is facilitated through jurisdictional legislation – that is to say, territorially defined powers.

Planning in and through territorial and relational spaces presents challenges that echo the wider, binary 'either/or' tensions previously mentioned: how can planning be bounded and unbounded, open and closed, a process and a product? Or perhaps planning necessarily involves thinking and working in terms of both territorial and relational spaces. Certainly, the 'relational turn' in the spatial sciences that explores social, porous and networked understandings of space and scale (e.g. Massey, 2005) has been recently accompanied by attempts to bring territory 'back in' (Jones, 2009; Allen and Cochrane, 2010). Through the lens of spatial and scalar restructuring, Cochrane (2012) has argued that regional politics draw on and employ a range of relational networks that stretch beyond regions, but are simultaneously lodged within them. Territory retains a strong focus for politics that are conducted in, through and against a set of institutions whose jurisdiction is precisely defined in territorial terms (Goodwin, 2013). Some go further and claim that territory remains the quintessential state space (Painter, 2010).

One way in which the seemingly intractable tensions between territorial and relational perspectives have been addressed in contemporary practice is through the emergence of alternative planning spaces, often framed as experiments and interruptions to the previous status quo. Alternative planning spaces are new spatial fixes or practices outside and alongside of the enduring scales of planning, which in the British context means mainly the local and national. Here, we have in mind the creation of new planning and regeneration *spaces*, for example, those that emerged post-devolution at the national (e.g. Scotland) or regional scale from the late 1990s or the national spaces of major infrastructure in England from 2008. We also include new *spatial practices*, such as the move to spatial planning in England from the early 2000s that sought to change the attitudes and approaches from regulation to growth management (Haughton *et al.*, 2010; Allmendinger and Haughton, 2012). During this period, we also saw the growing cross-fertilisation of professional disciplines and ideas, as planning was opened up to other professionals and as more planners found themselves employed in other sectors, from regeneration to design, property and environmental companies (Allmendinger and Haughton 2007, 2009). Often, alternative spaces and practices emerge together seeking, to greater or lesser degrees, to provide new fixes that suture the 'open' and 'closed' necessity of planning, or that shift the focus of planning towards facilitating growth and development.

A particularly significant class of alternative planning space involves what we have termed elsewhere 'soft spaces' (Haughton *et al.*, 2010). Soft spaces are 'informal or semi-formal, non-statutory spatialities of planning and regeneration, with associations and relations stretching both across formally established boundaries and scalar levels of planning and across previously entrenched sectoral divides' (Metzger and Schmitt, 2012, pp. 265–266).

At a theoretical level, the rise of alternative planning and regeneration spaces can be understood as one of many manifestations of the 'filling in' of the sub-national state apparatus that has accompanied the 'hollowing out' of the nation state (Goodwin *et al.*, 2005, 2006). The important point, here, is that while the nation state may have engaged in a dramatic horizontal and vertical reworking of its powers, it still retains its authority and legitimacy through its ability to determine (and to reconsider) where powers are re-located: what Jones (1997) has referred to as the strategic and spatial selectivity of the state. The state has not so much lost power as rethought how it uses and allocates responsibilities and resources. In this context, the emergence and disappearance of successive generations of alternative planning spaces is always in some respects a manifestation of state power.

Alternative planning and regeneration spaces can be seen as a continuing fea-ture of planning in the post-war period, yet there has been a marked shift in the use and significance of such spaces in recent years, as they have moved into the mainstream of planning tools and approaches, often with the encouragement of government and professional bodies. This chapter outlines the emergence, use, significance and future of such alternative spaces of planning, examining the claims of their liberating potential and of their use for closing out meaningful debate and democratic accountability. We argue that too much attention is some-times placed on the formal, visible, statutory forms of planning and not enough on the less visible, informal spaces and practices. In part this is understandable, given the subtle shift and long-term emergence into the mainstream of planning prac-tice and the deliberate desire to distract attention away from the significance and influence of such alternative spaces and practices. Yet, the clues to this shift have been clear for some time. The emergence and (usual) disappearance of alternative planning spaces has been accompanied by a new vocabulary and skills set for planners: positivist notions of control, regulation, modelling and prediction have given way to a post-positivist nomenclature and toolkit of partnership, govern-ance, collaboration, visioning and emergence. The upshot is the need for a holistic rather than partial view of what constitutes contemporary planning.

The development of alternative planning spaces

In terms of European planning, alternative, informal, cross-boundary or 'soft' spaces and approaches have been a feature of practice for many decades (Allmendinger *et al.*, 2015). Some are well known though rarely seen as alterna-tive spaces of governance. This section provides a brief and, admittedly, selective overview of these alternative spaces, predominantly from an English perspective: it would be impossible to cover in the space available the various planning and regeneration initiatives set in train in the past 60 years or so. Figure 5.1 illustrates some of the more high-profile alternative spaces of planning outside the 'hard' or more formal territorial spaces of planning from the 1940s onwards.

In the immediate aftermath of the Second World War, and in response to the proposals of the Greater London Plan in 1944 to create eight new towns around London, the new Attlee government quickly created the New Town Commission

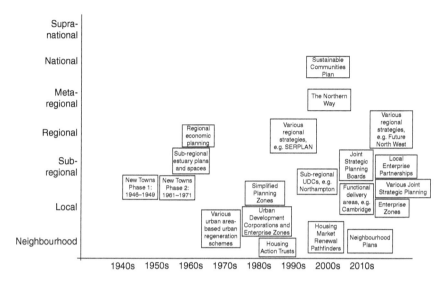

Figure 5.1 Key alternative spaces of planning from the 1940s onwards.

in 1945, chaired by Lord Reith. The 1946 New Town Act introduced the New Town Development Commission model, where New Towns would be run by boards appointed by central government and given devolved planning powers (HoC, 2002).

Apart from the bespoke, delivery-orientated spaces such as the New Town Development Corporations, there have been a variety of new, mainly central government-initiated alternative planning spaces, the most notable of which were the 'regional' and 'sub-regional' studies undertaken in the 1960s and early 1970s. The regional studies tended to be about 'economic planning', not simply land-use planning, using the boundaries of government standard regions. Sub-regional planning studies, however, had a more powerful semblance as alternative planning spaces. The inspiration for some of these was the Government Minister for Housing and Local Government in 1965, Richard Crossman, who saw them as ways of encouraging authorities in adjacent areas to set up *ad hoc* teams to prepare long-term broad-brush plans, without any direct connection to future local-government reform (Glasson, 1974, p. 223; Glasson and Marshall 2007, p. 37). One of the first examples was the Leicester-Leicestershire Study of 1969 led by J.B. McLoughlin, then a local planner, who later moved to Manchester University. He recorded his experience of undertaking the sub-regional study, noting how a unit was set up between the two local authorities which was also separate to them, meaning it had 'all the advantages of and close working relationships with and immediate support from the sponsors, yet at the same time was able to maintain an independence like that of a private consultant' (McLoughlin, 1969, p. 313). This is a theme that resonates with more recent soft-space literature. Other sub-regional studies in this period included the 1969

Teesside Study (led by private consultants), the Coventry-Solihull-Warwick Study published in 1971, the North Gloucestershire Sub-regional Study in 1970 and one for Reading-Wokingham-Aldershot-Basingstoke (Glasson, 1974; Glasson and Marshall, 2007; Ratcliffe, 1974).

Particularly notable were the estuary studies commissioned for the Humber, Tees, Tay and Severn (Frey, 1971), since all of these culminated in the creation of new units of territorial government: the county councils of Humberside, Teesside, Tayside and Avon. In this sense, the experiments in creating new regional formations through the sub-regional studies were essentially exercises in both relational and territorial thinking, but very quickly this was translated into a territorial tier of government, with hard boundaries and elected local government. This was very different to the generation of 'soft spaces' that was to follow.

The election of the Thatcher government in 1979 set in train a series of more substantial disruptions to previous planning practices, not least with the predisposition of Conservative politicians to distrust both planners and local government, especially in those urban areas where Labour tended to be in political control. The result was a series of highly localised experiments in a watered-down version of non-planning, most notably with Urban Development Corporations (UDCs), Enterprise Zones (EZs) and Simplified Planning Zones (SPZs). These created in different ways 'black holes' within the wider planning regimes of the time (Haughton *et al.*, 2013).

The UDCs became an especially potent symbol of this approach. They were formally introduced in the 1980 Local Government Planning and Land Act. Effectively, they were creatures of central government, led by government-appointed boards which were purposely dominated by private-sector interests. The 11 UDCs were ten-year experiments in regeneration, which attracted considerable government funding to pursue their work. They were given planning powers for their areas and were seen by critics as a Balkanisation of the local state (Haughton, 1999). While the UDCs were expected to liaise with local planning authorities, in reality the boundary of responsibilities in planning was blurred, leaving them considerable discretion over the extent to which they followed statutory plans or their own development documents (Lawless, 1988; Gaffikin and Warf, 1993). Local input into the planning controls and strategies in these areas was often minimal or carefully choreographed so as not to create delays in development. Indeed, the justification for such experimental planning space was that local control and input was part of the problem.

Similar logics prevailed in other parts of the local governance system, for instance with the introduction of Housing Action Trusts in this period to insert private-sector expertise into redeveloping problem areas. Training and Enterprise Councils (TECs), similarly, were private sector-led, quasi-autonomous non-governmental organisations (quangos), expected to develop and deliver for their areas programmes of training, small-business support and other aspects of economic-development policy. These early initiatives embodied legitimacy challenges for elected local government, providing alternative spaces for the delivery of national growth and regeneration priorities. For the most part, power and resources were shifted in favour of private-sector interests, though there was sufficient flexibility in the approach to allow community-based initiatives also to benefit, particularly where these were perceived to be challenging intransigent local governments, with well-known national examples including Coin Street in London and the Eldonians in Liverpool (Brindley *et al.,* 1996; Meegan, 1990). The huge academic and policy debate at that time about quangos and the non-elected local state focused on the democratic challenges that these bodies collectively represented (Shaw, 1990; Hart *et al.,* 1996).

These alternative spaces of deregulation were at one level insignificant, covering only a small fraction of the land area, but their symbolic significance was much greater. The dismantling of the regional planning apparatus from the late 1970s and the promotion of micro-spaces of redevelopment promulgated the shift in the purpose of planning from nested and hierarchical forms of governmental action to much narrower, supply-side constraint-focused regulatory planning. This amounted to alternative planning and regeneration spaces as experimental, insurgent or seditious pathfinders, disrupting the status quo and challenging the assumptions and worldview of planners and others.

If the 1980s and early 1990s amounted to a first distinctive turn in the nature of alternative planning and regeneration spaces, then the period from 1997 following the election of New Labour marked a second. The key feature here is that New Labour, while still distrustful of aspects of local government, nonetheless sought to build from local-government planning powers, developing additional growth and regeneration initiatives around them. In its initial period at least, New Labour appeared to be strongly motivated to do away with the so-called 'non-elected state', announcing that UDCs and TECs would be discontinued. While there had been a range of quasi-formal regional strategies emerging from the early 1990s, most notably for the southeast of England, the period from 1998 saw the re-emergence of the region as a strategic planning scale. Some bodies, such as the Regional Assemblies, were strongly rooted in local government, while others such as the private sector-led Regional Development Agencies (RDAs) seemed to be re-creating the quango state at new scales. This rescaling activity was accompanied by, and may have even helped shape, a further round of alternative strategy making, particularly around meta-strategy such as the Northern Way and the delivery of growth and housing through a range of delivery bodies and vehicles (Haughton *et al.,* 2010). The 2003 Sustainable Communities Plan was particularly significant in this respect, with its creation of Housing Market Renewal Pathfinders and the establishment of growth areas, the latter leading to a whole range of new delivery bodies at sub-regional level, including the creation of 'new generation' UDCs in some instances.

Area master-planning also became a widespread feature of the planning system, typically involving consortia of consultancies with different professional backgrounds being brought together to develop area plans by any other name, which might then get incorporated into local plans at a later stage. Regional planning was put on a statutory basis from 2004, with the regional planning bodies encouraged to develop more emphasis on sub-regional plans, especially where these involved cross-border issues. In addition, local authorities were encouraged to create Local Strategic Partnerships (LSPs) in their localities and to cooperate more formally with neighbouring authorities on selected policy areas by creating Multi-Area Agreements (MAAs).

The result of New Labour's reconfiguration of the sub-national governance landscape was a resurgence of new strategic bodies at neighbourhood, local, sub-regional and regional levels, all engaged to greater or lesser degrees with the process of local plan making. In short, New Labour started off challenging the legitimacy of the sub-national quango state only to reinvent it in its own image, with local government positioned as a key actor in the new arrangements, but, nonetheless, required to work with other local actors if they were to access government powers and funding in the broad areas of planning-related activities, such as economic development, regeneration and housing.

Against this long-term backdrop of evolution and change, English planning after 2010 began another of its regular bouts of upheaval and reform. The Coalition government, which came to power in 2010, dismantled the regional apparatus of its predecessor. Some of the post-2010 changes, notably the introduction of a National Planning Policy Framework (NPPF) and a presumption in favour of sustainable development, have been particularly controversial and contested (Allmendinger and Haughton, 2012, 2013). The election in 2015 of a Conservative government committed to a major expansion of house building by 2020 may see further reforms to the planning system, as localised housing shortages and widespread problems of affordability remain prominent political issues.

In terms of planning spaces, the abolition of the regional tier of plans and the introduction of neighbourhood plans, both under the guise of the localism agenda, have attracted only limited contestation (but see Swain *et al.,* 2012). Other changes such as the creation of the Infrastructure Planning Commission (IPC) introduced at the tail end of the last Labour government have been adopted and adapted by the Coalition. The IPC now exists, in a slightly modified form, as the Major Infrastructure Planning Unit within the Planning Inspectorate. In a parallel radical initiative, the government has created powers to transfer to the Planning Inspectorate planning decisions from local government, if it feels decisions are slow or otherwise problematic. In a similar vein, powers have been created such that if local plans are not agreed within a given short-timeframe, then the default planning framework will be the NPPF, not the local plan (Haughton and Hincks, 2013).

The era following the 2010 General Election and the emergence of Conservative-led governments, then, has been characterised by a radical round of spatial restructuring, with the abolition of regional spatial strategies and the emergence of various, voluntary sub-regional joint arrangements to provide strategic planning, the reintroduction of a form of EZ linked to private sector-led Local Enterprise Partnerships (LEPs) and a new emphasis on empowering neighbourhood planning.

It is also important to emphasise the growing European dimension to planning thought in England, in particular the EU's promotion of a variety of new multi-regional, trans-national alternative spaces (e.g. Faludi, 2010; Medeiros, 2011; Stead, 2014). Faludi (2013) identifies new spaces of planning as key to the EU's aim of territorial cohesion, overcoming the tensions between national territorial and functional cohesive spaces. Such cross-national border spaces of cooperation have increased significantly in recent years (Chilla *et al.*, 2012), with macro-regional strategies proposed for the Danube Basin, the Adriatic-Ionion Sea, the North Sea-English Channel and the Alpine Region (Knieling, 2011). In contrast to earlier attempts at creating new trans-national European regional formations, such as the Atlantic Arc (created in 1989), the recent initiatives are notable for including regions outside the EU. The significance of this is that they have become much more than exercises in finding new ways to get EU actors together as part of the 'European project' to promote greater internal integration.

Metzger and Schmitt (2012, p. 264) have explored the recent development of the European Union Strategy for the Baltic Sea Region (EUSBSR), describing it as 'one of the most radical innovations in European territorial management since the development of the ESDP (European Spatial Development Perspective) in the 1990s' (see also Knieling, 2011; Stead, 2014). The EUSBSR, along with other EU-driven macro-regions, represents part of an attempt to strengthen transnational territorial cooperation by collectivising, unsettling or challenging national sovereignties, allowing sometimes difficult or controversial issues around 'hard' boundaries or different legal systems to be addressed. For Faludi (2013), the increasing use of alternative planning spaces, such as the macro-regions, is part of an attempt at territorial cohesion by the EU, deliberately undermining what he sees as the inherent conservatism of subsidiarity and territoriality.

The role of challenging existing representations of space through the deployment of fuzzy boundaries has also been a feature of other alternative planning spaces, most notably in Wales where the creation of six new areas in the 2004 Wales Spatial Plan was seen by its proponents as essential to creating new thinking (see Haughton *et al.*, 2010; Heley, 2012). Work in Denmark has also highlighted how the use of fuzzy spatial representations at the national scale has helped avoid contestation:

> The concern with handling potentially volatile spatial politics seems to have caused an increasing 'fear' of spatial representations in Danish spatial planning.
>
> (Olesen and Richardson, 2011, p. 373)

In addition to what we might term 'functional planning justifications' and understanding of the emergence of alternative trans-national and trans-regional spaces, there is also a largely overlooked cultural dimension. Strategic spatial planning and the emergence of alternative spaces can be seen as ways of managing deeply embedded differences in national planning regimes (Othengrafen, 2010, 2012). The distinctions between, for example, zoning and discretionary-based national planning regimes, civil and common law-based legal frameworks, and different administrative traditions (centralised, federal, etc.) provide stark boundary effects and potential impediments to cross-border cooperation and integration. New, alternative spaces of planning provide flexible tools through which such differences can be managed.

Understanding alternative spaces of planning

From a longer-term perspective, recent changes can be seen as part of the cyclical to- and fro-ing of policy scale and scope within planning (Allmendinger and Haughton, 2007). Yet there is another dimension to change that needs to be borne in mind. The creation of new planning spaces such as the NPPF, Major Infrastructure Planning Unit, Neighbourhood Plans, LEPs and EZs, and the abolition of other spaces, constitutes an important though only partial dimension of planning practice. These established, legally sanctioned and visible spaces are complemented by a fissiparous and complex landscape of other, alternative planning spaces as the historical overview discussed made clear. The question then arises of whether we can discern any underlying pattern or commonalities? We outline, here, seven types of alternative planning spaces, which are not necessarily mutually exclusive (this section draws on a typology first outlined in Allmendinger and Haughton, 2010).

New formal or statutory tiers of government

From the late 1990s, devolution in the United Kingdom created a range of new, statutory spaces derived from rescaled, post-devolution planning functions. The main manifestations of this involved the regional planning arrangements in England that existed during the 2000s and remain extant in London, and the national spatial planning frameworks created in Scotland, Wales and Northern Ireland. Some of these new state spaces, such as the territories associated with regional spatial strategies, were created to help deliver strategic, coordinated planning, providing additional spatial sensitivity by generating informal sub-regional plans as part of their approach.

These 'plan within plans' highlighted the symbiotic nature of what we termed 'hard' and 'soft' spaces of planning. While the statutory regional spatial strategies are now being rescinded, the informal or soft sub-regional approaches have tended to remain and have evolved in places into formal, plans or spaces through various joint strategic arrangements (see Allmendinger *et al.*, 2016).

Informal or soft spaces of governance

Soft spaces can be used to create new spatial imaginaries intended to help shift attitudes, coordinate public and private actors and garner support for proposals. They represent a distinct class of alternative planning space and fall into three types.

The first is 'bottom-up functional'. Formal regional and local plans often map uneasily onto development opportunities or functional planning areas. To address this, local authorities and others have begun to prepare plans and other strategies to better reflect such functional geographies at various scales, alongside, though, sometimes 'outside of formal' plans. Examples include sub-regional planning statements and master-planning exercises, for instance. The emergence of bodies such as Cambridgeshire Horizons as delivery bodies between and across scales is a clear example of this.

The emergence of joint strategic-planning arrangements represents another example of alternative planning spaces. Such sub-regional arrangements vary, sometimes being advisory, soft spaces (e.g., Cambridgeshire Joint Strategic Plan), and in some places being formal, joint plans based on pooled sovereignty (e.g., the South Worcestershire Development Plan).

The second form of soft space, 'bespoke delivery spaces', can be distinguished from the first in terms of motivation. Formal or statutory plans and approaches can be characterised by their lengthy preparation times and inflexible processes. Establishing shadow plans and strategies on different scales allows planners and others to deliver development on different terms and over shorter timescales than through statutory systems. Research in the Thames Gateway highlighted examples where authorities were 'going through the motions' of statutory plan making while focusing attention on informal, delivery-focused shadow plans and master plans (Allmendinger and Haughton, 2009).

A third form of soft space, 'top-down functional spaces', has been driven by the Treasury in relation to sub-regional planning and economic development, and by the Department of Communities and Local Government in relation to housing market and travel-to-work areas, most evident in the Housing Market Renewal Pathfinders and the growth areas introduced as part of the Sustainable Communities Plan.

City-regions are a hybrid of top-down and bottom-up functional spaces, actively lobbied for by certain larger metropolitan areas, notably through the Core Cities Group. These ideas were then taken up by the 2007 sub-national economic-development review led by the Treasury, which saw city-regions as a mechanism for driving forward economic development (Varró, 2010). The Coalition government took on many of these ideas, supporting the creation of the Greater Manchester Combined Authority in 2012, giving it statutory powers for economic development, regeneration and transport. Subsequently there has been considerable interest within central government in the creation of a Northern Powerhouse, embracing not only Manchester but also other northern city-regions within a wider development corridor stretching across northern England.

Fuzzy spaces

The hard boundaries of most statutory plans and strategies do not sit well with more networked forms of space and governance. It is sometimes deemed helpful to create ambiguity through 'fuzzy boundaries', to enable flexible policy responses or to mask politically sensitive proposals. Examples include the six areas created in the Wales Spatial Strategy and the initial city-region proposals of the Northern Way (Haughton *et al.*, 2010; Heley 2012). LEPs sometimes also fall within the fuzzy category, since some have overlapping boundaries.

Spaces of emancipation

As noted earlier, there is a long tradition of local actors coming together to create their own strategies and delivery vehicles, often in exasperation at difficulties in dealing with a particular level of government – and sometimes funded by another level of government. Examples include Coin Street Community Builders in London and the Eldonians in Liverpool. Coin Street was backed by the Greater London Council (GLC) as an antidote to the mainstream national government approach of the time, while the Eldonians was very much a community response to the excesses of Militant Labour in Liverpool (Brindley *et al.*, 1996; Meegan, 1990; Leeming, 2002).

Another example is the community economic-development areas funded through the European Regional Development Fund as a way of ensuring that these funds were not being appropriated for national government programmes whose direct beneficiaries were not necessarily those most in need, for instance, when used as part of major infrastructure projects. The resulting 'pathways to integration' areas, as they were known on Merseyside in particular, were funded to develop their own governance systems and projects, targeted at the needs of their particular areas (Meegan and Mitchell, 2001).

Emancipatory potential can also sometimes be used to legitimate changes to mainstream planning policy. Neighbourhood planning in England since 2011 is framed as being growth supportive, with incentives being given to local communities to reward agreeing to development. Just as likely in some localities is that neighbourhood plans will be used to justify limiting new developments in some areas.

Private planning spaces

Since 2010, the creation of LEPs in England has provided another dimension to encouraging the emergence of 'private planning spaces', most remarkably the Atlantic Gateway in the North West (Dembski, 2012; Harrison, 2012). Here, Peel Holdings has assembled a group of public and private actors willing to cohere around their plans for a large sweep of land connecting Liverpool and Manchester. The boundaries of this archetypal fuzzy space are not clear, but, broadly, Atlantic Gateway follows the Manchester Ship Canal, which Peel Holdings own along with large swathes of adjacent development land. In 2013, the UK government announced that LEPs would have a leading role in helping determine housing targets for an area – targets that are given effect through component territorial plans for local planning authorities. This amounts to a 'fuzzy relationship' between the two bodies and, more specifically, between the larger scale LEPs and the constituent local authorities.

National spaces of delivery

Partly in response to problems of planning meeting objectives, we are beginning to witness the emergence of alternative spaces of delivery. The early 2000s witnessed the eco-town initiative, with a number of new settlements planned by central government to help address housing supply shortages. In addition, the IPC (now the Major Infrastructure Planning Unit), after its establishment in 2008, took responsibility for major infrastructure proposals away from local government and put it into national government. By partitioning major infrastructure and new housing settlements into the realm of national planning with bespoke structures of governance and distinct policy frameworks, successive governments have created discrete spaces focused on delivery.

Trans-national and other trans-boundary spaces

As we have already seen, European Commission initiatives have been used for some years to 'reach in' to local areas to help shape growth strategies and, indeed, to insist on strategies being created by 'social partners' at the regional scale, even in periods when national governments were not keen to support regional-scale actions. With the latest generation of European regional spaces 'reaching out' to neighbouring non-EU countries, a new era of European spatial thinking is now taking shape.

These alternative spaces emerge, evolve or disappear against the backdrop of territorial, mainstream planning spaces. They can be relatively enduring, sometimes 'filling in' gaps between mainstream planning spaces, sometimes challenging ,sometimes complementing them. Some initiatives can possess attributes from more than one of these categories – arguably it is in the nature of alternative spaces that they should in so many cases transcend attempts to neatly categorise them.

Conclusion

The emergence into the planning mainstream of alternative planning and regeneration spaces cannot be judged as a 'good' or 'bad' thing. Such spaces have no inherent properties, so they are never inherently progressive or regressive. They can be used to deliver on much needed development, coordinating disparate public and private bodies and improving the efficiency and effectiveness of planning. At the same time, alternative spaces can and have been used as ways of displacing political questions and issues, avoiding accountability and transparency and delivering on a growth agenda. Despite the notion that these alternative spaces are essentially functional tools that can be used for a variety of purposes, they do have more general consequences. In some situations, they have provided much-needed functional spaces of planning, but they have also undoubtedly added to the congestion and complexity of governance in general and spatial governance in particular. This congestion has been largely overlooked, particularly by the Conservative-led governments of 2010 onwards who are intent on deregulation and localism while also content to encourage new 'infill' practices and spaces to fill the vacuum that is being opened up.

We conclude with three points. First, while alternative planning spaces have been a recurrent and regular feature of planning in the United Kingdom, there are clear distinctions between the types of space that emerged from the 1940s through to the present. In the earlier examples, the various studies and alternative planning spaces were initiated and usually tightly controlled by central government. From around 2000, such spaces were initiated as much by local and regional actors as by central government. There is another dimension to this account, which is that the period from the 2000s onwards saw a punctuated or accelerated evolution in the emergence of alternative planning spaces. What distinguishes the more recent incarnations of spatial experimentation is the increase in their use at a range of scales and for a variety of purposes, their endorsement by central government and their acceptance by the planning profession as a legitimate and 'normal' part of the toolkit or armoury of planning (Allmendinger and Haughton, 2010, p. 811).

Second, there is also a change in the nature of the spaces themselves. The 1960s and 1970s' experiments in creating alternative planning spaces were all variants of creating new governmental spaces, effectively exercises in rethinking territorial government, leading to the creation of, for instance, new county councils. In the subsequent period, we have seen the growing use of governance bodies and new geographies to work at scales other than that of local-government units. In the earlier period, initiatives such as UDCs, EZs and SPZs were deliberately disruptive and challenging to the status quo, but they were also for the most part small scale and limited. The period from 2000 has seen a more widespread, overlapping, multi-sectoral and multi-scalar emergence of alternative planning and regeneration spaces and related governance bodies that reflect a more relational understanding of space, even as these new alternative spaces necessarily must also work with territorial forms of government as part of their quest to gain some form of legitimacy for their activities.

Finally, we feel the need to stand back from the history and development of alternative planning spaces and reflect on their significance and the nature of planning. There is not the space here to engage with all the consequences, so we will focus on three issues that we pose as questions. The first question is, what is now meant by planning in an era of fragmented, multiple spaces and overlapping practices? If, as we are reminded by central government, planning is a 'burden on business', which aspect of planning constitutes that burden – the territorial/statutory spaces or the emerging, alternative spaces blessed by the notion of localism? Has all that is solid melted into air? Second, what does it mean to be a planner in such an era? One of our primary concerns as academics is to take responsibility for the initial education of planners – but what skills and knowledge are required when a diminishing component of planning is the 'visible' and statutory element and a growing element is the less visible, informal planning? Finally, wearing a different hat as individuals within communities affected by planning, who – to paraphrase Henry Kissinger – do we phone if we wish to discuss planning in our area? Where does the transparency and accountability of alternative planning spaces lie?

References

Allen, J. and Cochrane, A. (2010) Assemblages of state power: topological shifts in the organization of government and politics, *Antipode*, 42, 1071–1089.

Allmendinger, P. and Haughton, G. (2007) The fluid scales and scope of UK spatial planning, *Environment and Planning A*, 39, 1478–1496.

Allmendinger, P. and Haughton, G. (2009) Soft spaces, fuzzy boundaries and metagovernance: the new spatial planning in the Thames Gateway, *Environment and Planning A*, 41, 617–633.

Allmendinger, P. and Haughton, G. (2010) Spatial planning, devolution and new planning spaces, *Environment and Planning C*, 28, 803–818.

Allmendinger, P. and Haughton, G. (2012) Post-political spatial planning in England: a crisis of consensus? *Transactions of the Institute of British Geographers*, 37, 89–103.

Allmendinger, P. and Haughton, G. (2013) The evolution and trajectories of neoliberal spatial governance: 'neoliberal' episodes in planning, *Planning Practice and Research*, 28, 6–26.

Allmendinger, P., Haughton, G., Knieling, J. and Othengrafen, F. (eds.) (2015) *Soft Spaces in Europe: Re-Negotiating Governance, Boundaries and Borders*, London: Routledge.

Allmendinger, P., Haughton, G. and Shepherd E. (2016) Where is planning to be found? Material practices and the multiple spaces of planning, *Environment and Planning C*, 34, 38–51.

Brindley, T., Rydin, Y. and Stoker, G. (1996) *Remaking Planning: The Politics of Urban Change*, London: Routledge.

Chilla, T., Evrard, E. and Schulz, C. (2012) On the territoriality of cross-border cooperation: 'institutional mapping' in a multi-level context, *European Planning Studies*, 20, 961–980.

Cochrane, A. (2012) Making up a region: the rise and fall of the South-East of England as a political territory, *Environment and Planning C*, 30, 95–108.

Dembski, S. (2012) *Symbolic Markers and Institutional Innovation in Transforming Urban Spaces*, Amsterdam: Amsterdam Institute for Social Science Research.

Faludi, A. (2010) *Cohesion, Coherence, Cooperation: European Spatial Planning Coming of Age?* London: Routledge.

Faludi, A. (2013) Territorial cohesion and subsidiarity under the European Union treaties: a critique of the 'territorialism' underlying, *Regional Studies*, 47, 1594–1606.

Frey, A. (1971) Estuary development feasibility: Tayside, Humberside and Severnside compared, *Area*, 3, 231–233.

Gaffikin, F. and Warf, B. (1993) Urban policy and the post-Keynesian state in the United Kingdom and the United States, *International Journal of Urban and Regional Research*, 17, 67–84.

Glasson, J. (1974) *Regional Planning*, London: Hutchinson Educational.

Glasson, J. and Marshall, T. (2007) *Regional Planning*, London: Routledge.

Goodwin, M. (2013) Regions, territories and relationality: exploring the regional dimensions of political practice, *Regional Studies*, 47, 1181–1190.

Goodwin, M., Jones, M. and Jones, R. (2005) Devolution, constitutional change and economic development: explaining and understanding the new institutional geographies of the British State, *Regional Studies*, 39, 421–436.

Goodwin, M., Jones, M. and Jones, R. (2006) Devolution and economic governance in the UK: rescaling territories and organizations, *European Planning Studies*, 14, 979–995.

Harrison, J. (2012) In what sense a new *non*-state space? Globalization, the politics of rescaling, and the new politics of city-regionalism. Available: http://papers.ssrn.com/sol3/papers.cfm?abstract_id=2110777 (accessed 25 August 2016).

Hart, T. Haughton, G. and Peck, J. (1996) Accountability and the non-elected local state: bringing Training and Enterprise Councils to local account, *Regional Studies*, 30, 429–441.

Haughton, G. (1999) Trojan horse or white elephant? The contested biography of the life and times of the Leeds Development Corporation, *Town Planning Review*, 70, 173–190.

Haughton, G. and Counsell, D. (2004) *Regions, Spatial Strategies and Sustainable Development*, London: Routledge.

Haughton, G. and Hincks, S. (2013) Austerity planning, *Town and Country Planning*, 82, 23–28.

Haughton, G., Allmendinger, P., Counsell, D. and Vigar, G. (2010) *The New Spatial Planning: Territorial Management with Soft Spaces and Fuzzy Boundaries*, London: Routledge.

Haughton, G., Allmendinger, P. and Oosterlynck, S. (2013) Spaces of neoliberal experimentation: soft spaces, postpolitics and neoliberal governmentality, *Environment and Planning A*, 45, 217–234.

Heley, J. (2012) Soft spaces, fuzzy boundaries and spatial governance in post-devolution Wales, *International Journal of Urban and Regional Research*, 37, 1325–1358.

HoC (House of Commons) (2002) *The New Towns: Their Problems and the Future*, Transport, Local Government and the Regions Committee, HC603-I, London: The Stationery Office.

Jones, M. (1997) Spatial selectivity of the state? The regulationist enigma and local struggles over economic governance, *Environment and Planning A*, 29, 831–864.

Jones M. (2009) Phase space: geography, relational thinking, and beyond, *Progress in Human Geography*, 33, 487–506.

Knieling, J. (2011) Metropolitan networking in the western Baltic Sea region: metropolitan region of Hamburg between multilevel governance and soft spatial development, in: Herrschel, T. and Tallberg, P. (eds.) *The Role of Regions: Networks, Scale, Territory*, pp. 195–214, Gothenburg: Region Skane.

Lawless, P. (1988) Urban Development Corporations and their alternatives, *Cities*, 5, 277–289.

Leeming, K. (2002) Community businesses – lessons from Liverpool, *Community Development Journal*, 37, 260–267.

McLoughlin, J.B. (1969) Simulation for beginners: the planting of a sub-regional model, *Regional Studies*, 3, 313–323.

Massey, D. (2005) *For Space*, London: Sage.

Medeiros, E. (2011) (Re)defining the Euroregion concept, *European Planning Studies*, 19, 141–158.

Meegan, R. (1990) Merseyside in crisis and in conflict, in: Harloe, M., Pickvance, C. and Urry, J. (eds.) *Place, Policy and Politics: Do Localities Matter?* pp. 87–107, London: Unwin Hyman.

Meegan, R. and Mitchell, A. (2001) Change and cohesion in urban regeneration policies 'it's not community round here, it's neighbourhood', *Urban Studies*, 38, 2167–2194.

Metzger, J. and Schmitt, P. (2012) When soft spaces harden: the EU strategy for the Baltic Sea Region, *Environment and Planning A*, 44, 263–280.

Olesen, K. and Richardson, T. (2011) The spatial politics of spatial representation: relationality as a medium for depoliticization? *International Planning Studies*, 16, 355–375.

Othengrafen, F. (2010) Spatial planning as expression of culturised planning practices: the examples of Athens and Helsinki, *Town Planning Review*, 81, 83–110.

Othengrafen, F. (2012) *Uncovering the Unconscious Dimensions of Planning: Using Culture as a Tool to Analyse Spatial Planning Practice*, Farnham, UK: Ashgate.

Painter, J. (2010) Rethinking territory, *Antipode*, 42, 1090–1118.

Ratcliffe, J. (1974) *An Introduction to Town and Country Planning*, London: Hutchinson Educational.

Shaw, K. (1990) The lost world of local politics revisited: in search of the non-elected local state, *Regional Studies*, 24, 180–184.

Stead, D. (2014) European integration and spatial rescaling in the Baltic Region: soft spaces, soft planning and soft security, *European Planning Studies*, 22, 680–693.

Swain, C., Marshall, T. and Baden, T. (eds.) (2012) *English Regional Planning 2010–2012: Lessons for the Future*, London: Routledge.

Varró, K. (2010) *After resurgent regions, resurgent cities? Contesting state geographies in Hungary and England, unpublished doctoral thesis, Nijmegen*, The Netherlands: Radboud University.

6 Multi-level geographies of trans-boundary cooperation in Catalonia

Governance, planning and 'cross-border spaces of regionalist engagement'

Claire Colomb, Francesc Morata Tierra, Antoni Durà Guimerà and Xavier Oliveras González

Introduction

This chapter discusses whether practices of trans-boundary cooperation in the European Union (EU) can lead to new types of spatial planning and territorial development strategies and new forms of trans-boundary territorial governance, focusing on the case of Catalonia in Spain. The generic term of 'trans-boundary cooperation' used here refers to (more or less institutionalised) forms of collaboration at different scales between sub-national authorities from two or more states,[1] aimed at the coordination and elaboration of common actions, projects, policies or strategies. Such forms of collaboration seek to overcome, at the local and regional level, the consequences of the continuous existence of state borders which demarcate different legal and administrative systems of health and education provision, labour market regulations and transport and territorial planning, to name but a few. Since the late 1980s, the process of European integration has given a significant impulse to practices of trans-boundary cooperation, thanks to the creation of EU programmes supporting cooperation across EU internal and external borders. Many local and regional authorities across the EU are now routinely involved in forms of cooperation across state borders. The increasingly proactive engagement of sub-central state actors in trans-boundary cooperation has occurred in parallel to the strengthening of the role of local and regional authorities in Europe: devolution and decentralisation processes have transformed them into key political actors and proactive agents of local and regional development (Keating, 1998; Pike *et al.*, 2006).

The chapter analyses how trans-boundary cooperation has been mobilised by the local and regional governmental actors of a particular region, Catalonia – one of Spain's Autonomous Communities – to support broadly conceived political, economic and cultural goals. The chapter first introduces the types of trans-boundary cooperation which have emerged in the EU since 1945, followed by an overview of the state of scholarship on the impact of trans-boundary cooperation on spatial planning, territorial development policies and governance. In the second part, the multiple types and geographies of trans-boundary cooperation in which

Catalan local and regional public actors have engaged over the past three decades are outlined.[2] Building on the social constructivist approach to cross-border cooperation proposed by Perkmann (2003) and others, we discuss whether the participation of Catalan public actors in various forms of trans-boundary cooperation has led to rescaled, innovative forms of spatial planning, territorial development and governance. In the final section, we show how the engagement of Catalan actors (in particular, the regional government) in such forms of cooperation is part of the search for a strengthened political and economic role for the region in the Mediterranean and in Europe, in the context of recurrent tensions with the Spanish central state over increasing claims for more regional autonomy.

Trans-boundary cooperation, territorial governance and spatial development policies in the EU

Trans-boundary cooperation was long the preserve of central state actors. In order to deal with specific cross-border issues, such as the coordination of transport infrastructure planning, in the 1960s and 1970s various bi- or multi-lateral governmental commissions, which were not open to local authorities, were established to support inter-state cooperation (such as the Benelux, the Nordic Council or the International Commission of the Pyrenees) (Perkmann, 2003). Sub-central levels of government are usually not legal subjects according to international law, and are therefore not allowed to conclude international treaties with foreign authorities. This explains why, until recently, trans-boundary cooperation between sub-national levels of government was based on informal arrangements (Perkmann, 2003), such as the first 'Euroregion' created in 1958 at the German-Dutch border. In 1980, the Council of Europe approved the Madrid Convention, which allows sub-central state actors to enter into formal cross-border cooperation agreements.

From the late 1980s onwards, the development of trans-boundary cooperation between local and regional state actors was given a major boost by the reform and expansion of EU Cohesion Policy, in particular by the creation of the European Territorial Cooperation (INTERREG) programmes in 1990. There are currently dozens of trans-boundary cooperation programmes funded under the so-called 'European Territorial Cooperation' objective of EU Cohesion Policy, which is divided into three strands of cooperation: cross-border, trans-national and inter-regional.[3] From the European Commission point of view, trans-boundary cooperation should seek to overcome 'border effects' and achieve the EU objectives of economic, social and territorial cohesion by encouraging local and regional authorities to address territorial and spatial development problems across state borders more effectively, such as flood risk in trans-national river basins. It has also been argued that the European Commission sees trans-boundary networking as a way to promote particular agendas and 'good practices' in policy fields where the EU does not have a formal legislative competence (Bomberg and Peterson, 2000), such as spatial planning and urban policy (Atkinson, 2001; Jensen and Richardson, 2004; Dabinett and Richardson, 2005; Dühr *et al.*, 2010).

Building on the analytical framework developed by Perkmann (2003), Oliveras González *et al.* (2010) provided an overview of the number and type of cross-border regional cooperation initiatives in the EU in the second half of the 2000s. Perkmann (2003, p. 156) defined such forms of cooperation as those whose main protagonists are public *sub-central governmental* authorities in different countries, who are concerned with *practical problem-solving* in a broad range of fields of everyday administrative life which involve a certain *stabilisation* of cross-border contacts, i.e. institution-building, over time. While there were only 20 such initiatives in the mid-1980s, this had increased to 73 by 2003 (Perkmann, 2003) and to 133 in 2007 (Oliveras González *et al.*, 2010), under various labels such as 'Euroregions', 'Eurodistricts' or 'Working Communities'.

The variety of trans-boundary cooperation forms in the EU

Several criteria can be used to distinguish between various forms of trans-boundary cooperation (Perkmann, 2003; Oliveras González *et al.*, 2010). First, the nature of the *key agents* giving an impulse to, and involved in, trans-boundary cooperation varies. Sub-central state actors play a key role, i.e. local and regional authorities, or sometimes intermediary tiers of government, such as Italian provinces or French *départements*. Other types of public or quasi-public actors often involved include regional development agencies, business associations, chambers of commerce and universities, while the participation of private-sector companies is less common. Second, the *topics* and *objectives* of trans-boundary cooperation can vary significantly, between generic, wide-ranging initiatives covering a particular cross-border area, and sectorial or thematic projects or networks. Third, the extent to which cooperation involves *geographically contiguous* actors across one (or more) national border(s) matters – or whether it entails networks between non-contiguous cities and regions. The latter is referred to as 'inter-regional cooperation' in the EU-funded territorial cooperation programmes and includes networks of cities and regions covering a specific theme (e.g. the European Regeneration Areas Network), geographical area (e.g. the Latin Arc) or the whole EU (e.g. Eurocities), for the purpose of lobbying and exchanges of expertise.

Within forms of cooperation between geographically contiguous actors, various *scales of cooperation* exist, where physical proximity matters to a different degree. What we refer to as 'micro-cooperation' involves actors located immediately alongside a national border (e.g. within a 50–100 km wide strip), and is referred to as 'cross-border cooperation' in the EU-funded INTERREG A programmes. Such forms of cooperation tend to involve primarily municipal and supra-municipal actors, sometimes provincial or regional actors (e.g. Eurodistricts or some of the small Euroregions). They accounted for two-thirds of the structures listed by Oliveras González *et al.* (2010) in 2007. The so-called 'Working Communities', or the larger Euroregions which have proliferated across Europe, correspond to a bigger scale of cooperation between regional authorities in two or more countries, referred to as 'macro-cooperation' by some authors (Perkmann, 2003; Oliveras González *et al.*, 2010), although it may be more appropriate to label them as 'meso-level regional cooperation', in light of the recent debates on 'European macro-regional strategies' at the EU level.[4]

Another important variable is the *existence of formal institutional structures* with legal status, as opposed to cooperation based on individual, time-limited projects or informal networks.[5] Cooperation may become institutionalised through the formation of new permanent structures composed of local or regional authorities on both sides of a border, which may take various forms in legal and organisational terms. Such structures have their own human, administrative and financial resources (albeit often limited) and are governed by specific decision-making processes based on political agreements between their members (Gabbe *et al.*, 2000). They offer an arena for the definition and implementation of concrete projects, often with EU funding, and have thus become legitimate partners in the implementation of EU Cohesion Policy in a context of multi-level governance (Perkmann, 2002). They materialise processes of 'solidification', whereby soft spaces of trans-boundary cooperation 'are transfigured into harder, more clearly regulated and governed, spaces through the establishment of more rigid and strictly formatted and regulated socio-material forms of spatial organization' (Metzger and Schmitt, 2012, p. 266). In 2006, an EU regulation established a new cooperation instrument with legal identity, the European Grouping of Territorial Cooperation (EGTC), composed of national, regional or local authorities, and/ or bodies governed by public law from two or more member states. By the end of 2013, 45 such EGTCs had been established in the EU (CoR, 2014). Yet, as will be discussed in the Catalan case, even when a formal cross-border structure is in place, the actual success of cooperation relies on the active engagement of specific 'policy entrepreneurs', networks and public and private actors who are willing to drive concrete projects. This can be captured by the notion of *cooperation intensity*, which Oliveras González *et al.* (2010) define as 'the strategic capacity gained by the cross-border structure and its degree of autonomy vis-à-vis the central state and other authorities'. The intensity of cooperation is additionally characterised by the existence of medium-term joint (territorial) strategies which go beyond a logic of individual projects (Colomb, 2007).

At this point, it is important to stress that forms of trans-boundary cooperation do not emerge in particular cross-border areas simply because of their potential 'regionness' (Perkmann, 2003, p. 157), that is to say, because of pre-existing economic, social, cultural or political links (such as a common language or integrated urban system). In some cases, it is the development of new forms and practices of cooperation, and of locally institutionalised frameworks for cross-border region building, which are supposed to lead to the creation of a stronger sense of trans-boundary regional identity and to trans-boundary networking and flow of all kinds: economic, environmental and cultural (Kramsch and Hooper, 2004). Oliveras González (2013), building on the social-constructivist approach proposed by Perkmann (2003) and others (e.g. Paasi, 1986, 2009, 2010; Gualini, 2003), conceptualises cross-border regions as the result of a socially constructed process in which some, or all, of the following elements converge: (a) a territory divided by a political border, but where similar territorial processes take place;

(b) some cross-border social, economic and/or environmental dynamics; (c) some inter-related territorial agents who mobilise to implement projects of mutual interest; (d) some projects carried out through cooperation; (e) a common identity, based on the same culture, language, symbology, history or shared territory; and (f) discourses and narratives (of geographical, historical, socio-economic and/or socio-cultural unity) that project the idea of sharing the territory, certain dynamics, projects and/or an identity.

The impact of trans-boundary cooperation on territorial governance and spatial development policies

The increasing number, variety, geographic and thematic scope of trans-boundary cooperation initiatives in Europe has generated a vast amount of research in geography, regional studies, political science, 'border studies', planning and sociology. While some authors argue that such initiatives are 'producing another soft, but institutionalised, comprehensive, stable and territorially-defined layer in the European "multi-level-system" [of governance]' (Blatter, 2004, online abstract, n.p.; Perkmann 2007a), others are more sceptical about the long-term structural impacts of such forms of cooperation on the rescaling of public policies, strategic planning and territorial-development strategies (Dühr and Nadin, 2007; Dühr *et al.*, 2010). If we take governance as concerned with reaching binding decisions in the public sphere (Kohler-Koch, 1999; Stead, 2014), it is rare that trans-boundary cooperation leads to a new scale of (institutionalised) governance. A broader definition of governance may be used, however. Blatter (2004), in his analysis of cross-border regions, builds on the two types of multi-level governance identified by Hooghe and Marks (2003) and distinguishes between 'territorial governance' (type I) and 'functional governance' (type II). Type I governance has been, historically, the most prevalent form when it comes to spatial planning, as most planning systems are 'based on the concept of territory as a neatly ordered space within definite boundaries', in which each scale has its own instruments such as land-use plans and strategic spatial plans (Stead, 2014, p. 1369). 'Functional governance', by contrast, is characterised by networked interaction and is oriented towards specific tasks or policy problems to be addressed through variable scales of intervention (Stead, 2014). The territories for action are defined not by intra- and inter-state administrative boundaries, but in terms of criteria such as functional relations (e.g. travel patterns) or environmental systems (e.g. river basins). Trans-boundary cooperation initiatives, in this understanding, potentially represent new informal, non-statutory 'soft planning spaces' with more or less 'fuzzy boundaries' (Allmendinger and Haughton, 2009; Haughton *et al.*, 2010, see also Chapter 5, this volume).

Approaches to and paradigms of spatial planning and territorial development policies vary across and within countries, and are shaped by distinctive historical, political, economic and social factors. In an era of globalisation and European integration, in which knowledge about the policies of other units of government travels more easily than ever, geographers and planners have begun to reconceptualise planning and territorial development policies as 'socially produced and circulated forms of knowledge addressing how to design and govern cities [and regions] that develop in, are conditioned by, travel through, connect, and shape various spatial scales, networks, policy communities, and institutional contexts' (McCann, 2011, p. 109). The process of economic and political integration in the EU has had a direct and indirect influence on spatial planning systems, policies and practices in EU member states (Dühr *et al.*, 2010, Table 23.1). The transformation of domestic policies (at the central or sub-central levels of government) which may arise as a result of the influence of the EU and its activities is referred to by political scientists as 'Europeanisation', which can happen through the formal implementation of binding EU legislation and decisions, or through 'soft', 'cognitive' and 'discursive' channels (Radaelli, 2004) which encourage policy change. Such channels include the 'Open Method of Coordination' (Faludi, 2004) and benchmarking (Bruno *et al.*, 2006), as well as various forms of trans-boundary cooperation designed to stimulate horizontal exchanges of 'good practice' between sub-central levels of government (Marshall, 2005; Colomb, 2007; Hachmann, 2011). The EU thus facilitates the mobility of urban, regional and territorial development policies and practices through its INTERREG programmes.

The assumption that trans-boundary cooperation can lead to policy learning and policy change[6] via the dissemination of 'good practice' has become accepted wisdom in international organisations (Bulkeley, 2006), the EU being no exception. However, few studies have managed to substantiate this assumption with conclusive empirical evidence, in part because there are serious methodological challenges in evaluating the learning processes at play within trans-boundary cooperation, and in establishing clear causal links between such forms of cooperation and observable changes in policies and practices within partner institutions, cities or regions (Colomb, 2007). Over the past decade, scholars have paid increasing attention to the qualitative impacts of EU trans-boundary cooperation programmes[7] (especially trans-national ones), arguing that they have contributed to the diffusion of certain policy ideas across European regions, to changes in urban, regional and spatial planning approaches, and to innovation in territorial governance (Janin Rivolin, 2004; Giannakourou, 2005; Janin Rivolin and Faludi, 2005; Pedrazzini, 2005; ESPON and Nordregio, 2005; Dabinett and Richardson, 2005; Dabinett, 2006; Hachmann, 2011).

Dühr *et al.* (2010, Chapter 22) have conceptualised the potential changes in spatial planning and territorial development policies arising from trans-boundary cooperation into three types: policy learning and change at the local or regional level; a trans-boundary rescaling of policies; and policy convergence (or Europeanisation) between the participating institutions. Past research on North West Europe has shown that while there is, in some cases, evidence of policy change at the local or regional level as a result of trans-boundary cooperation, there is scant evidence of a real trans-boundary rescaling of planning and territorial development strategies, or of a convergence of planning systems and territorial development practices (Dühr and Nadin, 2007; Dühr *et al.*, 2010, Chapter 23; Stead, 2013). The reasons for this lie with the various factors which influence trans-boundary cooperation activities, potentially facilitating or constraining the individual, intra-organisational and inter-organisational learning processes which occur within them (Colomb, 2007). Some of the factors which influence inter-institutional learning include differences in competences, administrative cultures and institutional capacity; political factors (e.g. the 'European' commitment of political leaders); or cultural and linguistic differences (Morata and Noferini, 2013), as will be discussed in the Catalan case. Within partner institutions, the existing institutional capacity (e.g. human, financial and technical resources; links and degree of trust between technical and political staff; interdepartmental cooperation; relationships with other tiers of government and other socio-economic actors) is often not adapted to the challenges posed by trans-boundary working.[8]

The multiple scales and forms of trans-boundary cooperation in Catalonia

Catalonia, with a population of 7.5 million in 2014, is one of the 17 Autonomous Communities of Spain. Catalonia has its own culture, language (Catalan[9]), and a long history of self-government. In the nineteenth and early twentieth century, Catalonia became, with the Basque Country, the epicentre of the Industrial Revolution in Spain. The region, which accounts for 16% of Spain's population, generated 18.7% of the Spanish Gross Domestic Product (GDP) in 2012 and, in European terms, is a relatively rich region.[10] The government of Catalonia – the *Generalitat* – was established in 1359, when Catalonia was a self-governing principality within the Crown of Aragon, a powerful Mediterranean power which ruled, at its most expansive, the territories which today form Eastern Spain, the Balearic Islands, part of Southern France, Corsica, Sardinia, Sicily, the South of Italy and part of Greece. In the thirteenth and fourteenth century, Catalonia was the leading economic and trading power of Western Mediterranean, thoroughly embedded in networks of cooperation with cities and regions across the Mediterranean (Durà Guimerà, 2012a, referring to Braudel, 1990). The Crowns of Aragon and Castile were united in 1469, leading to the territorial consolidation of the Kingdom of Spain in the sixteenth century. After the discovery of the Americas, trading flows shifted to the Atlantic and Catalonia lost its pivotal economic role, a decline which continued through to the eighteenth century with the consolidation of the Spanish state into a highly centralised system. Catalan self-government was disbanded in 1714, after Catalonia's defeat in the Spanish War of Succession. The *Nueva Planta* decrees of 1716 banned Catalan political institutions, rights and privileges and merged Catalonia as a province into the Crown of Castile. The border between Spain and France was established in 1659–60 by the *Treaty of the Pyrenees,* later further demarcated throughout the nineteenth century by the *Treaties of Limits.* The border splits the historic Catalan territory between Spain and France, in particular the Cerdanya valley. Between 1880 and 1930, mayors from both sides of the border occasionally convened assemblies to address cross-border issues of mutual interest (e.g. railways or water supply)

(Oliveras González, 2013). From the mid-1930s until 1980, however, cross-border cooperation was by and large halted by the authoritarian Franco regime in Spain.

After a short-lived restoration in 1931–39 under the Second Spanish Republic, Catalan regional self-government was finally restored after Franco's death and Spain's return to democracy in 1977. On the basis of the Spanish Constitution of 1978, the Spanish state has evolved into a highly decentralised 'State of Autonomies', characterised by a system of asymmetrical devolution between the central state and the 17 Autonomous Communities (each with its own 'Statute of Autonomy'). While the Basque Country and Navarre have full fiscal autonomy, Andalusia, Catalonia and Galicia do not, but have more powers than other Autonomous Communities (due to the existence of two modalities to achieve regional autonomy in the post-Franco transition years). The *Generalitat de Catalunya* has a high degree of legislative and executive power, albeit subject to central state control. The lower tiers of government in Catalonia include four provinces (Barcelona, Girona, Lleida and Tarragona) administered by the *Diputacións*,[11] 946 municipalities, 42 *comarques* (groupings of municipalities) and other inter-municipal cooperation structures.

The first cross-border cooperation initiative in the Iberian Peninsula started in the early 1980s with the Working Community of the Pyrenees. After Spain joined the EU in 1986, Catalan, Basque and Galician regional actors began to engage proactively in trans-boundary cooperation projects and initiatives. The creation of INTERREG programmes by the EU in 1990, and the effective opening of internal EU borders following the Schengen agreement of 1995, gave further impetus to trans-boundary cooperation in the Iberian Peninsula. France and Spain signed the Bayonne Treaty on cross-border cooperation in 1995, which allowed sub-central state actors to enter into cross-border cooperation agreements and structures. In 2013, there were 67 formal agreements of cross-border cooperation at the Portuguese-Spanish and Franco-Spanish borders (including both micro- and meso-level forms of cooperation, as defined previously) (Trillo-Santamaria and Lois González, 2014), as well as 11 approved cross-border EGTCs and four under construction.

As shown by Durà Guimerà and Oliveras González (2008, 2013) in their survey of agents and forms of territorial cooperation in the Mediterranean Arc (on the basis of Oliveras González, 2009), Catalonia is one of the most actively engaged regions in trans-boundary cooperation in South West Europe. There are specific reasons for this, which will be developed further in the final part of this chapter. Table 6.1 and Map 6.1 provide an overview of the most significant trans-boundary cooperation initiatives in which Catalan regional, provincial and local authorities have been involved over the past 30 years. These initiatives exhibit different degrees of institutionalisation and intensity. A complex layering of different scales and forms of trans-boundary cooperation has emerged, in which different sub-central levels of government are involved to varying degrees. We will focus on two scales of cooperation and outline their achievements and shortcomings to date: first, 'micro-level' cross-border cooperation alongside the Pyrenees; second, 'meso-level' Euroregional cooperation. The first represents a more bottom-up,

Table 6.1 Trans-boundary cooperation initiatives in which Catalan public authorities are involved, in chronological order by foundation date

Name	Date of creation	Scale/type of cooperation	Key actors	Degree of institutionalisation	Objectives and topics of cooperation
Comunitat de Treball dels Pirineus Working Community of the Pyrenees www.ctp.org	1983	Meso-level cross-border cooperation between contiguous regions	Spanish Autonomous Communities: Basque Country; Aragon; Navarra; Catalonia + French regions: Aquitaine; Languedoc Roussillon; Midi-Pyrénées + Principality of Andorra (since 2007)	1993–2005: association under French law (without legal personality) on the basis of an Agreement Protocol (limited funding and weak status) Since 2005: consortium under Spanish law (with legal personality) Since 2007: manages EU funds as Managing Authority for the INTERREG A France-Spain-Andorra Cross-border Cooperation Programme General secretariat in Jaca, Aragon Two-year rotating presidency. General assembly; executive committee; four thematic commissions (Infrastructure and Communication; Training and Technological Development; Culture, Youth and Sports; Sustainable Development)	Contribute to the development and protection of the Pyrenees through exchanges of good practice and joint actions to address shared issues (e.g. study of transport in the Pyrenees, publication of a tourist guide, conference on risks in the mountains, meetings of technology, research and innovation centres in the Pyrenees) Lobby relevant regional, national and European institutions

Quatre Motors per a Europa Four Motors for Europe www.4motors.eu (has lost momentum)	1988	Inter-regional cooperation network between non-contiguous regions	Launched at the initiative of the then-presidents of Baden-Württemberg, Lothar Speth, and Catalonia, Jordi Pujol Regional governments of Baden-Württemberg (DE); Catalunya (SP); Lombardia (IT); Rhône-Alpes (FR) + ad hoc cooperation with three other associated regions on particular projects (Wales, Flanders, Malopolska)	No permanent structure or secretariat Rotating one-year presidency between the four regions. Coordination committee meeting three times/year	Promote technological innovation and transfer; economic and trade links; cooperation in the fields of environment and culture Lobby EU institutions for a 'Europe of the Region' Economy group: joint missions abroad to promote the economic sectors of the four regions (e.g. in China, India, Russia)
C-6 Group of Regional Mediterranean Capitals (now inactive)	1990–98	Inter-city network (regional capitals of contiguous regions)	Proposal made by the then-Mayor of Barcelona, Pasqual Maragall, to the mayors of the neighbouring regional capitals. Quickly lost momentum due to rigid legal structure and rivalries (Morata 2007) Municipal governments of Montpellier (FR); Toulouse (FR); Zaragoza (SP); Barcelona (SP); València (SP); Palma de Mallorca (SP)	European Economic Interest Group (legal entity under European law)	Promote exchanges of experience through working groups led by each city (transport, tourism, culture and universities, sports, housing and urban planning, environment)

(*Continued*)

Table 6.1 (Continued)

Name	Date of creation	Scale/type of cooperation	Key actors	Degree of institutionalisation	Objectives and topics of cooperation
Euroregió Mediterrània Euroregion Mediterranean (Now defunct, replaced by the *Euroregió Pireneus-Mediterrània*)	1991–2001	Meso-level cross-border cooperation between contiguous regions	Members: Catalonia (SP); Languedoc-Roussillon (FR); Midi-Pyrénées (FR) Loss of momentum at the end of the 1990s following the controversial re-election of the president of the Languedoc-Roussillon region in 1998 with the support of National Front votes	'Regional association of cross-border cooperation'	Cooperate in economic, scientific and cultural development Lobby EU institutions
Arco Latino Latin Arc www.arcolatino.org	1999	Inter-regional cooperation network between sub-central (intermediate) levels of government	Around 60 intermediate authorities from Spain (provinces/diputacions in Catalonia + island councils of the Balearic islands), France (départements), Italy (provinces)	2002: non-profit association under French law	Cooperation initiatives in economic development, information and communications technology (ICT), transport, spatial planning, environment (water management), social integration, equal opportunities, culture and heritage Decentralized cooperation with local authorities South of the Mediterranean

Name / URL	Timeline	Type	Actors	Governance	Objectives
Euroregió Pireneus-Mediterrània Euroregion Pyrenees-Mediterranean www.euroregio.eu/	2004	Meso-level cross-border cooperation between contiguous regions	Catalonia (SP); Balearic Islands (SP); Languedoc-Roussillon (FR); Midi-Pyrénées (FR) Previously: Aragon (SP), which suspended its participation in May 2006 due to a disagreement with the Catalan government over the ownership of works of religious art	Political leaders of the four participating regions meet annually in a general assembly; 18 months rotating presidency between the regions Since 2009: EGTC (with legal personality) acting as operating arm for project management and staff contracting. Small budget based on contributions from member regions + some EU funding on a project basis. EGTC director based in Toulouse, EPM Secretariat based in Barcelona, one representative in Brussels + technical staff Thematic working groups made of political representatives and experts from the member regions	Transform the Euroregion into an ambitious economic space in the south of Europe devoted to research and technological innovation Create a dense network of infrastructure for its population Become a space of cultural and human interchanges Become the engine for sustainable development based on social and territorial inclusion (Founding declaration, 2004)
Cross-border Hospital of the Cerdanya www.hcerdanya.eu/	2003: feasibility study 2007: political agreement between key actors 2010: EGTC 2012: end of construction 2014: opening	Micro-level cross-border cooperation	France: French (national) Ministry of Health; Languedoc-Roussillon region; Communauté de Communes Capcir Haut Confluent Catalonia: Generalitat de Catalunya - Department of Health; Consell comarcal de la Cerdanya (17 municipalities); Municipality of Puigcerda	EGTC Management Board: meeting twice a year with 15 members representing the stakeholders involved at national, regional and local levels in France, Spain and Catalonia Executive committee: meeting every two to three weeks (three Catalans, two French)	First cross-border hospital built ex-novo in Europe serving the populations on both sides of the border Accompanied by a project for the integration of the health-care systems in the Cerdanya area

(*Continued*)

Table 6.1 (Continued)

Name	Date of creation	Scale/type of cooperation	Key actors	Degree of institutionalisation	Objectives and topics of cooperation
Eurodistricte de l'Espai Català Transfronterer Eurodistrict of the Catalan Cross-border Area www.eurodistricte.cat	2006/2009	Micro-level cross-border cooperation between contiguous local authorities	Territory covering 453 municipalities in the French département of Pyrénées-Orientales and the Catalan Province of Girona + six adjoining municipalities Members: all the local authorities and/ or associations and groupings of local authorities of the area (of which Perpignan, Figueres, Girona); Conseil Général des Pyrénées-Orientales ; Comarques (on the Catalan side); Diputació de Girona; Generalitat de Catalunya; Regional Natural Park of the Catalan Pyrenees	2006: framework agreement between Generalitat de Catalunya and Conseil Géneral des Pyrénées-Orientales 2009: creation of an EGTC (seat in Perpignan), with a technical director + team Rotating one-year presidency; assembly of members; advisory bodies and thematic working groups	Encourage a common cross-border spatial planning and sustainable development strategy and the structuring of a 'common employment, activity and residential basin' through concrete actions in the field of economy, services, transport and communications, tourism, education, culture and environment Support projects, search for EU funding, organise calls for proposals for cross-border projects (with funds from the Conseil Général and Generalitat)
Pirineus-Cerdanya EGTC	2011	Micro-level cross-border cooperation	Catalonia: Consell Comarcal de la Cerdanya (17 municipalities) France: Communauté de Communes Pyrénées-Cerdagne (16 municipalities)	Idea born in the 2000s through a joint waste water treatment plant and an INTERREG project 2011: creation of an EGTC with seat in Saillagouse, France Two-year rotating presidency	Support cooperation projects in four fields: infrastructure; water and environment; language, heritage and culture; economy and tourism

INTERREG A: cooperation programme Spain-France-Andorra (POCTEFA) www.poctefa.eu	(Created 1990) 2014–20: Fifth generation of programmes	Micro-level cross-border cooperation	Border territory corresponding to five Spanish provinces (of which two Catalan ones), five French départements + Andorra. Eligible actors: any public and non-profit organization in the eligible area (+ limited opportunities for private companies)	EU-funded programme under the European Territorial Cooperation strand of EU Cohesion Policy: Managing Authority + programming and steering committees with participating entities	Fund cross-border cooperation projects in a diverse range of fields. Total ERDF budget 2014–20: EUR 189.5 million
INTERREG B: trans-national cooperation programmes MED and SUDOE www.interreg-sudoe.eu www.programmemed.eu	(Created 1997) 2014–20: Fourth generation of programmes	Macro-level trans-national cooperation between large groupings of contiguous regions	Catalonia is part of - the South West Europe (SUDOE) programme covering the whole of Portugal and Spain + Southwestern France - the Mediterranean (MED) programme covering the territory of the sea-bordering regions of 13 countries. Eligible actors: any public and non-profit organization in the eligible area (+ limited opportunities for private companies)	EU-funded programmes under the European Territorial Cooperation strand of EU Cohesion Policy: trans-national projects. Managing Authority + programming and steering committees with participating entities	Fund trans-national cooperation projects in a diverse range of fields. SUDOE programme – total European Regional Development Fund (ERDF) budget 2014–20: EUR 100.4 million. MED programme – total ERDF budget 2014–20: EUR 224 million (+ EUR 9 million of Instrument for Pre-Accession Assistance (IPA))

(Continued)

Table 6.1 (Continued)

Name	Date of creation	Scale/type of cooperation	Key actors	Degree of institutionalisation	Objectives and topics of cooperation
INTERREG Europe (previously INTERREG C): inter-regional cooperation programme www.interreg4c.eu/	(Created 2000) 2014–20: Third generation of programmes	Macro-level inter-regional cooperation between non-contiguous regions	Eligible actors: any public and non-profit organization in the 28 EU member states + Norway and Switzerland	EU-funded programme under the European Territorial Cooperation strand of EU Cohesion Policy Managing authority + programming and steering committees with participating entities	Fund inter-regional cooperation projects in a diverse range of fields to improve policy learning, in particular in terms of the management of EU funds and regional development policies. Includes the thematic programmes INTERACT, URBACT and ESPON. Total ERDF budget 2014–20: EUR 359 million

Source: Compiled by the authors

Notes:

1   This table excludes

- very small-scale initiatives (twinning, consortia, agreements) between two towns across the Franco-Catalan border (e.g. Cap de Creus-Cap de Sant Vicenç, Salines-Bassegoda, Puigcerdà-Bourg Madame …);
- bilateral consortia or arrangements created by national and/or regional governments of the two countries for the construction and operation of a specific piece of cross-border infrastructure, e.g. high-speed railway line and road tunnels (Perthus, Bielsa);
- Europe-wide inter-city networks of various kinds (thematic and area-based), in which the city of Barcelona and other Catalan towns have been very active, supporting exchange of good practice and lobbying, for example, Eurocities;
- Europe-wide inter-regional networks (thematic and area-based), in which the Catalan government is an active member, supporting exchange of good practice and lobbying, such as the Association of Cross-Border European Regions and the Conference of Peripheral and Maritime Regions;
- sectorial networks of private, quasi-public or non-governmental actors, such as FERRMED (lobbying for the rail freight axis Scandinavia-Rhine-Rhone-Western Mediterranean), the Vives Universities Network of Catalan-speaking regions, the Network of Chambers of Commerce of the Euroregion EPM, or the Mediterranean Arc Euroregion (EURAM, a non-profit group of business people, professionals, and institutions founded in Valencia in 2000 to promote the idea of a trans-national, economic macro-region along the Mediterranean Arc);
- forms of decentralized cooperation with partners outside of the EU, in particular on the Southern rim of the Mediterranean, in which Catalan sub-central state actors have been active (e.g. the ARLEM (Assemblea Euromediterrània d'Autoritats Regionals i Locals) or the inter-city network MEDCITÉS).

locally led approach to cooperation, the second a more top-down, regionally led approach (Morata and Noferini, 2014, p. 9).

Cross-border cooperation alongside the Pyrenees

Since the 1980s, various forms of what we have termed 'micro-level' cross-border cooperation have emerged between the municipalities and intermediate levels of government on both sides of the Franco-Catalan border. Historically, the territories now located in the French *département* of Pyrénées-Orientales (Roussillon, Conflent, Vallespir, Capcir and Upper Cerdanya) were once part of the Principality of Catalonia (they are often referred to as 'North Catalonia'). Two specific sections of the border have witnessed the development of multiple cross-border cooperation initiatives: the Cerdanya area, a mountain valley, and the cross-border area close to the Mediterranean coast between the cities of Perpignan and Girona (see Map 6.1).

In Cerdanya, the political border between Upper Cerdanya/Capcir in France and Lower Cerdanya in Spain does not follow any obvious physical or geographical element. Cross-border cooperation on this mountainous plateau of 1,300 km² has been driven by several motivations: the resolution of conflicts about the management of natural resources; the desire to support economic development and common sectors (e.g. agriculture); the formation of a critical mass of population to attract supra-municipal services or infrastructure; and the joint management of risks (e.g. forest fires) (Oliveras González, 2013). These practical considerations have sometimes been accompanied by a discourse on (cross-border) Catalan cultural unity and identity, more often invoked by Catalan actors south of the border (Oliveras González, 2013). Häkli (2004) highlights the symbolic importance of the 'mountain imaginary' in Catalan collective identity and the sense of historical trans-boundary unity that the Pyrenees represent. He stresses how the uniting and dividing functions of the Pyrenees (both a cultural link and a physical divide) 'represent two opposite realities that are simultaneously present in any effort to create transboundary networks and organise cross-border governance' in Catalonia (p. 60).

In the villages located immediately at the border (Bourg-Madame-Puigcerdà and Estavar-Llívia), cross-border cooperation projects were developed in the field of tourism promotion, sports, culture, environment and economic development. Cross-border cooperation has been used as a tool of environmental conflict resolution for issues such as water management (Oliveras González, 2013), for example, through the construction in the 1990s of water-treatment plants serving several towns across the border, or through the launch in 2004 of a cross-border *contrat de rivière* involving the joint management of the Segre river by the two groupings of municipalities on each side of the border. Cooperation has also aimed at the shared creation, use and management of services and amenities, according to two complementary strategies which depend on whether such services existed prior to cooperation (a 'cross-border resizing') or whether they were created afresh (a 'cross-border sizing') (Oliveras González, 2013). The first strategy is exemplified

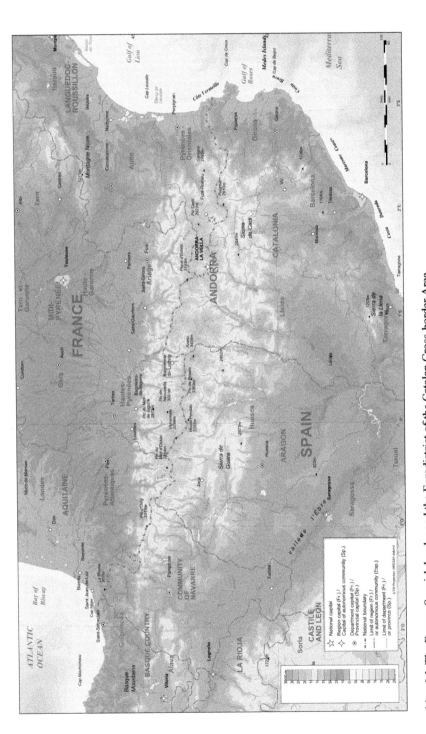

Map 6.1 The Franco-Spanish border and the Eurodistrict of the Catalan Cross-border Area.

Source: Pyrenees topographic map-en by Eric Gaba, derivative work: RedWolf - Pyrenees_topographic_map-fr. Licensed under Creative Commons CC BY-SA 3.0 via Wikimedia Commons, available at http://commons.wikimedia.org/wiki/File:Pyrenees_topographic_map-en.svg.

by the (ongoing) construction of a single cross-border slaughterhouse which will replace the existing sub-standard facilities on both sides of the border. The second is best illustrated by what has become the flagship project of Franco-Catalan cross-border cooperation: the construction of the first European cross-border hospital, the Hospital of Cerdanya, which opened in September 2014 in Puigcerdà (Catalonia), 1 km from the French border (indicated with a diamond shape on Map 6.1).

With 180 (multi-lingual) staff, the hospital provides care for a permanent population of 32,000 (which can quadruple during the winter and summer holidays) spread over 53 municipalities on both sides of the border. Sixty per cent of the construction costs (EUR 31 million) were funded by the ERDF; the rest was split between the Catalan regional government and the French national government (who also share the running costs at a height of 60% and 40%, respectively, proportionate to the population covered). The first plans for the hospital emerged in the late 1990s, but the planning, construction and management arrangements of the hospital have proven to be very complex, because of the number of actors and issues involved. This was particularly pronounced in the context of an asymmetry of competences: in France, health-care facilities are within the remit of the national Ministry of Health and its regional agencies; in Spain, they are a responsibility of the Autonomous Communities. The hospital management structure was set up in 2010 in the shape of an EGTC, the only legal structure which allows a state to co-own a public facility in another state, something normally impossible except in the case of embassies (Morata and Noferini, 2014). Complex issues of technical, financial and legal coordination between the French and Catalan health-care systems also had to be dealt with. The harmonisation of issues as trivial as meal times, the use of butter or olive oil, the ways in which patients should be addressed, or visiting times, had to be agreed (Morata and Noferini, 2014). The pioneering experiment of the cross-border hospital is widely considered a success by local and regional actors, residents and the media.

Building on these successful initiatives, a new structure was set up in 2011 to facilitate future cooperation in the Cerdanya area: the EGTC Pirineus-Cerdanya, which gathers the supra-municipal groupings of Spanish local authorities (*Consell Comarcal de la Cerdanya*) and French local authorities (*Communauté de Communes Pyrénées-Cerdagne*). The activities of the EGTC are currently being developed. This includes the preparation of a 'cross-border landscape plan' announced in May 2013, which involves a joint inventory of landscape features and awareness-raising activities. In spite of the multiple cross-border cooperation activities developed over the years, however, the cross-border dimension is still virtually absent from most of the *formal* urban planning strategies and documents of the municipalities of the Cerdanya on both sides of the border (MOT, 2008). In that sense, forms of cross-border cooperation are not (yet) embedded in routine, legally binding local planning (i.e. plan-making) and territorial management practices, which remain firmly driven by the authorities of administratively bounded 'hard planning spaces'.

Closer to the Mediterranean coast, the 'Eurodistrict of the Catalan Cross-border Area' has been given a new impulse in 2009 through the creation of an EGTC which aims at supporting the development of a truly cross-border employment and residential catchment area, through actions in the fields of the economy, services, transport and communications, tourism, education, culture and the environment. The Eurodistrict territory, around the cities of Perpignan, Figueres and Girona (see Map 6.1), contains the main motorway between France and Catalonia as well as the new high-speed train line connecting Paris and Barcelona. It is characterised by intense cross-border flows for shopping, leisure and tourism purposes, but there is little cross-border labour mobility. As noted by Kramsch and Hooper (2004, p. 6), 'generating positive cross-border regional economies of any sort has been one of the main aspects bedevilling cross-border regional development generally.' The objectives of the EGTC, based on a comprehensive study of the Eurodistrict territory (MOT, 2008), demonstrate the willingness of participating authorities to go beyond *ad hoc* projects to develop a joint cross-border spatial planning and sustainable development strategy. The extent to which this will be achieved remains to be seen as there is, to date, scarce evidence of its actual development. The activities of the Eurodistrict have been heavily slowed down by the financial crisis faced by Catalan municipalities since 2008.

Many of the cross-border initiatives mentioned here have received EU co-financing from the INTERREG A programme Spain-France-Andorra (POCTEFA). Under the four generations of POCTEFA programmes, hundreds of cross-border projects have been funded,[12] mainly involving public, quasi-public or non-profit actors. The first two generations of the POCTEFA programme (1990–93 and 1994–99) were managed by French and Spanish central government agencies, and funded projects with little cross-border content (Harguindéguy and Bray, 2009). In the third generation of INTERREG (2000–06), French regions and Spanish Autonomous Communities were devolved more responsibility for the management of the programme, a trend reinforced in 2007–13 as the Working Community of the Pyrenees took over its management. The Catalan regional government has played a more prominent role in project allocation and implementation than French regional actors, because Spanish Autonomous Communities have gained sufficient institutional capacity and resources to become real 'cross-border institutional entrepreneurs' (Perkmann, 2007b; Harguindéguy, 2007; Harguindéguy and Bray, 2009).

Euroregional cooperation

The Euroregion Pyrenees-Mediterranean (thereafter referred to as EPM) currently brings together the two Spanish Autonomous Communities of Catalonia and the Balearic Islands and the two French regions of Midi-Pyrénées and Languedoc-Roussillon (Map 6.2).[13] The EPM territory comprises 14 million inhabitants, 15% of the joint population of Spain and France (Morata *et al.*, 2008). It benefits from the presence of prosperous metropolitan centres – Barcelona, Montpellier and Toulouse – with advanced economic sectors and clusters. The EPM was built on previous cooperation initiatives: the earlier Euroregion and former C-6 network (see Table 6.1 and Morata, 1997). It was institutionalised in 2009 through the creation of an EGTC with legal standing, which can manage funds and projects. Yet the administrative management of the EPM, with the EGTC located in Toulouse and the Secretariat located in Barcelona, has proven complex and challenging.

The objectives of the EPM (Table 6.1) are primarily defined in terms of the search for economic competitiveness on the European stage. The EPM supports trans-boundary cooperation projects between public or private actors via technical assistance and subsidies granted through regular calls for proposals for Euroregional projects (fed by funds granted to the EGTC by the four participating regional governments). It has been particularly active in supporting projects and networks in the fields of culture (Perrin, 2012, 2015), higher education, sustainable development and economic sectors such as renewable energy, bio-, aircraft and nanotechnologies. It has also developed its own projects with INTERREG funding.[14] To date, however, no explicit joint economic-development or spatial planning strategy has been developed at the level of the Euroregion, although a study of the potential for a Euroregional sustainable development strategy was commissioned (Morata *et al.*, 2008).

Map 6.2 The Euroregion Pyrenees-Mediterranean, 2012.

Source: Sforzanda, Licensed under Creative Commons CC BY-SA 3.0 via Wikimedia Commons, available at http://commons.wikimedia.org/wiki/File:Carte_Euroregion_2012.jpg#/media/File:Carte_Euroregion_2012.jpg.

The experience of the EPM suggests that formal declarations of principle and the establishment of a legal structure for Euroregional cooperation (through an EGTC) have to be accompanied by a process of institutional capacity building characterised by the definition of common objectives, the integration of diverse interests and actors, the integration of uneven competences and resources, the management of internal and external interactions, the resolution of conflict and the ability to learn from previous successes and failures (Morata and Noferini, 2013, 2014). A Euroregion does not have structures of democratic representation, so it needs to derive its legitimacy from other sources. Its success is related to the vertical and horizontal cooperation between the actors of its territory, who can design and implement common strategies (Perkmann, 2002, 2007b). While regional authorities have a key role to play as catalysts for cooperation between economic and social actors, they rarely do so from scratch. The EPM has, indeed, successfully built on pre-existing functional networks and initiatives between key actors on both sides of the border which were already in place, such as universities,[15] the 40 chambers of commerce of the Euroregional territory, trade unions, port authorities, professional associations (e.g. from the tourism or agriculture sectors) and cultural institutions (Morata and Noferini, 2013, 2014).

Yet, the scope for action of the EPM has been limited by a number of challenges. First, its main protagonists are regional governments,[16] but the participation of some of the key actors necessary for the implementation of its objectives has been weak. The cities of Barcelona, Montpellier and Toulouse have not played a key role. More generally, local authorities have not been actively involved in EPM networks. On specific issues of strategic importance for the EPM (such as the Mediterranean rail corridor), it is the national governments of France and Spain who control investment in key infrastructure. Civil society organisations and the private sector have not sufficiently engaged with the EPM either. When it comes to the population of the EPM territory, the mental maps of the residents of each side of the border are still highly bounded by national spaces, in spite of occasional cross-border mobility practices. News coverage by the national and regional media tends to ignore what is happening across the border (Durà Guimerà, 2012a) – more so in France than in the Catalan media – and rarely includes regional cross-border cooperation initiatives. This is witnessed, more generally, across the EU: in spite of the physical removal of border controls and markers, there is often a profound indifference shown by locals towards their neighbours on the other side of the border (Kramsch and Hooper, 2004). In the Catalan case, a survey conducted by Häkli in 1999 to chart the attitudes of 'ordinary' Catalans showed a weak sense of cross-border identity or political community among the Catalan borderlanders and a lack of knowledge about existing initiatives of cross-border cooperation (Häkli, 2001, 2002, 2004). The Euroregion activities are 'characterized by their technocratic overtone, addressing mainly the political, economic and governmental elites that are involved in its functions' (Häkli, 2004, p. 61).

Second, the asymmetry of competences between Spanish Autonomous Communities and French regions influences the potential for cooperation. In various policy fields, the former have much more devolved powers than the latter. However, the French regions can levy funding for large projects more easily, without the approval of the central Ministry of Economy as is the case in Spain (Morata and Noferini, 2013, 2014). Third, changes in political leadership in the participating regions have led to changes in the attitude towards the Euroregional project. The experience of the predecessor of the EPM (*Euroregion Mediterranean*) shows the fragility of cooperation projects based only on (individual) political leadership and, thus, subject to the vicissitudes of electoral politics (Morata, 2007). Finally, there is little institutional interaction between the EPM and the cross-border cooperation initiatives described in the previous section, which remain relatively disconnected and poorly articulated with the Euroregional scale (Morata and Noferini, 2014).

Regionalist/nationalist claims and the 'symbolic use' of trans-boundary cooperation

There are various political factors which explain, in part, the proactive and dynamic role played by Catalan actors – in particular the *Generalitat* – in trans-boundary cooperation initiatives. One may, at first sight, assume that cooperation is based on the *a priori* existence of strong, historically rooted cross-border functional, cultural and linguistic relationships inherited from a (distant) shared past. As argued by Perkmann (2003, p. 157), the discursive dimension of cross-border regionalism is often dominated by an assemblage of 'common' cultural, ethnic or economic elements', although he stresses that 'there is no necessary or "natural" foundation' for any cross-border region. The Franco-Spanish border has actually proven to be less permeable than other borders of the French state (MOT, 2008), with low patterns of cross-border commuting or urbanisation. The highly centralist construction of the French and Spanish states, from the seventeenth century onwards, made the differences between both sides of the border very marked – in transport infrastructure, education and health systems, legislation, language and temporal rhythms (Oliveras González, 2013). Catalan virtually ceased to be spoken on the French side of the historic territory of Catalonia, due to the imposition of French over 'regional' languages in the nineteenth and early twentieth century, although it has recently undergone a revival under the influence of local cultural and political elites. Thus, the existence of separate languages on each side of the border has acted as a barrier to cross-border cooperation and population mobility for employment, business or education purposes.

The engagement of the Catalan regional government in trans-boundary cooperation should be seen as part of a wider process of mobilisation of 'Europe' in the context of recurrent conflicts with the central Spanish state, and of the search for a more pivotal political and economic role in the Western Mediterranean. It is consequently helpful to analyse trans-boundary cooperation activity as *one* of multiple strategies of region-building (Oliveras González, 2013, p. 43) – a strategy of 'unbounded regionalism' (Deas and Lord, 2006). This engagement can be interpreted as a form of 'para-diplomacy' which emerged in the late 1980s in those Spanish Autonomous Communities with regionalist agendas, followed in the 1990s by other Communities (Trillo-Santamaria and Lois González, 2014). Autonomous Communities have increasingly demanded more involvement in the Spanish domestic decision-making processes over EU affairs (Morata, 2010; Morcillo-Laiz, 2009).[17] The EU system of multi-level governance has actually opened new opportunities of 'regional mobilisation beyond the state' for Autonomous Communities, through permanent delegations in Brussels, coalitions built with other European regions to advocate a 'Europe of the regions', and participation in trans-boundary cooperation initiatives (Morata, 2010).

In that context, from the early 1980s onwards the main Catalan political parties have 'Europeanised' their discourse, viewing the EU both as an alternative institutional channel to promote their objectives and as an incentive for socio-economic and political modernisation (Giordano and Roller, 2002). This was clearly visible in the impetus given to the first Euroregion by the conservative-nationalist Catalan regional governments led by Jordi Pujol (1980–2003), and subsequently by the former Socialist Mayor of Barcelona (1982–97) and later by Catalan President (2003–06), Pasqual Maragall. Prytherch (2009) argues that in the Catalan-speaking Mediterranean littoral, a strong coincidence developed between the 'new' politics of economic, trans-boundary Euroregionalism and the 'old' politics of cultural regionalism and nationalism. By tracing the genealogy of Catalanist macro-regionalism over nearly a century, he argues that in the 1980s and 1990s, Catalanists 'discursively shifted the subject from Catalan nation-building to Mediterranean economic integration' (p. 139), reframing cultural community[18] in the less controversial terms of economic competitiveness and inter-connectedness through the 'new regionalist' politics of the economic Euroregion (see also Keating, 2001; Häkli, 2002; Durà Guimerà and Oliveras González, 2013).

Kramsch and Hooper (2004, p. 3) argue that 'common among all euroregional initiative ... is an attempt to re-inscribe border areas formerly considered marginal and peripheral to the territorial projects of nation-states to those of centrality and dynamism at the very heart of Europe'. This is particularly the case in regions with strong regionalist/nationalist political movements. In a study of the Euroregional and cross-border strategies of the Basque Country, Catalonia and Galicia (the three Spanish Autonomous Communities which have a distinct historical, linguistic and cultural heritage and regionalist/nationalist parties), García-Álvarez and Trillo-Santamaría (2013, p. 108) show that while external action and cross-border cooperation in most Autonomous Communities are fundamentally viewed in terms of strengthening economic and territorial development, in others (such as those governed by nationalist parties) these actions are mixed with other types of political and territorial discourses and projects, such as those geared towards national construction itself.

Their analysis highlights a dialectical relationship between *cross-border regional spaces* and *cross-border spaces of regionalism/of regionalist engagement* (building on Cox, 1998 and MacLeod and Jones, 2007). The Basque Country and Catalonia exemplify the mobilisation of a 'cross-border space of regionalist engagement' by regional governments that include regionalist or nationalist parties. This process contains a politico-cultural ingredient which contrasts with the more functional approach to cross-border cooperation promoted by the European Commission. It also gives rise to suspicion or opposition in the adjacent Autonomous Communities governed by parties of other political leanings (García-Álvarez and Trillo-Santamaría, 2013). When the Catalan President Maragall planned to (re)establish the Pyrenees-Mediterranean Euroregion in 2003, his vision included Aragon, Catalonia, the Balearic Islands and the Valencian Community, as well as the French regions of Languedoc-Roussillon and Midi-Pyrénées. Besides geo-economic arguments, Maragall legitimised his proposal by referring to the historical territory of Catalonia under the Crown of Aragon. His Euroregional proposal triggered a fierce opposition by the regional government of the Valencian Community, then ruled by the centralist, conservative People's Party (PP), which strongly denigrated what it perceived to be an attempt to give reality to the concept of the 'Catalan Countries' (*Països Catalans* – the linguistic-cultural area where Catalan is spoken, in France, Spain, Andorra and Italy (Sardinia)). The Valencian President branded the initiative as a 'real danger for the institutional and territorial stability of Spain' (García-Álvarez and Trillo-Santamaría, 2013, p. 110), demonstrating the strong reaction which the politics of cross-border cooperation can provoke if mixed with regionalist/nationalist projects and arguments over identity. The EPM eventually went ahead without the Valencian Community.

Between 2003 and 2010, a coalition of left-wing parties[19] governed Catalonia and pursued the pro-European agenda initiated by previous governments, in particular through the revival and active support of the Pyrenees-Mediterranean Euroregion (Morata and Noferini, 2014). This was accompanied by cooperation with a wider range of Spanish and French regional actors to lobby national governments and the EU for key infrastructure investments in passenger and freight rail to connect the cities of the Mediterranean Axis (Algeciras, Murcia, Valencia, Barcelona, Perpignan, Montpellier, Marseille) to those of the Transalpine Axis (Lyon, Turin, Milan). The political economy of large-scale infrastructure investments has played an increasingly contentious role in the tensions between the Spanish central state and the Catalan government over the past decade (Colomb *et al.*, 2014) in the context of a 'radial state' characterised by the historical convergence of major transport networks towards Madrid (Bel, 2010). The Mediterranean rail corridor, which would strengthen the economic position of Catalonia, was eventually approved by the EU in 2013 as one of the Trans-European Transport Network priority projects. The high-speed train link between Barcelona and France (via Perpignan) began operating in 2013 and will most likely have territorial impacts in terms of cross-border mobility flows which have yet to be analysed.

Since the 2008 financial crises, the economic difficulties which have affected Spain have led to significant cuts in public expenditure at all levels of government. This has negatively affected the political willingness and financial capacity of Spanish and Catalan local and regional actors to participate in trans-boundary cooperation initiatives, as they struggle to deliver core services.[20] The year 2010 marked a major turning point in the Catalan political landscape. The Catalan Statute of Autonomy agreed in 1979 was revised in 2006 and agreed by the Spanish Parliament, by the Catalan Parliament and by popular referendum in Catalonia. Following a challenge by the conservative, centralist Spanish Popular Party (PP), in 2010 the Spanish Constitutional Court declared significant parts of the new Catalan Statute of Autonomy 'unconstitutional'. This led to extensive public protests in Catalonia, subsequently repeated on an annual basis on 11 September, the National Day of Catalonia. The share of votes for secessionist parties in Catalonia subsequently increased, and a significant fraction of the Catalan parties that were nationalist but did not support independence (i.e. *Convergència i Unió*, CiU) began to support 'the right to decide' of the Catalan people. The tensions between the Catalan and Spanish governments further increased after 2011, as the PP won the Spanish general election. At the 2012 regional elections, political parties advocating the Catalans' right to self-determination represented nearly two-thirds of the Catalan Parliament. A non-binding 'popular consultation' on Catalan independence was organised in November 2014, but it was declared illegal by the Spanish central government. The regional elections of September 2015 were dominated by the question of the Catalans' 'right to decide'. The dominance of this issue on the political agenda of the Catalan (centre-right) nationalist government led by CiU, combined with the austerity politics of the Spanish and Catalan governments, mean that the political and financial support to trans-boundary cooperation initiatives has faltered to a degree. The Catalan government has instead developed proactive forms of European and international 'para-diplomacy' (through a new organisation for external action, *Diplocat*) focused on generating support for the Catalans' right to self-determination among key national governments, e.g. France, Germany, the United Kingdom and the United States. This has partly weakened the political attention previously given to regional trans-boundary cooperation initiatives like the Euroregion.

Conclusion

This chapter has discussed how various forms and scales of trans-boundary cooperation have been mobilised by the local and regional governmental actors of Catalonia for various purposes. In that process, pragmatic considerations – such as the need to access EU funding or to cooperate with others on pressing policy issues – have often been accompanied by political, symbolic and cultural ones. Over the past two decades, the Franco-Catalan border has witnessed a multiplicity of 'micro-level' cross-border cooperation initiatives primarily driven by municipal governments. In some cases, these initiatives have successfully resolved concrete problems (e.g. service delivery in mountain areas) through small-scale, innovative and effective forms of collective action and pooling of resources (Gualini, 2003). In parallel, successive Catalan governments have supported 'meso-level' transboundary cooperation within the framework of the Euroregion – an engagement which cannot be separated from their search for more autonomy in the context of conflicts with the Spanish central state.

In spite of the (overall) strong political support by Catalan regional leaders and recent processes of institutionalisation through the creation of a number of EGTCs, trans-boundary cooperation projects and initiatives to date have not been anchored in broader cross-border or Euroregional territorial development and spatial planning strategies drawn jointly by the relevant authorities. There are technical and political difficulties involved in the development of institutionalised forms of cooperation that go beyond a 'logic of projects', as many cooperation initiatives have been slowed or impeded by political disagreements, differing administrative cultures, funding shortages and the permanence of linguistic or legal barriers (Oliveras González, 2013). Empirical evidence additionally shows a disconnection between micro- and meso-level trans-boundary cooperation initiatives, which are led by different actors. In the Catalan case, the multiple forms and scales of trans-boundary cooperation have led to new spaces of EU fund management and project development, new spaces of discursive 'cross-border regionalist engagement' (García-Álvarez and Trillo-Santamaría, 2013) and, in some cases, new spaces of 'soft planning' and small-scale innovation addressing specific territorial development issues (such as water management or health-service provision). But as witnessed in other parts of Europe – notably North West Europe (Dühr and Nadin, 2007) – they have not led to a trans-boundary rescaling or transformation of 'hard', statutorily defined planning spaces and strategies, or to a change in territorial governance paradigms which would fundamentally reshape the existing division of competences between (sub-central) tiers of governments.

Notes

1   The use of the term 'trans-boundary' as a generic umbrella concept is deliberate: it aims to distinguish it from more specific terms (e.g. 'cross-border') which refer to a particular *scale* of cooperation across state borders in the language of EU Cohesion Policy, as explained later.
2   This chapter synthesises the findings of separate research projects carried out by the authors. Claire Colomb (a planner and sociologist) researched 'Transboundary territorial cooperation, policy learning and the Europeanisation of urban and spatial planning policies in the Mediterranean area' with the support of an EU Marie Curie Intra-European Fellowship she held as a visiting fellow (2010–12) at the University Institute of European Studies, Autonomous University of Barcelona. Francesc Morata Tierra (a political scientist) directed a study on 'The Pyrenees-Mediterranean Euroregion: Perceptions, Expectations and Policy Networks' (2005–07) and was the coordinator of the Spanish research network on trans-boundary territorial cooperation in the Iberian peninsula (RECOT). Antoni Durà Guimerà (a geographer) investigated the construction of the Mediterranean Arc macro-region (the Mediterranean coast extending from the south of the Iberian Peninsula to southern Italy) as a geo-economic space in collaboration with Xavier Oliveras González (a geographer), whose doctoral research involved an in-depth survey of the territorial cooperation organizations and initiatives in the Mediterranean Arc during the 1951–2008 period.
3   The European Territorial Cooperation programmes only receive a small part (€10.1 billion, i.e. 2.8%) of the total budget for EU Cohesion Policy in 2014–20. See van Lierop, 2016.
4   The EU formally launched a new initiative to support 'macro-regional strategies' between member states and third countries in (large) geographical areas, which

addresses 'common challenges for which increased cooperation is crucial (e.g. environmental, climate or connectivity issues) and common opportunities for which increased cooperation is of mutual interest' (CEC, 2013, p. 3). An EU Strategy for the Baltic Sea Region was adopted in 2009, one for the Danube Region was adopted in 2011 and one for the Adriatic and Ionian Region was under development in 2014. The complex governance arrangements of these macro-regional strategies present considerable challenges, as does the limited involvement of sub-national actors (Dühr, 2011). There have been some debates about a macro-regional strategy for the Mediterranean Arc (Durà Guimerà, 2012b), which will not be discussed here.

5 In the framework of EU-funded INTERREG programmes, hundreds of trans-boundary cooperation projects have been developed on an *ad hoc* basis. Often their lifespan is limited to the few years of the funding period and the partnership put in place does not survive to the end of the funding. In some (rare) cases, projects have led to stable or institutionalised forms of cooperation.

6 Policy learning is defined by the political scientist Hall (1993, p. 278) as 'a deliberate attempt to adjust the goals and techniques of policy in response to past experience and new information'. Such learning might occur at different 'levels and settings', from a mere change in 'instrument settings' in light of new knowledge to changes in policy instruments and settings, or even to 'paradigm shifts' involving wholesale changes in instruments and the hierarchy of goals (Hall, 1993).

7 Their work builds on the prior studies which have investigated the *qualitative* impacts of EU regional policy in terms of institutional capacity building, policy change and innovations in regional and local governance (e.g. Brugué *et al.*, 2001, on Catalonia; Pasquier, 2005, on Spain and France; Gualini, 2001, 2004, on Italy).

8 Simple details like the impossibility for a public administration to transfer funds abroad or for a local authority officer to make international phone calls have been crucial barriers to trans-boundary cooperation.

9 And Aranese, a variety of Occitan spoken in the Val d'Aran.

10 Its regional GDP (in Purchasing Power Standards (PPS) per inhabitant) was 113% of the EU28 average in 2011 (Eurostat figures, http://epp.eurostat.ec.europa.eu/tgm/table.do?tab=table&plugin=1&language=en&pcode=tgs00006).

11 The provinces were created by the Spanish state in the first half of the nineteenth century. Particularly relevant here is the technical support offered by the *Diputacións* to Catalan municipalities for participation in European territorial cooperation projects.

12 In the 2007–13 programming period, this programme received EUR 168 million of European Regional Development Funds (ERDF), which co-funded 260 cross-border projects.

13 In December 2014, the French Parliament approved a reform of the French regions to decrease the total number of regions from 22 to 13 through a series of merges which took effect on 1 January 2016. The two regions Midi-Pyrénées and Languedoc-Roussillon were merged into a new region, Occitanie Pyrénées Méditerranée.

14 In 2014, the EPM was awarded the Committee of the Regions' award for the best EGTC in the EU for its CreaMed project (funded by the INTERREG IV SUDOE programme), a network between the associations of business incubators of the four regions.

15 The University Network of the Pyrenees-Mediterranean Euroregion was set up by the vice-chancellors of 13 universities of the Mediterranean Arc – today it is called *Institut Joan Lluís Vives* and has 20 partner universities.

16 Within the regional governments themselves, it is usually the European Affairs department that deals with the activities of the EPM, which means that other sectorial departments are often not very exposed to it (Morata and Noferini, 2014).

17 The Spanish central government is responsible for voting on the adoption of EU decisions whose implementation the Autonomous Communities are actually responsible for (a situation common in federal or decentralised EU states). In 2004, an agreement was reached between the central government and the Autonomous Communities to widen

the participation of the latter in four formations of the Council of the EU and their working groups (see Morata, 2010).
18 The emergence of the Euroregional idea cannot be entirely separated from wider debates about integrating the Catalan-speaking regions of the Mediterranean Arc (see Prytherch, 2009), an idea central to pan-Catalanist pro-independence movements. The para-diplomacy of the Generalitat de Catalunya over the past 20 years has had a strong cultural dimension, particularly targeted at the French part of Catalonia, through actions to promote the Catalan language (Castex-Ey, 2014).
19 The Socialist Party of Catalonia (PSC), Republican Left of Catalonia (ERC) and Initiative for Catalonia Greens (ICV).
20 The existence of EU funding continues to be an important incentive, although it has to be match funded by other sources.

References

Allmendinger, P. and Haughton, G. (2009) Soft spaces, fuzzy boundaries, and metagovernance: the new spatial planning in the Thames Gateway, *Environment and Planning A*, 41, 617–633.

Atkinson, R. (2001) The emerging 'urban agenda' and the European Spatial Development Perspective: Towards an EU urban policy? *European Planning Studies*, 9, 385–406.

Bel, G. (2010) *España, Capital París*, Barcelona: Destino.

Blatter, J. (2004) From 'spaces of place' to 'spaces of flows' territorial and functional governance in cross-border regions in Europe and North America', *International Journal of Urban and Regional Research*, 28, 530–548.

Bomberg, E. and Peterson, J. (2000) *Policy Transfer and Europeanisation: Passing the Heineken Test?* Queen's Papers on Europeanisation, No. 2/2000.

Braudel, F. (1990) *La Méditerranée et le monde méditerranéen à l'époque de Philippe II*, Vol. 1: 'La part du milieu', Paris: Armand Colin (1949).

Bruno, I., Jacquot, S. and Mandin, L. (2006) Europeanisation through its instrumentation: benchmarking, mainstreaming and the open method of co-ordination … toolbox or Pandora's box? *Journal of European Public Policy*, 13, 519–536.

Brugué, Q., Gomà, R. and Subirats, J. (2001) Multi-level governance and Europeanization: the case of Catalonia, in: Featherstone, K. and Kazamias, G. (eds.) *Europeanization and the Southern Periphery*, pp. 95–118, London: Routledge.

Bulkeley, H. (2006) Urban sustainability: learning from best practice? *Environment and Planning A*, 38, 1029–1044.

Castex-Ey, J.-F. (2014) *L'action du Gouvernement Catalan en Catalogne Française (2000/2014). Une Politique Extérieure du Dedans*, Paris: Les impliqués.

Colomb, C. (2007) The added value of transnational cooperation: towards a new framework for evaluating learning and policy change, *Planning Practice and Research*, 22, 347–372.

Colomb, C., Tomaney, J. and Bakke, C. (2014) *Shaping the Territory in Scotland, Catalonia* and *Flanders*, Working Paper No. 5, UCL European Institute, London: UCL Online. Available: www.ucl.ac.uk/european-institute/analysis-publications/publications/WP5_Colomb.pdf (accessed 25 July 2016).

Cox, K. (1998) Spaces of dependence, spaces of engagement and the politics of scale, or: looking for local politics, *Political Geography*, 17, 1–23.

CEC (Commission of the European Communities) (2013) *Report from the Commission to the European Parliament, the Council, the European Economic and Social Committee and the Committee of the Regions Concerning the Added Value of Macro-regional*

Strategies, Brussels, 27.6.2013 COM(2013) 468 final. Available: http://ec.europa.eu/regional_policy/sources/docoffic/official/communic/baltic/com_added_value_macro_region_strategy_en.pdf (accessed 25 July 2016).

CoR (Committee of the Regions) (2014), EGTC Monitoring Report 2013. Towards the New Cohesion Policy, Brussels: CoR Online. Available: https://portal.cor.europa.eu/egtc/Events/Documents/EGTC_MonitoringReport_2013_Paper_pdf.pdf (accessed 25 July 2016).

Dabinett, G. (2006) Transnational spatial planning-insights from practices in the European Union, *Urban Policy and Research*, 24, 283–290.

Dabinett, G. and Richardson, T. (2005) The Europeanisation of spatial strategy: shaping regions and spatial justice through governmental ideas, *International Planning Studies*, 10, 201–218.

Deas, I. and Lord, A. (2006) From a new regionalism to an unusual regionalism? *Urban Studies*, 43, 1847–1877.

Dühr, S. (2011) *Baltic Sea, Danube and Macro-Regional Strategies: A Model for Transnational Cooperation in the EU?*, Studies and Research 86, Paris: Notre Europe Online. Available: www.eng.notre-europe.eu/011-2815-Baltic-Sea-Danube-and-macro-regional-strategies-a-model-for-transnational-cooperation-in-the-EU.html (accessed 25 July 2016).

Dühr, S. and Nadin, V. (2007) Europeanization through transnational territorial cooperation? The case of INTERREG IIIB North-West Europe, *Planning Practice and Research*, 22, 373–394.

Dühr, S., Colomb, C. and Nadin, V. (2010) *European Spatial Planning and Territorial Cooperation*, London: Routledge.

Durà Guimerà, A. (2012a) La cooperació territorial transpirinenca en el context de l'Arc Mediterrani, *Treballs de la Societat Catalana de Geografia*, 74, 59–77.

Durà Guimerà, A. (2012b) Macroregions in the Mediterranean: a new strategy for development and peace, paper presented at the Association of American Geographers Annual Meeting, New York, USA, 24–28 February.

Durà Guimerà, A. and Oliveras González, X. (2008) *A Typology of Agents and Subjects of Regional Cooperation: The Experience of the Mediterranean Arch*, IUEE Working Papers On Line (WPOL), No. 23.

Durà Guimerà, A. and Oliveras González, X. (2013) A typology of agents and subjects of regional cooperation: the experience of the Mediterranean Arc, in: Bellini, N. and Hilpert, U. (eds.) *Europe's Changing Geography: The Impact of Inter-regional Networks*, pp. 101–23, London: Routledge.

ESPON and Nordregio (2005) *ESPON 2.2.1: The territorial effects of the Structural Funds. Annex Report C: The Contribution of INTERREG to Polycentric Development*, Luxembourg: ESPON.

Faludi, A. (2004) The open method of co-ordination and 'post-regulatory' territorial cohesion policy, *European Planning Studies*, 12, 1019–1033.

Gabbe, J., Malchus, V. and Martinos, H. (2000) *Practical Guide on Cross Border Cooperation*, 3 ed., Gronau, Germany: Association of European Border Regions.

García-Álvarez, J. and Trillo-Santamaría, J.-M. (2013) Between regional spaces and spaces of regionalism: cross-border region building in the Spanish 'state of the autonomies', *Regional Studies*, 47, 104–115.

Giannakourou, G. (2005) Transforming spatial planning policy in Mediterranean countries: Europeanization and domestic change, *European Planning Studies*, 13, 319–331.

Giordano, B. and Roller, E. (2002) Catalonia and the 'Idea of Europe': competing strategies and discourses within Catalan party politics', *European Urban and Regional Studies*, 9, 99–113.

Gualini, E. (2001) 'New programming' and the influence of transnational discourses in the reform of regional policy in Italy', *European Planning Studies*, 9, 755–771.

Gualini, E. (2003) Cross-border governance: inventing regions in a trans-national multi-level polity, *DISP*, 152, 43–52.

Gualini, E. (2004) *Multi-Level Governance and Institutional Change: The Europeanization of Regional Policy in Italy*, Aldershot, UK: Ashgate.

Hachmann, V. (2011) From mutual learning to joint working: Europeanization processes in the INTERREG B programmes', *European Planning Studies*, 19, 1537–1555.

Häkli, J. (2001) The politics of belonging: complexities of identity in the Catalan borderlands, *Geografiska Annaler B: Human Geography*, 83, 5–13.

Häkli, J. (2002) Transboundary networking in Catalonia, in: Kaplan, D. and Häkli, J. (eds.) *Boundaries and Place: European Borderlands in Geographical Context*, pp. 70–92, Lanham, MD: Rowman and Littlefield.

Häkli, J. (2004) Governing the mountains: cross-border regionalization in Catalonia, in: Kramsch, O. and Hooper, B. (eds.) *Cross-Border Governance in the European Union*, pp. 56–69, London: Routledge.

Hall, P. (1993) Policy paradigms, social learning and the state, *Comparative Politics*, 25, 275–296.

Harguindéguy, J. B. (2007) Cross-border policy in Europe: Implementing INTERREG III-A, France–Spain, *Regional and Federal Studies*, 17, 317–334.

Harguindéguy, J. B. and Bray, Z. (2009) Does cross-border co-operation empower European regions? The case of INTERREG III-A France-Spain, *Environment and Planning C*, 27, 747–760.

Haughton, G., Allmendinger, P., Counsell, D. and Vigar, G. (2010) *The New Spatial Planning: Territorial Management with Soft Spaces and Fuzzy Boundaries*, London: Routledge.

Hooghe, L. and Marks, G. (2003) Unraveling the central state, but how? Types of multilevel governance, *American Political Science Review*, 97, 233–243.

Janin Rivolin, U. (2004) *European Spatial Planning: La Governance Territoriale Comunitaria e le Innovazioni dell' Urbanística*, Milano: Franco Angeli.

Janin Rivolin, U. and Faludi, A. (2005) The hidden face of European spatial planning: innovations in governance, *European Planning Studies*, 13, 195–215.

Jensen, O. B. and Richardson, T. (2004) *Making European Space: Mobility, Power and Territorial Identity*, London: Routledge.

Keating, M. (1998) *The New Regionalism in Western Europe: Territorial Restructuring and Political Change*, Cheltenham: Edward Elgar.

Keating, M. (2001) Rethinking the region: culture, institutions and economic development in Catalonia and Galicia, *European Urban and Regional Studies*, 8, 217–234.

Kohler-Koch, B. (1999) The evolution and transformation of European governance, in: Eising, R. and Kohler-Koch, B. (eds.) *The Transformation of Governance in the European Union*, pp. 14–35, London: Routledge.

Kramsch, O. and Hooper, B. (2004) Introduction, in: Kramsch, O. and Hooper, B. (eds.) *Cross-border governance in the European Union*, pp. 1–21, London: Routledge.

McCann, E. (2011) Urban policy mobilities and global circuits of knowledge: toward a research agenda, *Annals of the Association of American Geographers*, 101, 107–130.

MacLeod, G. and Jones, M. (2007) Territorial, scalar, networked, connected: in what sense a 'regional world'? *Regional Studies*, 41, 1177–1191.

Marshall, A. (2005) Europeanization at the urban level: local actors, institutions and the dynamics of multi-level interaction, *Journal of European Public Policy*, 12, 668–686.

Metzger, J. and Schmitt, P. (2012) When soft spaces harden: the EU strategy for the Baltic Sea Region, *Environment and Planning A*, 44, 263–280.

Morata, F. (1997) The Euroregion and the C-6 Network: the new politics of subnational cooperation in the West-Mediterranean macro-region, in: Keating, M. and Loughlin, J. (eds.) *The Political Economy of Regionalism*, pp. 292–305, London: Frank Cass.

Morata, F. (2007) *La cooperació territorial de les regions. L'experiència de Catalunya*, IUEE Working Papers Online (WPOL), No. 17.

Morata, F. (2010) Europeanization and the Spanish territorial state, in: Scully, R. and Wyn Jones, R. (eds.) *Europe, Regions and European Regionalism*, pp. 134–154, Houndmills, UK: Palgrave Macmillan.

Morata, F. and Noferini, A. (2013) The Pyrenees-Mediterranean Euroregion: functional networks, actor perceptions and expectations, in: Bellini, N. and Hilpert, U. (eds.) *Europe's Changing Geography: The Impact of Inter-regional Networks*, pp. 171–190, London: Routledge.

Morata, F. and Noferini, A. (2014) *Gobernanza y capacidades institucionales en la frontera pirenaica*, Working Paper No. 326, Institut de Ciències Polítiques i Socials, Barcelona: UAB.

Morata, F., Cots, F. and Roca, D. (2008) A Sustainable Development Strategy for the Pyrenees-Mediterranean Euroregion: Basic Guidelines, Barcelona: Consell Assessor per al Desenvolupament Sostenible de Catalunya (CADS); Generalitat de Catalunya.

Morcillo-Laiz, A. (2009) *Contentious regions in the European Union: National parties and the Coordination of European policies in Federal member states*, Baden-Baden: Nomos.

MOT Mission Opérationnelle Transfrontalière and Universitat de Girona (2008) *Livre Blanc de l'Eurodistrict, pour un avenir transfrontalier*. Available: www.eurodistricte. cat/fr/documentation/livre-blanc-de-leurodistrict-pour-un-avenir-transfrontalier-2008 (accessed 25 July 2016).

Oliveras González, X. (2009). La construcció metageogràfica de l'Arc mediterrani, unpublished PhD thesis, Universitat Autònoma de Barcelona.

Oliveras González, X. (2013) Cross-border cooperation in Cerdanya (Spain-France border), *Boletín de la Asociación de Geógrafos Españoles*, 62, 435–440.

Oliveras González, X., Durà Guimerà, A. and Perkmann, M. (2010) Las regiones transfronterizas: balance de la regionalización de la cooperación transfonteriza en Europa (1958–2007), *Documents d'Anàlisi Geogràfica*, 56, 21–40.

Paasi, A. (1986) The institutionalisation of regions: a theoretical framework for understanding the emergence of regions and the constitution of regional identity, *Fennia*, 164, 105–146.

Paasi, A. (2009) The resurgence of the region and regional identity: theoretical perspectives and empirical observations on regional dynamics in Europe, *Review of International Studies*, 35, 121–146.

Paasi, A. (2010) Commentary: regions are social constructs, but who or what 'constructs' them? Agency in question, *Environment and Planning A*, 42, 2296–2301.

Pasquier, R. (2005) 'Cognitive Europeanization' and the territorial effects of multilevel policy transfer: local development in French and Spanish regions, *Regional and Federal Studies*, 15, 295–310.

Pedrazzini, L. (2005) Applying the ESDP through INTERREG IIIB: a southern perspective, *European Planning Studies*, 13, 297–317.

Perkmann, M. (2002) Euroregions. institutional entrepreneurship in the European Union, in: Perkmann, M. and Sum, N.-L. (eds.) *Globalization, Regionalization and Cross-border Regions*, pp. 103–24, Houndmills, UK: Palgrave.

Perkmann, M. (2003) Cross-border regions in Europe: significance and drivers of regional cross-border co-operation, *European Urban and Regional Studies*, 10, 153–171.

Perkmann, M. (2007a) Construction of new territorial scales: a framework and case study of the EUREGIO cross-border region, *Regional Studies*, 41, 253–266.

Perkmann, M. (2007b) Policy entrepreneurship and multilevel governance: a comparative study of European cross-border regions, *Environment and Planning C*, 25, 861–879.

Perrin, T. (2012) Regionalism and cultural policies: distinctive and distinguishing strategies, *Journal of Contemporary European Studies*, 20, 459–475.

Perrin, T. (2015) Creative regions on a European cross-border scale: policy issues and development perspectives', *European Planning Studies*, 23, 2423–2437.

Pike, A., Rodríguez-Pose, A. and Tomaney, J. (2006) *Local and Regional Development*, London: Routledge.

Prytherch, D. (2009) New Euroregional territories, old Catalanist dreams? Culture and economy in the discursive construction of the Mediterranean Arc, *European Urban and Regional Studies*, 16, 131–145.

Radaelli, C. (2004) Europeanisation: solution or problem, *European Integration online Papers* (EIoP), 8. Available: http://eiop.or.at/eiop/texte/2004-016a.htm (accessed 25 July 2016).

Stead, D. (2013) Convergence, divergence, or constancy of spatial planning? Connecting theoretical concepts with empirical evidence from Europe, *Journal of Planning Literature*, 28, 19–31.

Stead, D. (2014) The rise of territorial governance in European Policy, *European Planning Studies*, 22, 1368–1383.

Trillo-Santamaría, J. M. and Lois González, R. (2014) Estrategias para cuestionar el control central del espacio estatal. Acción exterior y cooperación transfronteriza, *Scripta Nova*, XVIII, 493, 1–22.

van Lierop, C. (2016) *European Territorial Cooperation*, Briefing Note, European Parliamentary Research Service, Luxemburg: European Parliament. Available: www.europarl.europa.eu/EPRS/EPRS-Briefing-586666-European-Territorial-Cooperation-FINAL.pdf (accessed 20 October 2016).

Part III

Mobility and circularity in urban–regional policy

7 Business improvement districts in the United Kingdom

Territorialising a 'global' model?

Kevin Ward and Ian Cook

Introduction

> By getting out of the way and letting councils and communities run their own affairs we can restore civic pride, democratic accountability and economic growth – and build a stronger, fairer Britain. It's the end of the era of big government: laying the foundations for the Big Society.
>
> (Pickles, quoted in *Inside Government* 2010, n.p.)

> [A]ll contemporary expressions of territory … are, to varying degrees, punctuated by and orchestrated through a myriad of trans-territorial networks and relational webs of connectivity.
>
> (MacLeod and Jones, 2007, p. 1186)

There are few individuals who have had an economic-development policy named after them. Mary Portas became one such person when 12 successful Portas Pilot Towns were announced by Britain's Coalition government in May 2012. It was announced that public-private partnerships in Bedford, Croydon, Dartford, Bedminster (Greater Bristol), Liskeard, Margate, Market Rasen, Nelson, Newbiggin-by-the-Sea, Stockport, Stockton-on-Tees and Wolverhampton would receive a small government grant, as well as advice and training from government and 'industry leaders' such as Portas herself. This, it was hoped, would stimulate 'innovative ideas about how to transform their local high street into a social place, bustling with people, services and jobs' (*Inside Government*, 2012, n.p.). Portas, of course, is a well-known individual in the United Kingdom, from her career in retailing, most noticeably at Harvey Nichols, her appearances on television in *Mary Queen of Shops* and subsequent follow-ons, and the independent review into the future of high streets in the United Kingdom that she was commissioned to write by the former Coalition government.

The Portas Review was published at the end of 2011. It set out 28 'practical' recommendations, all geared towards increasing consumer spending and lowering vacancy rates on the high street. The aim, Portas (2011, p. 17) claimed, was to get 'town centres running like businesses', helping them combat long-standing competition from out-of-town and online retailers, as well as the post-2008 recession. While much of what was recommended was about altering existing methods of financing the management of high streets, the report does note a number of existing successes. One is particularly interesting in the context of this book because it relates to issues of territorial governance. As Portas (2011, p. 21) notes

> There is one model, already in place, which has begun to make important inroads: Business Improvement Districts (BIDs), where local businesses contribute to realising a jointly produced plan, funded by uplift in business rates.

Business Improvement Districts (BIDs) are public-private partnerships, first established in England in 2004, which focus typically on cleaning, security and marketing, funded by a mandatory levy on (selected) businesses in a designated area. Commenting on the successes (and failures) of BIDs, Portas makes the case for an increase in their powers:

> New Super-BIDs would develop a dynamic strategic vision for their towns. Super-BIDs should be about more than just 'grime and crime' and should work in much more of a strategic partnership to shape the thriving high streets of the future I want to see.
>
> (Portas, 2011, p. 22)

The Portas Review argued that these new 'super-BIDs' would be the kinds of initiatives the Coalition government should wish to see emerge under the Localism Act. She has not been alone in linking BIDs to the localism agenda (see also Jones, Chapter 2, this volume). Her words echo a number of other commentators such as regeneration practitioner Chris Brown (2011, n.p.) who blogged that 'BIDs are perfectly positioned for localism being designed at a neighbourhood scale'. Portas (2011, p. 22), however, goes further than most by suggesting that the government

> should look at how duly-constituted BIDs could be enabled to exercise the new community rights to buy assets and run services provided by the Localism Act. Provided that they can demonstrate local support and accountability, the new Super-BIDs should have the same rights as local authorities to use Compulsory Purchase Orders and enter and upgrade strategic properties, bringing empty property back into use. Super-BIDs should also be able to lead business-led neighbourhood planning exercises to develop a vision for their high streets.

The government response, *High Streets at the Heart of Our Communities*, was published the following year (DCLG, 2012). Despite claiming that '[w]e fully support these recommendations' (p. 9), it took only some on board, such as the establishment of the Portas Pilot Towns. With regards to BIDs, however, the response shied away from the creation of Porter-style 'super-BIDs'. Instead, it committed to setting aside just £500,000 from which prospective BIDs could request a loan to aid the costs of establishment. This was not quite the endorsement for which Portas and others in the UK BID community had been hoping. Nevertheless, it was a clear signal from the Coalition government that they saw economic and political value in BIDs.

This example, therefore, speaks to how a particular pre-existing 'model', in the words of Portas (2011), of territorial governance has been reinterpreted and repackaged by certain policymakers and practitioners as embodying the beliefs, ideologies and logics of New Localism. The centrepiece of New Localism – if you will excuse the oxymoron – is the Localism Act 2011 (HM Government, 2011). This, for Andrew Stunell, ex-Communities Minister, is about paving 'the way for the long overdue push of powers out of Whitehall to councils and neighbourhoods across the country, and giv[ing] local communities real control over housing and planning decisions' (quoted in *Inside Government*, 2010, n.p.). Despite the BID model first being introduced into the United Kingdom by the then-Labour government in 2004, BIDs have been lauded by both the Coalition and subsequent Conservative administrations as an instance of proto-New Localism: an example of the type of 'local' initiative they wish to encourage in the context of the systemic dismantling and restructuring of all levels of government (Clarke and Cochrane, 2013; Deas, 2013). BIDs, then, are in the process of being cast as a model for territorial governance, and not for the first time, as the model has been one which has moved across national borders, from one location to another (Cook, 2008; Hoyt, 2006; Ward, 2006).

In light of these recent developments, this chapter will critically examine the development, implementation and evolution of BIDs in the United Kingdom. The chapter is organised into five sections. The second section sets out how to understand the relational and territorial geographies behind the introduction of BIDs in the United Kingdom as a form of territorial governance. It draws on recent urban-policy mobilities research, the goal of which, in part, has been to unite traditional urban political studies where the emphasis is on 'territory' with more recent work on relational understandings of 'the urban'. The third section introduces BIDs and sets out the model's global geographies and histories. This reveals its Canadian origins, the work done to construct it as a US model and the range of actors involved in creating the conditions where BIDs could be introduced into the United Kingdom. The fourth section turns to the experiences of BIDs, first in England and Wales and then, more recently, in Scotland and Northern Ireland. This reveals the model's introduction across a growing number of towns and cities over the last decade. It ends by exploring the roles being played by BIDs in the context of the financial crisis and the UK government's programmes of austerity and New Localism.

The conclusion to the chapter makes two points in relation to the wider objectives of this book. First, we argue that theorising territorial governance in an increasingly inter-dependent context requires an approach that is sensitive to both networks and territories. If there were ever a time to account for the change in the nature of urban politics on the basis of analysis generated solely from within cities and the countries of which they are a part, then that time has surely passed

(Ward, 2011). Second, the form BIDs have taken in the United Kingdom reflects both the contexts through which the policy has travelled as well as those in which the policy has been introduced. Territorial models that are moved from one geographical location to another are adapted, modified, transformed and translated as part of that movement, and are made to 'fit' within their wider institutional and political environment (and, in turn, potentially transform that very same institutional and political environment through their presence).

Moving models

> [W]hat is commonly defined as 'urban politics' is typically quite heterogeneous and by no means referable to struggles with, or among, the agents structured by some set of social relations corresponding unambiguously to the urban.
>
> (Cox, 2001, p. 756)

Underpinning many of the accounts of the 'old urban politics' of collective consumption and social reproduction, and those on the 'new urban politics' of economic development, is a territorial understanding of the urban as a bounded entity, a city or a town, often within the geographical remit of local government. Work in recent years, however, has sought to rethink what, and where, we mean by the urban. Scholars such as Brenner (2004) and Jonas (2006) have shown that the urban is connected to, and even made up of, a multiplicity of spatial scales. Others have sought to bring territorial understandings of the urban into dialogue with recent interpretations of place as being open, porous and inter-connected (Amin, 2004, 2007; Massey, 2005). More concretely, this work has begun to explore the complex ways in which boundaries and fixities interact with inter-urban networks and mobilities to make and re-make the urban and urban policy (see, for example, Allen and Cochrane, 2007; Jacobs, 2012). Such understandings of cities as sites 'of intersection between network topologies and territorial legacies' (Amin, 2007, p. 103) show the elements of 'elsewhere' that go into the assembling of 'urban politics'. This can involve elements of other cities' experiences, models and success stories, for example.

Attempts to bridge urban territoriality and relationality can be found in recent work on urban policy mobilities, which examines the ways in which 'best practice' models are constructed and mobilised between different cities (see, for instance, Baker *et al.*, 2015; McCann, 2011; McCann and Ward, 2010, 2011, 2013; Peck and Theodore, 2010, 2015; Temenos and McCann, 2013; Ward, 2006). These studies, as Temenos and McCann (2013, p. 345) note, focus on the 'tension between policy as fixed, territorial, or place-specific, on the one hand, and dynamic, global and relational on the other' (see also McCann and Ward, 2010). As part of this, the work has three particularly useful insights. First, it illustrates the diverse set of actors and 'informational infrastructures' involved in the circulation of ideas, expertise and models. Informational infrastructures, in the words of McCann (2008, p. 12), are made up of 'institutions, organisations and technologies that, in various ways, frame and package knowledge about best policy practices, successful cities, and cutting-edge ideas and then present that information to specific audiences'. Perhaps the best known of these technologies are best-practice guides (Moore, 2013), conferences (Cook and Ward, 2012) and study tours (Cook and Ward, 2011; Cook *et al.*, 2014, 2015; González, 2011). These are important, not least because they actively connect some people and some places. They anoint and represent some models as 'best practice' and help lubricate their movement, while downplaying or ignoring others.

Second, the literature shows that 'comparison, learning and sharing' relationships often have a degree of path-dependency. The example of the frequent borrowing of policy ideas by UK policymakers from the United States is a case in point. In recent decades, we have seen UK policymakers drawing on a number of ideas from the United States – such as the Urban Development Action Grant, welfare-to-work, 'broken windows' policing, John Schools, BIDs and Tax Increment Financing (see Baker *et al.*, 2015; Cook, 2015; Dolowitz *et al.*, 1999; Jones and Newburn, 2007; Peck and Theodore, 2001; Ward, 2010; Wolman, 1992). This trans-Atlantic traffic is not surprising; as Dolowitz *et al.* (1999) note, policies often circulate between places with political infrastructures or ideologies that are perceived to be similar. Nevertheless, and as the literature makes clear, such relationships are rarely static. What is more, the movement of models often involves a complex assemblage of ideas, places and relationships (Cook and Ward, 2011; McCann and Ward, 2013).

Following on, the third point made in this literature is that the movement of policy is never a literal copying and pasting from place A to place B (Cook and Ward, 2012). As Peck and Theodore (2010, p. 170) note, 'mobile policies rarely travel as complete "packages", they move in bits and pieces – as selective discourses, inchoate ideas, and synthesised models – and they therefore "arrive" not as replicas but as policies already-in-transformation.' The assembling of ideas and their re-territorialisation is once again a messy, selective and contingent process (Baker, 2013).

While there is now an extensive literature on policy mobilities, we know little about the longer-term experiences of (once) mobile policies. What happens to policies several years after they have 'arrived'? How are they embedded (and re-embedded) over time and what are the consequences for the wider policymaking machinery? This chapter explores this through an analysis of the emergence and evolution of BIDs in England and Wales and, subsequently, Scotland and Northern Ireland.

Introducing BIDs into the United Kingdom

> [Business Improvement Districts] ... have been doing localism for a long time.
> (Pitkeathley, quoted on Future of London 2012, n.p.)

To celebrate the tenth anniversary of BID legislation in the United Kingdom, the London-based Association of Town Centre Management (ATCM) led a study tour of BIDs in the East Coast of the United States for its members in October 2013. Over four days, they visited New York, Philadelphia and Pittsburgh, where they met BID CEOs, as well as consultants and contractors who work with US BIDs. They also toured BID areas and saw BIDs 'at work'. On the final evening, the visitors convened as a group to pinpoint the key lessons learned and how they could translate these into actionable agendas for their work in the United Kingdom. This, of course, was not a holiday but, as the accompanying brochure put it, a 'unique investment opportunity' (see Figure 7.1). At a cost of £1,500 per delegate (excluding VAT and the cost of international travel and subsistence), the study tour began in New York on the same afternoon as the International Downtown Association's '59th Annual Conference and World Congress', also in New York, came to an end. Members of the ATCM study tour, suffice to say, were encouraged to attend the four-day conference beforehand at an additional cost. The existence of this visit embodies themes that underpin the history of BIDs in the United Kingdom, including the North American influence, the prominence of the ATCM, and the role of policy tourism in shaping the BID agenda. Before we examine the emergence of BIDs in the United Kingdom, we now explore the different elements of BIDs and their geographical origins.

The BID model has five core elements to it. First, BIDs govern particular spaces. Although the size of the districts varies, their geographical boundaries are always clearly defined, even if their shadow falls over a more nebulous surrounding area. Second, they are funded primarily by a tax on businesses within their district (although many have additional funding streams). Third, the money raised through the tax – or levy as many practitioners and policy-makers call it – is not redistributed throughout the city, region or nation, but is 'ring-fenced' to be spent on issues within the district. Fourth, the spending decisions are made by representatives of the district's business community, frequently alongside a small number of public officials, on BID boards. For MacDonald (2000, p. 401), this means that 'BIDs involve businesses as never before in the day-to-day operation of cities' (see Cook, 2009; Rasasinghe, 2013), and that they are more 'flexible' than their local government equivalents (Levy, 2001; Mallett, 1994). Fifth and finally, BIDs usually focus on managing public spaces rather than overseeing property-led redevelopment projects (Mallett, 1994).

While BIDs are not necessarily defined by the services they provide, these are the most outwardly visible element to what they do, particularly to the general public. Although they undertake a wide variety of activities, there are common services that BIDs tend to focus on (Mitchell, 2008; Ward, 2007):

1   public space cleaning and maintenance, in terms of basic service provision and monitoring the appearance of the streetscape;
2   securing public spaces and businesses, often through the hire of security guards to coordinate with local police and via the installation of surveillance technologies; and

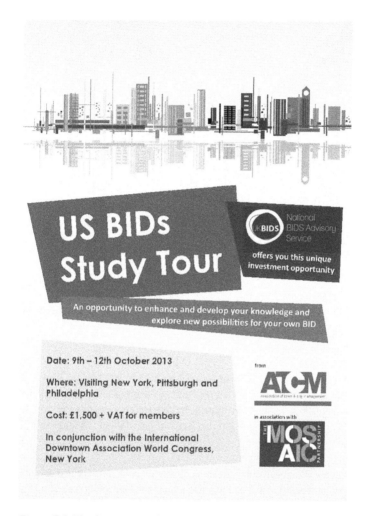

Figure 7.1 The front cover of a brochure advertising the ATCM's 2013 study tour.
Source: www.atcm.org.

3   marketing the BID area and organising events to compete with other areas inside and outside of the city (for an example, see Figure 7.2).

For people on the street, BIDs are frequently personified by the presence of 'clean teams', horticulturists and security-guards-come-goodwill-ambassadors (Cook, 2010; Ward, 2006). However, it is important to note that not every BID focuses on all three service areas, not all employ street personnel and fewer still place equal emphasis on the three service domains. Nonetheless, these partnerships are heavily involved in the day-to-day management of the public spaces

Figure 7.2 A free public screening of *Life of Pi* as part of the 'Monument Movies' series in Newcastle City Centre co-organised by NE1 BID and Tyneside Cinema.

of business districts. BIDs are often 'not sexy or monumental', as one journalist in Philadelphia's *The Plain Dealer* put it (Montgomery, 2005, p. C1). Instead, they focus on mundane, repetitive local government-like services (Ward, 2007). However, these services are heralded by their proponents as important ingredients in improving the 'quality-of-life' and the 'experience economy' and, hence, the profitability within business districts (Briffault, 2010–11; MacDonald, 2000; Mitchell, 2008).

It is possible to trace the introduction of BIDs in England and Wales, Scotland and Northern Ireland to various pieces of governmental legislation and regulations. The most noticeable of these are the Local Government Act 2003 (covering England and Wales), the Planning etc. (Scotland) Act 2006 and the Business Improvement Districts Act (Northern Ireland) 2013. However, the story of the introduction of BIDs in the United Kingdom involves much more than the passing of legislation; their existence stretches back much further and reflects a much more complex process in which variants of the BID model have spread to different countries.

BIDs, it may (or may not) be surprising to hear, did not emerge in the United States, but in Canada. To be precise, the first BID emerged in a suburban commercial district in Toronto when the Bloor-Jane-Runnymede Improvement Area, now known as Bloor West Village, was established in 1970. Facing competition from nearby malls, local businesses and public bodies in the district drew together plans for a business district financed by a mandatory levy on property owners in the district (Hoyt, 2006). BIDs subsequently spread across parts of Canada and then into the United States, to New Orleans, in 1975.

Although a recent and accurate count of BIDs in North America does not exist, it is generally believed that several hundred have emerged subsequently in the United States and Canada. By June 2013, New York City alone had 67 BIDs while Toronto had 74. BIDs have also emerged in a number of countries elsewhere, namely Jamaica, Serbia, Albania and South Africa, before arriving in the United Kingdom, and subsequently appearing in Germany, Ireland and the Netherlands (Cook, 2008; Cook and Ward, 2012; Hoyt, 2006; Peyroux *et al.*, 2012; Ward, 2006, 2011).

BIDs in the United Kingdom developed out of the Town Centre Management (TCM) movement that began to grow substantially in the 1990s (Cook, 2008). Promoted by the ATCM and the Conservative government of the time, TCM involved public-private partnerships forming and governing city and town centres. They were often involved in cleaning and marketing services (similar to BIDs) and were financed by local government and voluntary contributions from businesses within the area. TCM's introduction was accompanied by rhetoric asserting the private sector's ability to bring efficiency, innovation and market sensitivity to governance structures – and ultimately business profitability to its localities (Cook, 2008, 2009). Nevertheless, a number of its supporters grew frustrated with one of the fundamental features of TCM: the *voluntary* nature of business contributions was seen to encourage inadequately small and unpredictable incomes for TCM schemes (despite often being accompanied by grants from local councils). 'Free-riding' by businesses – enjoying the benefits of services paid for by other businesses without contributing themselves – was viewed as a widespread problem (Medway *et al.*, 1999, 2000). The small income generated by TCM schemes together with the considerable time and effort that staff needed to dedicate to encouraging donations – 'begging bowl' activities – were seen to impact negatively on the quality and quantity of services provided.

Simultaneously, news of the growing numbers of North American BIDs and their supposed successes was increasingly reaching senior officials at the ATCM. Indeed, the 1996 World Congress in Coventry, co-organised by the International Downtown Association and the ATCM, was a pivotal moment in 'showcasing' BIDs to ATCM and Whitehall officials. At the event, US BID officials were invited to speak of their 'successes' in transforming dirty, unsafe, emptying and unprofitable downtowns into thriving and profitable places that consumers and businesses wanted to populate (Cook, 2008). These achievements were attributed, in no uncertain terms, to the *mandatory* basis on which BIDs levied funding from constituent property owners.

Over the years that followed, trans-Atlantic dialogue continued, whether through personal communication, visits or conferences (see, for example, Travers and Weimar, 1996). As part of this, the apparent success and transferability of BIDs became increasing obvious to the ATCM and the Labour government elected in 1997. Yet, it was certainly not the Canadian experience that captured the attention or imagination. Nor was it the trans-US experience. Rather, it was the experience of a small number of downtown BIDs in the East Coast cities of New York City (primarily), Philadelphia and Washington, DC that became sites of 'best practice' and study tours (and, of course, it is the East Coast that officials visited in late 2013). A number of BID officials from these cities were repeatedly brought to the United Kingdom at the end of the 1990s and at the beginning of the 2000s to advise government officials in England and Wales (Cook, 2008; Ward, 2006, 2011).

Using the devolved powers granted to it after its establishment in 1999, the Scottish Parliament was also able to decide on whether or not to introduce BIDs. As well as consulting with business and government officials in Scotland (see Peel and Lloyd, 2005), political elites and leading policy actors looked elsewhere to see what lessons could be learnt. News of the various stages of the development of BIDs in England and Wales reached senior officials at the Scottish Parliament and ministers in the Executive, as well as at the Scottish section of the ATCM. Furthermore, government representatives visited BIDs and events in England and the United States, and liaised with officials at Whitehall and at the ATCM. There was a sense that BIDs were successful elsewhere and that they were transferable to Scotland. Speaking at the opening of a public consultation on BIDs, Andy Kerr, the then-Minister for Finance and Public Services, envisaged BIDs as

> a potentially powerful tool and ... relevant to all businesses and all types of areas. They can benefit city centres, town centres, industrial estates, business parks and anywhere where local authorities and businesses see an opportunity to stimulate economic growth. Business Improvement Districts have already been successful elsewhere. You only have to look at Times Square in New York to see the massive improvements they can make to the look and feel of an area ... The power will be with the business community to make a real difference in their local area.
>
> (Quoted in *Local Government Chronicle*, 2003, n.p.)

Kerr's comments echoed those of BID advocates south of the border, such as the then-Minister of State for Local Government, Nick Raynsford, who proclaimed that

> BIDs give businesses and councils an exciting opportunity to work together to improve their own areas ... BIDs will breathe new life into our towns and cities, making them better places to live, work and play ... contributing to a healthy economy.
>
> (Quoted in Hanlon, 2003, p. 16)

Kerr's words were also echoed by then-Minister for Social Development, Nelson McCausland, in a debate in the Northern Ireland Assembly. Speaking a decade after Kerr, McCausland positioned BIDs as a recession-fighting policy tool (an enemy unseen by Kerr and Raysnford):

> [The Business Improvement Districts] Bill will be an important addition to the toolkit of measures available to help hard-pressed traders during the continuing difficult economic situation. This is not a one-size-fits-all approach.

The BIDs legislation will simply provide a framework that will allow local traders to work closely with their local council to develop solutions to their unique situation, with the aim of attracting more shoppers and consumers into the BID area to explore what is on offer and spend money in local businesses.

(Hansard Debate, 11 February 2013)

For Kerr, Raynsford and McCausland, BIDs were not only locally sensitive and flexible but also business-led and profitable investments for local businesses. These sentiments, of course, resonate with the ways in which urban-development practitioners and advocates in the United States represent BIDs (see, for example, Levy, 2001; MacDonald, 2000; Mitchell, 2008). Across the United Kingdom, the DNA of BIDs resonated with the neoliberal approach to urban policy increasingly advocated within Whitehall, the Scottish Parliament and the Northern Ireland Assembly. The model reflected the emphasis in urban and regional policy on improving the 'business climate' and bolstering the competitiveness of towns and cities, attracting inward investment and promoting partnership working between the public and private sectors (Boyle *et al.*, 2008; Imrie and Raco, 2003; Murtagh and Shirlow, 2012; Ward, 2006).

Of course, the BID model did not remain fixed as it was prepared for introduction into the United Kingdom. The most important change concerned who would be responsible for paying the mandatory levy. While property owners are the ones who pay the BID levy in the United States, in England and Wales the Labour government decided that it was simpler to make business occupiers pay instead. This was because in the United Kingdom business occupiers already paid business rates, whereas property owners did not. Therefore, it would reduce the administrative 'burden' if the BID levy was collected by local councils as a surcharge of business rates (Cook, 2008). The BID levy would then be ring-fenced and transferred to the BIDs. Predictably, this raised questions about equity, with concerns that property owners may benefit from increases in rental and property prices as a result of BID operations without making any financial contributions themselves. Again, 'free-riding' was cited as a problem, but in a different form.

In Scotland, the Scottish Parliament also followed this logic by making the occupiers contribute, but provisions were made in the legislation to allow individual BIDs also to place a mandatory levy on property owners alongside business occupiers, should they wish. At the time of writing, however, these provisions have only been drawn on by two 'live' BIDs: the Inverness BID and the Clackfirst BID in Clackmannanshire. With these developments in Scotland in mind, the Coalition government announced plans for 'property-owner BIDs', voted for and paid for by property owners, to be introduced in England and Wales (DCLG, 2014). These would operate separately to existing 'ratepayer' BIDs, and they could feasibly operate in the same geographical areas as ratepayer BIDs. How this will work in practice continues to remain unclear.

In order to operate, BIDs in England, Wales and Scotland must pass a 'dual key test' in a ballot of businesses due to pay the levy in the proposed district. First, the BID must receive a 'yes' vote from a majority of voters. Second, the businesses that vote yes must together comprise a higher rateable value (i.e. estimated property rental value) than all those who voted against it (Cook, 2009). In England and Wales, it is business occupiers in the district who vote. In Scotland, if property owners are included in those who pay the levy, they must also be given a vote. A further difference in the voting procedures is that in Scotland, unlike south of the border, BID ballots require a 25% turnout in number and in rateable value. In Northern Ireland, BID legislation blends aspects of the voting procedures of England, Wales and Scotland: BIDs must pass the dual key test; only business occupiers vote and pay the BID levy; and there is a minimum turnout threshold of 25% in both number and rateable value.

All BIDs across the United Kingdom are time limited to a maximum of five years (with the overwhelming majority operating for five years). If they seek to continue beyond this, they must be re-elected through another renewal ballot (which is identical to a new ballot). It is through references to these voting procedures that proponents of BIDs argue they are both accountable and democratic. Such claims, however, have been questioned by critics, who argue that the democratic accountability of BIDs extends only to businesses and not to the wider community (Briffault, 2010–11; Hochleutner, 2003).

The evolution of BIDs in the United Kingdom

Kingston First was the first British BID to be 'voted in'. It was approved after an election in 2004 and began operating in 2005, in the centre of Kingston-upon-Thames, an outer borough of London. Three years later, proposals for a series of BIDs in Scotland were approved in ballots of local businesses. This time it was Enterprising Bathgate which went 'live' a few months after the vote. By the end of 2012, there were 145 BIDs in operation in the United Kingdom, with 126 in England, 17 in Scotland and two in Wales. BIDs remain in their infancy in Northern Ireland; the Ballymena Business Improvement District became the first official Northern Irish BID after a ballot of businesses in April 2015. A year earlier, seven pilot BIDs were established in Northern Ireland (including the one in Ballymena) – echoing experience in Scotland and England and Wales.

The spatial distribution of BIDs in the United Kingdom is somewhat uneven, although the overall number is growing. The city with the largest concentration of BIDs in the United Kingdom is London, which had 25 by the end of 2012, while other metropolitan cities such as Edinburgh and Birmingham also have more than one BID. Rural areas and small and medium-sized towns have also seen BIDs established. As a result, the number of new BID locations in the United Kingdom showed a steady increase each year between 2005 and 2012, with an average of just over 18 new BIDs annually. The total numbers of BID ballots – including those for new BIDs and renewals – was stable at an average of 28 per year between 2005 and 2009. However, in 2011 and 2012, there were 67 and 75 BID ballots respectively, a large number of which concerned renewals.

The application of the 'dual key test' has meant that the majority of BID proposals are approved. Until the end of 2012, 79% (208) of the 263 ballots which took place in the United Kingdom resulted in the approval of BID proposals, 21% (44) led to rejections and one (discussed later) was declared void (see Figure 7.3). Success at the ballot box is, therefore, not guaranteed. In Glasgow city centre, for example, a proposed BID led by the local Chamber of Commerce was narrowly rejected in the ballot, with 48% in favour by turnout and 59% in favour by rateable value. The legislation across Scotland, Northern Ireland and England and Wales allows BID proposers to institute a fresh ballot after rejection. This was an opportunity not taken in Glasgow, but several other stalled schemes have done so (with some successful and others unsuccessful for a second time).

Focusing on the renewal ballots, until the end of 2012 a total of 52 BIDs in the United Kingdom successfully renewed their mandate for a second term. Paddington BID and the New West End Company (both in London), meanwhile, were approved for a third term. Typically, a BID will arrange a renewal ballot to take place in the final year of its current term, with operations resuming the day after the current term ends. This ensures continuity of service, but not all BIDs are able to pass the dual key test at the renewal ballot. In 2011, Keswick saw the first rejection of a proposed BID renewal, a result that was subsequently repeated elsewhere (for example, in Sleaford, Hams Hall and twice in Altham). Nevertheless, in total 92% of BIDs passed the dual key test at renewal ballots up until the end of 2012.

One of the BIDs that failed at the renewal ballot was the Bolton Industrial Estate Partnership. The circumstances were somewhat unusual. After almost five years in operation, the BID received 51% voting yes by number and 55% by rateable value at a renewal ballot in 2011. However, two businessmen in the district appealed against the decision arguing that the margin between the numbers of businesses voting yes (90) and those voting no (88) was too narrow to justify levying a

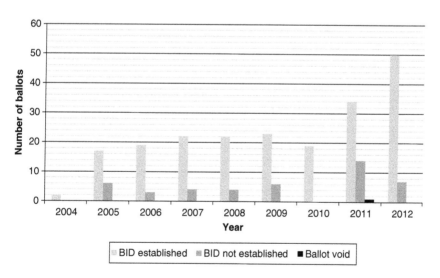

Figure 7.3 Outcome of BID ballots in the United Kingdom by year (2004–12).

Source: Data provided by ATCM.

charge on all businesses in the area. The Department for Communities and Local Government agreed and vetoed the BID ballot (something which it has not done before or since) through the powers vested in it via the Local Government Act 2003 (*Bolton News*, 2011). Following the veto, the BID ballot was repeated, but on this occasion only 36% of businesses by number voted in favour of renewal. In Coventry, meanwhile, another BID ended its operations in more unpredictable circumstances. This time, the Coventry Best for Business BID, established in 2007 to cover 84 industrial estates across the city, saw hundreds of businesses refuse to pay the levy and experienced a takeover of the board. Subsequently, the new board decided to end BID operations in year four of the five-year term (Reid, 2010). The experiences in Bolton and Coventry, therefore, pose difficult questions about how appropriate the existing 'dual key' test is for establishing a BID and also how, and in what circumstances, a BID should no longer operate.

Turnout at BID ballots is also useful to reflect on, not only because a threshold of 25% is required for BID adoption in Scotland and Northern Ireland but also because it can shed some light on the levels of support for BIDs among businesses. Of the 234 ballots between 2004 and 2012 whose turnout figures have been collated, 86 saw a turnout of 50% or more and only nine matched or exceeded the turnout of the UK General Election in 2010 (65%). At the other end of the spectrum, it is worth highlighting that all BIDs in Scotland exceeded the 25% threshold for turnout, the lowest being 34% (for the Inverness City BID in 2008) and 37% in rateable value (Edinburgh Grassmarket in 2012). In England and Wales meanwhile, where data on turnout are patchier, we found only one BID, in Argall, that had a turnout of less than 25%. Of course, there may be others with turnouts of less than 25% whose turnout data were not available.

The level of popularity of BIDs with businesses in the United Kingdom becomes a little clearer when looking at the voting preferences of all the *eligible* voters (as opposed to those actually voting). From the available data, only 19 out of the 234 ballots achieved a figure of 50% or more of all eligible businesses. The highest percentage was 76% for the Segensworth Estates BID in Winchester. The lowest, however, was Evolve Eastbourne with 13%. The former was approved and the latter rejected, but it is entirely feasible that a BID could be established with just over 25% of eligible voters taking part. In total, 72% of ballots had a figure between 20% and 40% of eligible voters voting 'yes'. Again, these figures should be viewed with caution. However, we should be equally cautious when looking at much of the rhetoric that asserts that BIDs are the sole, unambiguous voice of business in their locality (Rasasinghe, 2013) when the majority of BIDs in the United Kingdom received a 'yes' vote from less than 40% of eligible voters (Cook, 2009).

In addition to these issues of adoption, termination and voter turnout, it is also important to consider how the organisational structures of BIDs have developed since 2004. As BIDs were framed as a remedy for the financial problems within TCM, it is not a surprise that the vast majority of UK town centre BID partnerships, such as NE1 in Newcastle-upon-Tyne, are effectively reformed TCM with the pre-existing TCM scheme being converted into a BID after a successful vote.

Nevertheless, other BID schemes have emerged independently of TCM. The majority of these independent BIDs are located on business parks or industrial estates – places in which advocates in England and Wales did not expect BIDs to emerge. Yet, following the introduction of industrial-estate BIDs in Winsford and Bolton in 2005, BIDs in industrial estates and business parks have been actively promoted by the ATCM, British BIDs and Business Improvement Districts Scotland (BIDS). A good-practice guide by BIDs (n.d., p. 5), for instance, claims that BIDs in industrial estates and business parks 'can address problems and issues identified by local businesses with solutions that they believe are right ... BIDs are not all talk – they deliver real results'. However, as the examples of Bolton and Coventry show, support from local businesses cannot be guaranteed.

Of course, when considering the evolution of BIDs in the United Kingdom, we must consider the effects of the recession and the associated austerity measures. The economic and political contexts in which BIDs operate in the United Kingdom have changed in important respects. The first few BIDs in the United Kingdom pursued their strategies against a backdrop of relative buoyancy in the *national* economy, even if this did not extend to all locations. Fifty-seven BIDs were approved in England and Wales prior to the first of the bank bailouts in the United Kingdom – Northern Rock on 17 February 2008 – while the first BID in Scotland (Enterprising Bathgate) was voted in less than a month later. Even at that stage, it is unlikely that those in the UK BID community, much like economic and political commentators more generally, would have foreseen the extent of the financial crisis and the subsequent retrenchment and restructuring in public services.

Little is known about the effects of the recession on the organisation and the strategies of BIDs. What we do know is that the United Kingdom has experienced a number of businesses, including high-street retailers, entering administration, closing or streamlining their operations. The cost of the recession to the United Kingdom's retailers has been estimated to be around £23 billion (Thomas, 2013). In the face of this, supporters have argued that BIDs ought to be seen as mechanisms through which local economies can stabilise and then grow (Reilly, 2009; Houstoun n.d.). Nevertheless, businesses are finding themselves under significant financial pressures. Looking to cut their costs, it might reasonably be expected that businesses look at their discretionary costs – such as the annual sums they pay to their BID. At the same time in the United Kingdom, public-sector budgets have been cut as part of the UK government's austerity programme. This has meant that the non-core expenditure of local authorities, such as the funding of BID activities, has come under scrutiny. Taken together, the combination of the financial crisis and the state-led austerity programme has made the operating climate for UK BIDs harsher.

The figures discussed on BID adoption and termination suggest that there has not been a wholesale abandonment of the BID concept in the United Kingdom. In fact, BID numbers continue to grow steadily. But such an observation does not tell us much about what has happened inside BIDs during the recession. The clearest insight into this, so far, has been provided by De Magalhães (2012, p. 173) who, in a study of BIDs in the United Kingdom, argues that 'the recession and spending cuts have had some impact on most BIDs, but so far this impact has been manageable and the model itself has shown a large degree of resilience'. BIDs, he contends, have been hit harder by reduced or terminated funding from local government, Regional Development Agencies (RDAs) (abolished in 2012) and other regeneration 'pots' than by reduced business levies. Furthermore, as BIDs are supposed to be complementary, or additional, to existing public services, De Magalhães reasons that BIDs have also become vulnerable to potential reductions in the non-statutory services that local authorities, the police and other public-sector bodies provide, such as marketing, decorations, wardens, CCTV and so on. With their overall budgets diminished, De Magalhães notes that in the renewal business plans of BIDs assessed as part of his research, there was a tendency to focus more on core services such as cleaning, marketing and security.

What the longer-term implications are for BIDs as a form of territorial governance is not yet clear. The UK government sees elements of its version of localism in the institutional makeup of BIDs (DCLG, 2012), largely because they are viewed as 'more focused and flexible forms of governance than large municipal bureaucracies' (Levy, 2001, p. 129). However, an increasing number of BIDs will be required to undertake renewal ballots over the next few years, and this will compel them to demonstrate their value added to the businesses who pay the levy. Local authorities may continue to see their budgets reduced and thus are likely to have fewer resources to fund BID activities and services. This represents a challenging operating environment for BIDs.

Conclusion

The establishment of BIDs in the United Kingdom constituted a departure from previous strategies to oversee the governance of town and city centres. The fragmented approaches of the past were rendered more coherent by the creation of TCM partnerships in a number of cities and towns during the 1980s. This set the institutional territorial context for the introduction of BIDs, which despite their Canadian origins were promoted in the United Kingdom as being based on a US model, deemed both successful and transferrable. This model was amended to 'fit' the British context and has subsequently become a significant feature in many towns and cities in the United Kingdom. However, as this chapter has shown, their introduction and evolution have been geographically uneven. And while BID numbers are growing in the United Kingdom, their future remains unclear in the context of sluggish macro-economic conditions and ongoing austerity, even if they have been re-packaged as a form of 'best practice' New Localism.

The borrowing from elsewhere embodied in the trans-national and trans-urban mobility of the BID model underscores the extent to which there is a need to theorise 'the urban' as 'both a place (a site or territory) and as a series of unbounded, relatively disconnected and dispersed, perhaps sprawling activities, made in and through many different kinds of networks stretching far beyond the physical extent of the city' (Robinson, 2005, p. 763). While issues of territory remain important in urban and regional studies, as other chapters in this book demonstrate, the ways in which they are significant (and how best to capture their importance) continue to represent an intellectual challenge in the context of an increasingly inter-connected urban world.

References

Allen, J. and Cochrane, A. (2007) Beyond the territorial fix: regional assemblages, politics and power, *Regional Studies*, 41, 1161–1175.

Amin, A. (2004) Regions unbound: towards a new politics of place, *Geografiska Annaler: Series B Human Geography*, 86, 33–44.

Amin, A. (2007) Re-thinking the urban social, *City*, 11, 100–114.

Baker, T. (2013) Grounding the policy exemplar: territorial politics, global models and urban homelessness in Australia, paper presented at Association of American Geographers annual conference, Los Angeles, March.

Baker, T., Cook, I., McCann, E., Temenos, C. and Ward, K. (2016) Policies on the move: the transatlantic travels of Tax Increment Financing, *Annals of the American Association of Geographers*, 106, 459–469.

Bolton News, The (2011) Scrap CCTV system for industrial estates, *The Bolton News*, 17 August.

Boyle, M., McWilliams, C. and Rice, G. (2008) The spatialities of actually existing neoliberalism in Glasgow, 1977 to present, *Geografiska Annaler: Series B, Human Geography*, 90, 313–325.

Brenner, N. (2004) *New State Spaces: Urban Governance and the Rescaling of Statehood*, Oxford: Oxford University Press.

Briffault, R. (2010–11) The Business Improvement District comes of age, *Drexel Law Review*, 3, 19–33.

Brown, C. (2011) How business improvement districts fit into localism, *Regeneration and Renewal*, 19 January. Available: www.placemakingresource.com/article/1050254/business-improvement-districts-fit-localism (accessed 27 July 2016)

Business Improvement Districts Scotland (n.d.) *Business Parks and Industrial Estates: Benefiting from Business Improvement Districts*, Edinburgh: Business Improvement Districts Scotland. Available: www.bids-scotland.com/images/stories/bids%20business%20parks%20singles.pdf (accessed 27 July 2016).

Clarke, N. and Cochrane, A. (2013) Geographies and politics of localism: the localism of the United Kingdom's coalition government, *Political Geography*, 34, 10–23.

Cook, I. (2008) Mobilising urban policies: the policy transfer of US Business Improvement Districts to England and Wales, *Urban Studies*, 45, 773–795.

Cook, I. (2009) Private sector involvement in urban governance: the case of Business Improvement Districts and Town Centre Management partnerships in England, *Geoforum*, 40, 930–940.

Cook, I. (2010) Policing, partnerships and profits: the operations of Business Improvement Districts and Town Center Management schemes in England, *Urban Geography*, 31, 453–478.

Cook, I. (2015) A vengeful education? Urban revanchism, sex work and the penal politics of John Schools, *Geografiska Annaler: Series B, Human Geography*, 97, 17–30.

Cook, I. and Ward, K. (2011) Trans-urban networks of learning, mega-events and policy tourism: the case of Manchester's Olympic and Commonwealth Games projects, *Urban Studies*, 48, 2519–2535.

Cook, I. and Ward, K. (2012) Conferences, informational infrastructures and mobile policies: the process of getting Sweden 'BID ready', *European Urban and Regional Studies*, 19, 137–152.

Cook, I., Ward, S. and Ward, K. (2014) A springtime journey to the Soviet Union: postwar planning and policy mobilities through the Iron Curtain, *International Journal of Urban and Regional Research*, 38, 805–822.

Cook, I., Ward, S. and Ward, K. (2015) Post-war planning and policy tourism: the international study tours of the Town and Country Planning Association, 1947–61, *Planning Theory and Practice*, 16, 184–285.

Cox, K. (2001) Territoriality, politics and the 'urban', *Political Geography*, 20, 745–762.

DCLG (Department for Communities and Local Government) (2012) *High Streets at the Heart of Our Communities: The Government's Response to the Mary Portas Review*, London: DCLG.

DCLG (Department for Communities and Local Government) (2014) *Property Owners and Business Improvement Districts: Summary of Consultation Responses and Government Response*. London: DCLG.

Deas, I. (2013) Towards post-political consensus in urban policy? Localism and regeneration under the Cameron government, *Planning Practice and Research*, 28, 65–82.

De Magalhães, C. (2012) Business Improvement Districts and the recession: implications for public realm governance and management in England, *Progress in Planning*, 77, 143–177.

Dolowitz, D., Greenwold, S. and Marsh, D. (1999) Policy transfer: something old, something new, something borrowed, but why red, white and blue? *Parliamentary Affairs*, 52, 719–730.

Future of London (2012) *Business Improvement Districts on the Rise*, London: Future of London. Available: www.futureoflondon.org.uk/2012/12/07/business-improvement-districts-on-the-rise/ (accessed 27 July 2016).

González, S. (2011) Bilbao and Barcelona 'in motion': how urban regeneration 'models' travel and mutate in the global flows of policy tourism, *Urban Studies*, 48, 1397–1418.

Hanlon, J. (2003) Time to place your BIDs, *Local Government Chronicle*, 21 November, pp. 16–17.

Hansard Debate (2013)11 February 2013. Available: www.niassembly.gov.uk/assembly-business/official-report/reports-12-13/11-february-2013/ (accessed 27 July 2016).

HM Government (2011) *Localism Act*, London: The Stationery Office.

Hochleutner, B. (2003) BIDs fare well: the democratic accountability of Business Improvement Districts, *New York University Law Review*, 78, 374–404.

Houstoun, L. (n.d.) BIDs face the recession, Urban Public Spaces and Business Improvement Districts blog. Available: http://lhoustoun.wordpress.com/business-improvement-districts-2/bids-face-the-recession/ (accessed 27 July 2016).

Hoyt, L. (2006) Importing ideas: the transnational transfer of urban revitalization policy, *International Journal of Public Administration*, 29, 221–243.

Imrie, R. and Raco, M. (2003) (eds.) *Urban Renaissance? New Labour, Community and Urban Policy*, Bristol: Policy Press.

Inside Government (2010) Announcement: Localism Bill starts a new era of people power, *Inside Government*. Available: www.gov.uk/government/news/localism-bill-starts-a-new-era-of-people-power (accessed 27 July 2016).

Inside Government (2012) Policy: improving high streets and town centres, *Inside Government*. Available: www.gov.uk/government/policies/improving-high-streets-and-town-centres (accessed 27 July 2016).

Jacobs, J. (2012) Urban geographies I: still thinking relationally, *Progress in Human Geography*, 36, 412–422.

Jonas, A. E. G. (2006) Pro scale: further reflections on the 'scale debate' in human geography, *Transactions of the Institute of British Geographers*, 31, 399–406.

Jones, T. and Newburn, T. (2007) *Policy Transfer and Criminal Justice: Exploring US Influence over British Crime Control Policy*, Maidenhead: Open University Press.

Levy, P. (2001) Paying for public life, *Economic Development Quarterly*, 15, 124–131.

Local Government Chronicle (2003) Business Improvement Districts highlighted, *Local Government Chronicle*, 23 September. Available: www.lgcplus.com/business-improvement-districts-highlighted/1255131.article (accessed 27 July 2016).

McCann, E. (2008) Expertise, truth, and urban policy mobilities: global circuits of knowledge in the development of Vancouver, Canada's 'four pillar' drug strategy, *Environment and Planning A*, 40, 885–904.

McCann, E. (2011) Urban policy mobilities and global circuits of knowledge: towards a research agenda, *Annals of the Association of American Geographers*, 101, 107–130.

McCann, E. and Ward K. (2010) Relationality/territoriality: toward a conceptualization of cities in the world, *Geoforum*, 41, 175–184.

McCann, E. and Ward, K. (2011) *Mobile Urbanism: Cities and Policymaking in the Global Age*, Minneapolis, MN: Minnesota University Press.

McCann, E. and Ward, K. (2013) A multi-disciplinary approach to policy transfer research: geographies, assemblages, mobilities and mutations, *Policy Studies*, 34, 2–18.

MacDonald, H. (2000) BIDs really work, in: Magnet, M. (ed.) *The Millennial City: A New Perspective for 21st Century America*, pp. 383–403, Chicago, IL: Ivan R. Dee.

MacLeod, G. and Jones, M. (2007) Territorial, scalar, networked, connected: in what sense a 'regional world'? *Regional Studies*, 41, 1177–1191.

Mallett, W. (1994) Managing the post-industrial city: Business Improvement Districts in the United States, *Area*, 26, 276–287.

Massey, D. (2005) *For Space*, London: Sage.

Medway, D., Alexander, A., Bennison, D. and Warnaby, G. (1999) Retailers' financial support for town centre management, *International Journal of Retail and Distribution*, 27, 246–255.

Medway, D., Warnaby, G., Bennison, D. and Alexander, A. (2000) Reasons for retailers' involvement in town centre management, *International Journal of Retail and Distribution*, 28, 368–378.

Mitchell, J. (2008) *Business Improvement Districts and the Shape of American Cities*, Albany, NY: State University of New York Press.

Montgomery, C. (2005) Downtown draw: businesses consider 'improvement district', *The Plain Dealer*, 12th April, C1.

Moore, S. (2013) What's wrong with best practice? Questioning the typification of New Urbanism, *Urban Studies*, 50, 2371–2387.

Murtagh, B. and Shirlow, P. (2012) Devolution and the politics of development in Northern Ireland, *Environment and Planning C*, 30, 46–61.

Peck, J. and Theodore, N. (2001) Exporting workfare/importing welfare-to-work: exploring the politics of Third Way policy transfer, *Political Geography*, 20, 427–460.

Peck, J. and Theodore, N. (2010) Mobilizing policy: models, methods, and mutations, *Geoforum*, 41, 169–174.

Peck, J. and Theodore, N. (2015) *Fast Policy: Experimental Statecraft at the Threshold of Neoliberalism*, Minneapolis, MN: Minnesota University Press.

Peel, D. and Lloyd, G. (2005) A case for Business Improvement Districts in Scotland: policy transfer in practice? *Planning, Practice and Research*, 20, 89–95.

Peyroux, E., Pütz, R. and Glasze, G. (2012) Business Improvement Districts (BIDs): the internationalization and contextualization of a 'travelling concept', *European Urban and Regional Studies*, 19, 111–120.

Portas, M. (2011) *The Portas Review: An Independent Review into the Future of our High Streets*, London: Department for Business, Innovation and Skills.

Rasasinghe, P. (2013) Business Improvement Associations and the presentation of the business voice. *Urban Geography*, 34, 242–260.

Reid, L. (2010) Deal struck to axe hated business tax, *Coventry Evening Telegraph*, 25 June, p. 7.

Reilly, J. (2009) Is there a place for BIDs in the current economic climate? *Talking BIDs*, February, 1. www.atcm.org/images/files-ukbids/public_html/files/files/Talking BIDsFebruary2009 (Accessed 14 November 2016)

Robinson, J. (2005) Urban geography: world cities, or a world of cities, *Progress in Human Geography* 29, 757–765.

Temenos, C. and McCann, E. (2013) Geographies of policy mobilities, *Geography Compass*, 7, 344–357.

Thomas, C. (2013) UK retailers have lost £23bn since the start of the recession, *The Huffington Post*, 18 February. Available: www.huffingtonpost.co.uk/2013/02/15/uk-retailers-have-lost-23bn-since-the-start-of-recession_n_2694916.html (accessed 27 July 2016).

Travers, T. and Weimar, J. (1996) *Business Improvement Districts: New York and London*, London: The Greater London Group, London School of Economics and Political Science.

Ward, K. (2006) 'Policies in motion', urban management and state restructuring: the translocal expansion of Business Improvement Districts, *International Journal of Urban and Regional Research*, 30, 54–75.

Ward, K. (2007) Business Improvement Districts: policy origins, mobile policies and urban liveability, *Geography Compass*, 1, 657–672.

Ward, K. (2010) Entrepreneurial urbanism and Business Improvement Districts in the state of Wisconsin: a cosmopolitan critique, *Annals of the Association of American Geographers*, 100, 1177–1196.

Ward, K. (2011) Policies in motion and in place: the case of Business Improvement Districts, in: McCann, E. and Ward, K. (eds.) *Mobile Urbanism: Cities and Policymaking in the Global Age*, pp. 71–96, Minneapolis, MN: University of Minnesota Press.

Wolman, H. (1992) Understanding cross national policy transfer: the case of Britain and the US. *Governance*, 5, 27–45.

8 'Where it's at'

Fashions and fads in British local economic-development policy

Alex Lord

Introduction

A common trope in much of the writing on sub-national economic-development policy in the United Kingdom is that it is characterised by experimentation (Deas *et al.*, 2000; Deas and Ward, 1999; Wilks-Heeg, 1996). In this sphere, perhaps more so than many others, policymakers are said to have toyed with the aims, objectives, methods and, particularly, the spatial scale at which policy is designed and delivered (Peck and Theodore, 2012). However at the same time, it is widely acknowledged that, on close inspection, the degree to which the latest policy experiment genuinely represents new thinking is often overstated and dependent upon a very myopic view of history (Deas, 2013; Lord and Tewdwr-Jones, 2014). This idea that continuity rather than change is the best way of understanding what can superficially appear to represent policy innovation is reinforced by the territorial preferences of policymakers. It is from this perspective that we can draw some parallels between the new regionalism of the 1990s and early 2000s (HM Treasury, 2001), and earlier policy and practice dating to the 1920s (Wannop and Cherry, 1994). Experimentation with a new city-regionalism from the early 2000s similarly echoes earlier trials with metropolitan county councils (see SURF, 2004; Leach and Game, 1991; see also, conceptually, Geddes, 1915). And the 'new localism', the expression in vogue after 2010, represents in some respects the second or third time this spatial scale has formed the basis for policy reform (DoE, 1977; Imrie and Raco, 1999; Stoker, 2004; Pickles, 2010). Academics have enjoyed pointing out how little of the novel is genuinely new (Cochrane, 1999; Jones and Ward, 2002).

The question that remains is not why we feel the need to experiment in urban policy in the first place but, rather, why we feel the need to *re*-experiment. Remembering Einstein's famous quip that insanity can be defined as 'doing the same thing over and over again and expecting different results' seems appropriate here: why would a new experiment with city-regionalism, for example, built on similar terms to previous attempts, yield qualitatively different results?

Amongst the possible explanations is an ideological faith in a change to the formula – using a similar palette of ingredients but emphasising more strongly one of the flavours. For example, formal, even contractual, cross-sector partnership working versus the discursive desire to elevate one partner, such as the private sector, to a position of dominance might elucidate differences of impulse between, in the case of the latter, Conservative policy in the 1980s and, in the case of the former, that of New Labour post-1997 (see Russell, 2010; Thornley, 1991). The results are institutions, policies and prescriptions that bear the discursive imprint of a particular government's preferences and contribute to the impression of a 'style' of urban economic-development policy specific to a time and place.

But changes in style are often superficial. What might be said to remain beneath the surface are deeper continuities that manifest in many different ways. For example, the 'new' urban experiment is frequently peopled by the same individuals employed in the last one. These 'usual suspects' (Harding, 1999; Sherlock *et al.*, 2004) often have intimate knowledge of a particular urban context and the issues peculiar to it and, therefore, may retain an impulse to continue their work irrespective of what changes they (probably correctly) expect to be ushered in by transitory government.

An alternative interpretation is that superficial experimentation is essential to masking the truth that sub-national policy mutates so frequently because it is charged with confronting intractable problems fundamentally born of wealth inequality. Repeatedly tinkering with the terms of the game, the names of the agencies and the scale at which they deliver their work, it is argued, is consequently best understood as a device to cope with the localised, urban effects resulting from the internal contradictions at the heart of the national economic system. This interpretation of urban-regeneration policy as a core aspect of a state's approach to crisis management has been the subject of sustained academic research (Jones and Ward, 2002; for some interesting case studies, see England and Ward, 2007) and may well fundamentally explain the circumstances that result in the latest urban experiment jostling for room with the last.

Despite general support for this view, in this chapter an alternative way of understanding the wax and wane of urban experiments is considered: the idea that in urban regeneration policy, just as in other walks of life, fashions repeat. To explore this idea, a brief outline of recent experimentation in urban-regeneration policy is sketched within the context of the literature on how trends form, take root and pass. Thereafter, a specific focus is taken on the case history of one particular UK experiment: Urban Regeneration Companies (URCs).

A history of fads: British policy for sub-national territories

Short-lived enthusiasms, or fads, have been the subject of academic work for many years. Seminal moments in the literature on the sociology and psychology of fashion trends can be found in the likes of Simmel (1904), Sapir (1931) and Meyersohn and Katz (1957). Much of this work served to lay the foundations for subsequent modern studies of how crazes take root in fields as superficially diverse as youth culture (Savage, 1997; more generally see, Crane and Bovone, 2006; Davis, 1992; Entwistle, 2000, 2009) and, in the case of Sorokin's (1956) *Fads and Foibles in Modern Sociology*, academia.

Elsewhere, studies from business economics and management have speculated on models of how trends begin, take root and diffuse. Notions such as fads behaving as 'cascades' (Bikhchandani *et al.*, 1992) turn on the logic that trendsetters (or 'early adopters' in the subject-specific language) might be enlisted to help establish a trend that, through various corporate strategies, could be sustained and manipulated by product-placement strategies and celebrity endorsements (Reynolds, 1968). For more mainstream economics, a trend is understood descriptively as a transitory deviation from the mean that might occur for a variety of reasons, sometimes observed in combination. Faddishness in this sense is used to explain stock-market bubbles and price volatility in secondary markets (such as antiques and curiosities) created by chain reactions of behavioural conformity (also known as the 'bandwagon' or 'stampede effect') (Camerer, 1989).

With respect to local economic development, the fashion for one type of policy over others displays a similar cyclical logic. Moreover, as in other areas where fashion is an important consideration, sometimes the next big thing genuinely is new in the sense of being previously untested. For example, as noted by Ward and Cook in Chapter 7, the Bloor West Business Improvement District in Toronto operating since 1970 sets the precedent against which all subsequent experiments with the concept are measured (see also Hoyt and Gopal-Agge, 2007). On other occasions, however, what is evident is repetition of something from the past, but with a twist. An example in this respect is the Housing Market Renewal Pathfinder initiative, introduced in 2002 ostensibly to correct market failure evident in the form of abandonment in low-demand neighbourhoods across large swathes of urban England outside London. In some respects, this was an initiative of a piece with earlier moments of demolition and replacement, particularly those of the 1950s and 1960s (and in some cases with similar effects – see Allen, 2007; see, also, Yelling, 2000). However, Housing Market Renewal was pitched as an experiment; the desire for it to be thought of as such was explicitly signalled by the pioneering implications of the epithet 'pathfinder'. The initiative was presented using a political lexicon intended to differentiate it from its predecessors ('housing market renewal' rather than 'slum clearance'). It also differed from earlier initiatives in that its delivery was not guided by the planning system with local authorities in the lead, as in most previous periods, but by the national regeneration agency, the Homes and Communities Agency, in concert with 'preferred developers' from the private house-building industry.

Perhaps the feeling that these urban interventions that have decades-long implications and wreak lifechanging effects are, in some sense, experimental stems from the fact that they are often delivered by limited-life agencies that have no direct democratic underpinning. This limited lifespan makes it easy for an incoming government to abolish such agencies, to give a stay of execution or to offer the local authority the option to subsume the agency and its headcount into its mainstream, democratically legitimated suite of activities. There is then often a period in which a fresh set of institutions are introduced, setting the new fashion but with the echo of last season lingering in both the legacy agencies yet to be fully wound up and, sometimes, in the germ of the idea that underpinned their work (Cochrane, 1999). The result is a landscape of interrupted interventions and disembodied institutions, the leftovers of last year's big idea. For example, the creation of English Regional Development Agencies (RDAs) in 1999 has been understood as broadly consistent with the work of the Urban Development Corporations (UDCs) in the 1980s and 1990s (Deas and Ward, 1999), even if the Conservatives' scalar preoccupation with the problems of the 'inner-city' that informed the spatial scale for most of the UDCs was clearly qualitatively different to the strategic, regional remit of the RDAs.

From this perspective, the proclamations made by politicians that suggest a genuine break with the past and lasting alterations to the business model on which urban-regeneration policy proceeds should be treated with caution. The election of 2010 and the subsequent thinking of the UK Coalition government on urban planning serves as a good case study. Amongst the first actions of Eric Pickles on his appointment to the position of Secretary of State for Communities and Local Government was to give local authority planning – the most consistent player in the long-term struggle to effect urban regeneration – a makeover. All references to 'spatial planning' and 'regions' were airbrushed from official documentation as these concepts were regarded as being symbolically linked with Labour policy on planning. In their wake, the 'local' came to be reified as the scale at which planning should take place. The backdrop to this outlook is bound up with the idea of a 'big society', understood within the Conservative Party as redolent of long-standing Tory values of civic duty and voluntarism. This was presented as the rediscovery by the Conservatives of the philosophy of Burke (1790) and the One Nation politics of Disraeli, and as a softening of the free-market preoccupations of the party since the 1980s. 'Red Tories' (see principally Blond, 2010) have argued that this brand of bottom-up communitarian conservatism represents a genuine break from the argument that 'there is no alternative' to laissez-faire economics.

The territorial dimension to this form of Conservatism is 'the local', often presented as an alternative to other, now less fashionable, spatial scales such as the region:

> Communities will no longer have to endure the previous government's failed Soviet tractor style top-down planning targets ... I promised to get rid of them and today I'm revoking regional plans with immediate effect – hammering another nail in the coffin of unwanted and an unaccountable regional bureaucracy. They were a national disaster that robbed local people of their democratic voice, alienating them and entrenching opposition against new development.
>
> I want to make something very clear. Localism means much more than a tug of war of political power between Whitehall and the Town Halls. It's a fundamental shake up of the balance of power in this country. So power goes right back to the people who elected us.
>
> (Pickles, 2010, n.p.)

Whether localism really will constitute a 'fundamental shake up' will only become apparent in time. However, the early signs suggest that, like other moments in the fashion history of urban policy, the fad will pass as its internal contradictions are exposed and political pragmatism takes over. Indicators to this effect include the fact that accommodations made to the National Planning Policy Framework (NPPF), the guidance that sets the tone for the formulation and implementation of planning policies, resulted in part from lobbying by right-wing newspapers opposed to new development in the wealthy home counties where their readership, and the Conservative Party's core vote, happen to reside (*Daily Telegraph*, 2011a, 2011b). Also, Local Economic Partnerships (LEPs) designed to succeed the RDAs are not actually 'local' in the same sense as the rest of the localism agenda at all, but rather in most cases operate at a city-regional scale largely as a result of the advice of Tory grandee, Michael Heseltine (2012).

What remains is the impression that we seem to be endlessly intrigued by the possibilities of 'experimenting' with a new para-state architecture that will, in all likelihood, be just another passing fad. The end state is a whirl of short-lived interventions implemented by an array of institutions, some the outmoded remnants of a previous set of experiments, some the latest bespoke addition. To begin to explain this cycle of experimentation and re-experimentation, it is helpful to return to one of the central questions in work that has sought to understand the life cycle of fads in other walks of life: are trends determined by some semi-mystical set of forces, popularly wrapped up in the idea of a *zeitgeist*, that is then 'discovered' by a handful of early adopters before being disseminated more widely? Or is the *zeitgeist* deliberately formed and manipulated by an elite set of opinion formers?

The idea that trends are purposely determined clearly resonates with any common-sense interpretation of how fashions in, say, popular music or clothing come to predominate. But it does not explain why a fashion might *repeat*. Again, this issue mirrors the wider debate regarding whether the *zeitgeist* is genuinely the result of an invisible hand or is a conscious commercial construct. The former outlook would attribute mass-market demand for a past fashion to be revisited to a collectively shared will for a memory to be repeated; the latter implies that a conglomerate of business interests – manufacturers of products, celebrities paid for their endorsements, the media – conspire to create trends, although possibly in some quarters under a form of false consciousness that conflates being a trendsetter as a response rather than a spur to the trend. An impulse to re-visit a past trend is, therefore, understood as a capricious fancy allied to important circumstantial factors such as global commodities' prices and currency fluctuations.

For those who believe in this latter interpretation that fashions are determined by the whim of opinion formers, the query of how trends come and go in urban policy begs the question: to what extent is this also an elite pastime? If it is, we would need to ask who are the equivalents to the elite marketers that create and propagate fads in fashion with respect to urban and regional policy – Peck's (1995) 'movers and shakers'. Furthermore, to what extent are the trends that emerge indicative of a commercial pulse within the urban-regeneration industry in the same way that setting this season's 'new black' is determined by the fashion industry? To begin to explore these questions, it makes sense to look at a particular policy experiment explicitly designed to formalise elite actor relationships across public and private sectors in urban regeneration: URCs.

The last next big thing: URCs as emblem and artefact

The desire to deliver urban-development policy through effective partnership working between public and private sectors has been a consistent objective shared by governments since (at least) the Urban Programme and Community Development Projects of the late 1960s and early 1970s (Higgins *et al.*, 1983). However, the idea that local urban-development policy should be *made*, rather than simply delivered, by partnerships of this form dates primarily to the UDCs introduced by the Local Government, Planning and Land Act (1980). These nominally private sector-led agencies in places such as Merseyside, Trafford Park near Manchester and, most famously, London's Docklands were charged with catalysing development through a programme of land assembly and remediation to encourage private-sector investment in areas characterised by capital flight. The first wave in London's Docklands and Merseyside dating from 1981 were followed in 1987 by five more (The Black Country, Cardiff Bay, Teesside, Trafford Park and Tyne and Wear), a third wave in 1988–89 (Bristol, Sheffield, Central Manchester and Leeds) and, finally, Birmingham Heartlands and Plymouth in 1992–93.

The story of the UDCs has been told at length (see, for example, Lawless, 1989; Imrie and Thomas, 1999; Deas *et al.*, 2000). Controversies include their preoccupation with physical regeneration over social inclusion (Brownill, 1990; Brownill *et al*, 1996; Robinson and Shaw, 1991), although their remit from central government was always to focus on creating the conditions for development. Furthermore, their ambiguous position with respect to the planning system raised questions, as the vesting of some development control powers with the UDCs potentially grated against their need to accord to statutory local plans. However, most fundamentally, it was the UDCs' democratic legitimacy that caused most concern. As agencies with appointed boards, the UDCs' lack of a democratic mandate, coupled with their institutional separation from the traditional animator of urban policy, the local authority, exercised many academics (Batley, 1989; Lawless, 1991; Stoker, 1991; Thornley, 1991). In practice, evidence would suggest that UDCs worked closely with local authorities and may even have been instrumental in encouraging a more collaborative form of urban politics and decision making (Raco, 2005).

Whatever their effects, further post-industrial decline associated with macroeconomic restructuring, coupled with the national recession of the early 1990s, contributed to the impression that, a decade from its establishment, the UDC experiment was in jeopardy. Although all 13 UDCs limped on through, first, the property-market crash of 1989 and, second, the wider recession of the early 1990s, they began to be wound up beginning with Leeds in 1995, followed by the majority of the remainder in 1997–98, and Cardiff Bay in 2000. Long before this formal end of the experiment, focus had shifted to competitively allocated funding of a more project-based nature through the Single Regeneration Budget (SRB) (Rhodes *et al.*, 2003). However, it was speculated that the longer-term impacts of the UDCs would be far reaching, largely because of their effect of bringing business into urban policy. It was from this perspective that Harding *et al.* (2000, p. 990) speculated that 'the formal involvement of the private sector within urban (and other sub-national) institutions and policy processes has become sufficiently well established to survive a change in the party control of the UK national government with relative ease'.

Around the same time as this conjecture, an opportunity for empirical testing emerged in the shape of the Urban Task Force's (1999, paragraph 4.24) re-discovery of an urgent need to 'redevelop and bring investment back to the worst areas in our cities and towns'. The response of the first Blair government was immediate, with the establishment of three pilot URCs in Sheffield, Manchester and Liverpool in the same year. All three covered a different geography – Liverpool concentrated on the city centre and Manchester concentrated on the deprived east part of the city – but each was focused on a small area, typically a city centre or a handful of wards. A subsequent government-commissioned review (Amion Consulting, 2001) of the initial work of the pilot URCs gave clear backing to the idea that focused, property-led activity through a concerted public-private vehicle was a necessary addition to the institutional apparatus on the logic that responsibility for the depressed condition of many urban centres was the shared public/private result of 'market failures in many areas of our towns and cities and of the inability of past public sector interventions to correct these failures and create lasting improvements' (Amion Consulting, 2001, p. 6). Said to underpin this failure to effect sustained urban regeneration was a lack of coordination between public and private activities: 'not only had the market mechanism failed ... but importantly ... past public sector interventions had not been able to correct these problems' (Amion Consulting, 2001, p. 21). In other words, URCs were aimed explicitly at areas where 'local authorities had been unable to engage fully with the private sector as a result of past mistrust and poor relations' (Amion Consulting, 2001, p. 22). This breakdown of trust was said to require a formal partnership between a business-led board and representation from the three principal public funders of area-based regeneration initiatives covering all three tiers of formal governance: the national regeneration agency, English Partnerships, alongside the relevant RDA and the local authority (ODPM, 2004). As a result of their composition and the fact that they were to be business-led, it was maintained that these organisations would be at arm's length from local government and so would be able to adopt a business-like approach attuned to the needs of the local private sector.

This logic had startling parallels to the earlier rationale for UDCs: an independent agency tied to a specific geography (a UDA – Urban Development Area under the old UDCs) where a concerted focus was said to be required to stimulate private-sector investment. Further echoes can be found in the logic that the agency must be business led and focus on bringing the private sector back into an area that it had previously shunned, and that it should have an appointed board that seeks to consolidate land holdings. The formal partnership of the three principal statutory landholders – the local authority, the RDA and English Partnerships – within the URC represents a systemic difference between these agencies and the formally separate UDCs. However, this must be balanced against the corresponding implication that this meant the agency with statutory planning controls (for both development management *and* the authorship of local planning policy) occupied a formal, strategic position within this otherwise business-orientated, para-state agency. By contrast, the principle (if not the practice, CLES, 1990; Raco, 2005) of the UDCs' full separation from their local authorities arguably represented less potential for a conflict of interest.

At the time of their launch, the association between URCs and UDCs was not widely acknowledged. Despite significant parallels – in goals, scale and structure – a collective amnesia seemed to prevail that instead allowed URCs to be endorsed as a genuine departure from previous attempts to effect physical regeneration in specific small areas and, therefore, a model that might be extended elsewhere. Perhaps the best articulation of this identification of URCs as a new and, of course, 'experimental' trend that might catch on was offered by the official academic reviewers of the three pilot URCs: 'the initial phase of this new experiment appears to hold out considerable promise for the URC "model" as a vehicle for strategic planning and for the delivery of large regeneration programmes' (Parkinson and Robson, 2000, p. 15). Government approval was unequivocal: 'URCs are regarded as effective organisations for delivering focused physical development that is important for the successful regeneration of areas in need … there should be no arbitrary limit placed on the number of URCs supported by the national programme' (ODPM, 2004, p. 8). Perhaps unsurprisingly given this endorsement, by 2005 URCs were *de rigeur*, with 22 established across England and Wales. Many faithfully followed the fashion's originators in Sheffield, Manchester and Liverpool, including URCs in Hull (Hull Citybuild) and Sunderland (Sunderland Arc) that clearly fit the stereotype of cities struggling with the long-term effects of de-industrialisation. Others adopted the URC model but with bespoke adaptations, as in areas lacking the intense deprivation evident in the major cities (such as Gloucester Heritage) or areas characterised by much lower levels of urbanisation (such as Cornwall's CPR Regeneration covering Camborne, Pool and Redruth).

Subsequent evaluations followed for the first URCs, on the basis that they were the most longstanding and, therefore, context, cause and effect could be most readily disentangled (Liverpool Vision – SQW, 2005; New East Manchester – EIUA, 2005; Sheffield One – EIUA, 2007). However by the time of this latter review in 2007, the macro-economic circumstances had begun to change significantly with the first moments of the global financial crisis and the beginning of the deepest recession since the Great Depression. Again, as with the UDCs, the work that the URCs had overseen was undermined, and a gradual impression emerged that the fashion had begun to pass. The result was a rebadging of some of the URCs. Sheffield One was re-christened Creative Sheffield, with a new city-regional 'City Development Company' (CDC) established in 2008, mirroring similar moves from Aberdeen (Aberdeen City Council, 2006) to Southampton

(Southampton City Council, 2007). This was a shift that had explicit support from central government:

> Sheffield City Council has built on the track records of existing bodies, including the urban regeneration company (URC), Sheffield One, to establish a new city development company, Creative Sheffield, to spearhead the economic transformation of the city. Other places have developed, or are developing, new holistic economic development vehicles, combining functions such as housing strategy with a wider economic role. The Government believes there is considerable potential in this approach. Economic development companies operating at the city or city-regional level are a well established concept in countries including the United States, Canada, the Netherlands and Germany.
>
> (CLG, 2007, p. 7)

However, the CDC experiment was short-lived, running only for around two years after trailblazers like Sheffield emerged. As always one or two – such as Liverpool Vision – endured during the subsequent decade, but in a different institutional context as a result of the disbandment of other bodies. First, English Partnerships was wound up and its remit passed to the Homes and Communities Agency in 2008. Second, the RDAs were abolished in the wake of June 2010's emergency budget. Nevertheless, the content of the CLG quote is important as it helpfully identifies some of the important actors in determining fashions in urban policy: the trendsetters in both central and local government and their position in a network of international experience that makes certain policies cross some, but not other, national boundaries (see also McCann and Ward, 2011; Ward and Cook, Chapter 7, this volume).

However, just like the fashion industry more generally (Young, 2002), policy opinion formers could only work within the context of what the international and macro-economy would permit. CDCs were a more short-lived focus of enthusiasm than either URCs or UDCs, not because there was something qualitatively wrong with the idea of anchoring an economic-development agency to a metropolitan geography; in the shape of government and academia, they had support from two-thirds of the triumvirate of opinion formers necessary for the fashion to take hold. But the apparent absence of support from business meant that CDCs were never able fully to take root. The depth of the recession, and particularly the seizure experienced in markets for credit, meant that the often highly geared property sector was unable or unwilling to engage in the formulation and delivery of urban policy.

Dépêche mode: fast fashions in territorial policy recycling

The analysis in this chapter suggests that the urban-regeneration industry is affected in large measure by macro-economic well-being. Fashions for one form of policy over another closely follow macro-economic trends. The brief history presented demonstrates that the experience of URCs, for the most part broadly operational between 1999 and 2011, was not dissimilar to the earlier UDCs, particularly during the early 1990s, when deteriorating local economic circumstances limited the scope for effective land and property-led regeneration. Both initiatives were strongly pro-cyclical and reliant on a helpful macro-economy for their effectiveness.

This observation provides one insight into why there might be continuity between two experiments of very similar duration 20 years apart. But it neither explains what forces combined to animate a desire to re-visit the earlier experiment, nor why it was necessary to sublimate the parallels between the old and the new by reinforcing the idea that URCs were in some sense 'experimental' when palpably they were not. The audit trail points to a nexus of central and local government, private planning consultancies and influential academics combining to provide intellectual ballast for the creation of URCs (Amion Consulting, 2001; CLG, 2006, 2007; Parkinson, 2007; SQW, 2005). These were the equivalents of the opinion formers in the glossy magazines who set trends in mainstream fashion. At the same time, the decision to embark on the URC experiment was also informed by networks outside the United Kingdom, to which domestic policy-makers looked in the search for evidence to support policy reform. URCs, using precisely the same title, also operated in the Netherlands over a similar period as in the United Kingdom (Kort and Klijn, 2011), although it is difficult to establish if the direction of influence was from the Netherlands to Britain or vice versa.

Investigations of this issue – what makes policy prescriptions travel across international borders and contribute to the idea that the policy has 'legs' – are now well established (Theodore and Peck, 2011). This import/export model of urban policy must, then, also be contextualised among existing work that sees this, and the impulse to re-visit previous experiments, as 'policy recycling' (Jones and Ward, 2002). The result is the 'circularity of policy responses', (Wilks-Heeg, 1996, p. 1263) in which urban policy intervention becomes cyclical as a result of repeated re-experimentation. Sometimes this involves the redeployment in modified form of previous policy experiments, as in the case of UDCs/URCs. Sometimes it involves the revision of policy imports so that they are more attuned to domestic circumstance, as in the case of many of the urban-regeneration initiatives transferred from the United States to Britain in the 1980s (Lawless, 1989). In all cases, the precise shape of policy import is governed by whatever the wider economic climate will permit. From this perspective, the impulse to badge each new wave of interventions as innovative is analogous to the sham of fashion. Genuine innovation is as rare in urban policy as it is in the high street stores; however, the necessity to keep up the pretence is indicative of the same thing: the trendsetter has run out of ideas. So it is that the 'fundamental shake up' on which Eric Pickles and his civil servants embarked in 2011 echoes the 'revolution in urban policy' (DoE, 1991) 20 years earlier. The intervening period in which URCs emerged can also be viewed as part of this faux experimentation, as Jones and Ward (2002, p. 488) argue:

> Take for instance the … urban White Paper, *Our Town and Cities: The Future* (DETR, 2000), in which the British state embraces, 'third way'

politics as the friendly face of neo-liberalism, but in the process exacerbates the contradictions of capitalism through its own interventions. This revolutionary framework calls for a 'new vision for urban living' largely founded on modernist assumptions on the need to get the 'design and quality of the urban fabric right' (Urban Task Force, 1999: Chapter 2). This is not revolutionary at all; its policy gene is a document (with a similar title) published twenty years ago (DoE, 1980) and key elements of the 'urban renaissance' are heavily reminiscent of the last urban White Paper, *Policy for the Inner Cities*.

The continuity across these supposedly distinct phases of urban policy is provided by the logic of neoliberalism. Fashions in urban policy are determined, as Wacquant (1999, p. 323) describes it, by

> parties, politicians, pundits and professors who yesterday mobilized, with readily observable success, in support of "less government" as concerns the prerogatives of capital and the utilisation of labour, [and who] are now demanding, with every bit as much fervour, "*more* government" to mask and contain the deleterious social consequences, in the lower regions of social spaces, of the deregulation of wage labour and the deterioration of social protection.

(emphasis in original)

The same net result, albeit from a very different perspective, is offered by Cheshire (2006, p. 1234):

> Both governments and the academic community have been complicit in this abnegation of responsibility. The basic research has not been done and the government has not funded it; the academic community has let its belief systems and egos run away with themselves so that we have become barkers for flawed policies rather than dispassionate investigators, analysts and collectors of evidence … we need a much more detailed understanding of how cities work before we impose policies.

The real-world effects of this repetition of urban experiments are more than just the alphabet soup that marks UDCs' mutation into URCs, CDCs and then LEPs. The lasting impacts are disrupted interventions and unsustained investment in urban areas, resulting from what Peck (2002) calls 'fast policy' – more colloquially known as policy made 'on the hoof' – which obeys the whimsy of *dépêche mode*, or fast fashion. Given the apparently fickle nature of fashion it would seem foolish to prophesise the next turn for policy experimentation. However, there is enough evidence here to suggest that should a property boom come again, it will be accompanied by an experimental public-private agency with a name easily collapsed into a three-letter acronym and deployed at a sub-city geography. And it will last approximately 11 years.

References

Aberdeen City Council (2006) *Delivering City-wide Regeneration: Overview and Next Steps*, Aberdeen: Aberdeen City Council.

Allen, C. (2007) *Housing Market Renewal and Social Class*, Oxford: Routledge.

Amion Consulting (2001) *Urban Regeneration Companies: Learning the Lessons*, London: Department for Transport, Local Government and the Regions.

Batley, R. (1989) London Docklands: an analysis of power relations between UDCs and local government, *Public Administration*, 67, 167–187.

Bikhchandani, S., Hirschleifer, D. and Welch, I. (1992) The theory of fads, fashion, custom and cultural change as informational cascades, *Journal of Political Economy*, 100, 992–1026.

Blond, P. (2010) *Red Tory: How Left and Right Have Broken Britain and How We Can Fix It*, London: Faber and Faber.

Brownill, S. (1990) *Developing London's Docklands: Another Great Planning Disaster?* London: Paul Chapman.

Brownill, S., Razzaque, K., Stirling, T. and Thomas, H. (1996) Local governance and the racialisation of urban policy in the UK: the case of the UDCs, *Urban Studies*, 33, 1337–1356.

Burke, E. (1790) *Reflections on the Revolution in France*, Oxford: Oxford Paperbacks.

Camerer, C. (1989) Bubbles and fads in asset prices, *Journal of Economic Surveys*, 3, 3–41.

Cheshire, P. (2006) Resurgent cities, urban myths and policy hubris: what we need to know, *Urban Studies*, 43, 1231–1246.

CLES (Centre for Local Economic Strategies) (1990) *Inner City Regeneration: A Local Authority Perspective*, Manchester: CLES.

CLG (Communities and Local Government) (2006) The Role of City Development Companies in English Cities and City Regions: A Consultation, London: CLG.

CLG (Communities and Local Government) (2007) The Role of City Development Companies in English Cities and City Regions, London: CLG.

Cochrane, A. (1999) Just another failed urban experiment? The legacy of the Urban Development Corporations, in: Imrie, R. and Thomas, H. (eds.) *British Urban Policy*, 2nd Edition, pp. 246–258, London: Sage.

Crane, D. and Bovone, L. (2006) Approaches to material culture: the sociology of fashion and clothing, *Poetics*, 34, 319–333.

Daily Telegraph (2011a) Hands off our land: latest, 21 September. Available: www.telegraph.co.uk/news/earth/hands-off-our-land/8752127/Hands-Off-Our-Land-latest.html (accessed 17 January 2012).

Daily Telegraph (2011b) Planning minister's in pact with developers over reforms, 11 September. Available www.telegraph.co.uk/news/earth/hands-off-our-land/8756477/Planning-ministers-in-pact-with-developers-over-reforms.html (accessed 14 September 2011).

Davis, F. (1992) *Fashion, Culture and Identity*, Chicago: University of Chicago Press.

Deas, I. (2013) Towards post-political consensus in urban policy? Localism and the emerging agenda for regeneration under the Cameron government, *Planning Practice and Research*, 28, 65–82.

Deas, I. and Ward, K. (1999) The song has ended but the melody lingers: regional development agencies and the lessons of the urban development experiment, *Local Economy*, 14, 114–132.

Deas, I., Robson, B. and Bradford. M. (2000) Rethinking the urban development corporation 'experiment': the case of Central Manchester, Leeds and Bristol, *Progress in Planning*, 54, 1–72.

DoE (Department of the Environment) (1977) *Policy for the Inner Cities*, London: HMSO.

DoE (Department of the Environment) (1991) Michael Heseltine outlines new approach to urban regeneration, Press Release 138, 11 March, London: Department of the Environment.

EIUA (European Institute for Urban Affairs) (2005) New East Manchester Evaluation, Liverpool: EIUA, Liverpool John Moores University.

EIUA (European Institute for Urban Affairs) (2007) Sheffield One Evaluation: Final Report, Liverpool: EIUA, Liverpool John Moores University.

England, K. and Ward, K. (eds.) (2007) *Neoliberalization: States, Networks, Peoples*, London: Blackwell.

Entwistle, J. (2000) *The Fashioned Body: Fashion, Dress and Modern Social Theory*, Cambridge: Polity Press.

Entwistle, J. (2009) *The Aesthetic Economy of Fashion. Markets and Values in Clothing and Modelling*, New York: Berg.

Geddes, P. (1915) *Cities in Evolution*, London: Williams and Norgate.

Harding, A. (1999) North American urban political economy, urban theory and British research. *British Journal of Political Science*, 29, 673–698.

Harding, A., Wilks-Heeg, S. and Hutchins, M. (2000) Business, government and the business of urban governance, *Urban Studies*, 37, 975–994.

Heseltine, M. (2012) *No Stone Left Unturned in Pursuit of Growth*, London: BIS.

Higgins, J., Deakin, N., Edwards, J. and Wicks, M. (1983) *Government and Urban Poverty*, Oxford: Blackwell.

HM Treasury (2001) *Productivity in the UK: The Regional Dimension*, London: HM Treasury.

Hoyt, L. and Gopal-Agge, A. (2007) The business improvement district model: a balanced review of contemporary debates, *Geography Compass*, 1, 946–958.

Imrie, R. and Raco, M. (1999) How new is the new local governance? Lessons from the United Kingdom, *Transactions of the Institute of British Geographers*, 24, 45–63.

Imrie, R. and Thomas, H. (1999) *British Urban Policy: An Evaluation of the Urban Development Corporations*, London: Sage.

Jones, M. and Ward, K. (2002) Excavating the logic of British urban policy: neoliberalism as the 'crisis of crisis management', *Antipode*, 34, 473–494.

Kort, M. and Klijn, E. (2011) Public-private partnerships in urban regeneration projects: organizational form or managerial capacity, *Public Administration Review*, 71, 618–625.

Lawless, P. (1989) *Britain's Inner Cities*, London: Paul Chapman.

Lawless, P. (1991) Urban policy in the Thatcher decade: English inner-city policy, 1979–1990, *Environment and Planning C*, 9, 15–30.

Leach, S. and Game, C. (1991) English metropolitan governance since abolition: an evaluation of the English metropolitan county councils, *Public Administration*, 69, 141–170.

Lord, A. and Tewdwr-Jones, M. (2014) Is planning 'under attack'? Chronicling the deregulation of urban and environmental planning in England, *European Planning Studies*, 22, 345–361.

McCann, E. and Ward, K. (eds.) (2011) *Mobile Urbanism: Cities and Policy Making in the Global Age*, Minneapolis, MN: University of Minnesota.

Meyersohn, R. and Katz, E. (1957) A natural history of fads, *American Journal of Sociology*, 62, 594–601.

ODPM (2004) *Urban Regeneration Companies: Policy Stocktake*, London: ODPM.

Parkinson, M. (2007) *The Birmingham City Centre Masterplan: The Visioning Study*, Liverpool: European Institute for Urban Affairs, Liverpool John Moores University.

Peck, J. (1995) Moving and shaking: business elites, state localism and urban privatism, *Progress in Human Geography*, 19, 16–46.

Peck, J. (2002) Political economies of scale: fast policy, interscalar relations and neoliberal workfare, *Economic Geography*, 78, 331–360.

Peck, J. and Theodore, N. (2012) Follow the policy: a distended case approach, *Environment and Planning A*, 44, 21–30.

Pickles, E. (2010) Making the planning system work more efficiently and effectively, press release, 6 July, London: Department for Communities and Local Government. Available: www.gov.uk/government/news/eric-pickles-puts-stop-to-flawed-regional-strategies-today (accessed 27 June 2013).

Raco, M. (2005) A step change or a step back? The Thames Gateway and the rebirth of the Urban Development Corporations, *Local Economy*, 20, 141–153.

Reynolds, W. (1968) Cars and clothing: understanding fashion trends, *Journal of Marketing*, 32, 44–49.

Rhodes, J., Tyler, P. and Brennan, A. (2003) New developments in area-based initiatives in England: the experience of the Single Regeneration Budget, *Urban Studies*, 40, 1399–1426.

Robinson, F. and Shaw, K. (1991) Urban regeneration and community development, *Local Economy*, 6, 61–72.

Robson, B. and Parkinson, M. (2000) *Urban Regeneration Companies: A Process Evaluation*, Manchester: Centre for Urban Policy Studies, School of Education, Environment and Development, University of Manchester.

Russell, H. (2010) *Research into Multi-Area Agreements: Long-term Evaluation of LAAs and LSPs*, London: Department for Communities and Local Government.

Sapir, E. (1931) Fashion, in: Aseljgman, E. (ed.) *Encyclopedia of the Social Sciences VI*, pp. 139–141, New York: Macmillan.

Savage, J. (1997) *Teenage: The Creation of Youth, 1875-1945*, London: Pimlico.

Sherlock, K., Kirk, E. and Reeves, A. (2004) Just the usual suspects? Partnerships and environmental regulation, *Environment and Planning C*, 22, 651–666.

Simmel, G. (1904) Fashion, *International Quarterly*, 10, 130–155.

Sorokin, P. A. (1956) *Fads and Foibles in Modern Sociology*, Chicago: Henry Regnery Company.

Southampton City Council (2007) *Report to PUSH Economic Development Panel*, Southampton: SCC.

SQW (2005) *An Evaluation of Liverpool Vision Ltd*, Stockport: SQW.

Stoker, G. (1991) *The Politics of Local Government*, London: Macmillan.

Stoker, G. (2004) New localism, progressive politics and democracy, in: Gamble, A. and Wright, T. (eds.) *Restating the State*, pp. 117–129, Oxford: Blackwell.

SURF (Centre for Sustainable Urban Futures) (2004) *Releasing the National Economic Potential of Provincial City-regions: The Rationale for and Implications of a 'Northern Way' Growth Strategy*, Salford: Centre for Sustainable Urban and Regional Futures.

Theodore, N. and Peck, J. (2011) Framing neoliberal urbanism: translating 'commonsense' urban policy across the OECD zone, *European Urban and Regional Studies*, 19, 20–41.

Thornley, A. (1991) *Urban Planning Under Thatcherism: The Challenge of the Market*, London: Taylor and Francis.

Urban Task Force (1999) *Towards an Urban Renaissance*, London: E & FN Spon.

Wacquant, L. (1999) How penal common sense comes to Europeans: notes on the transatlantic diffusion of the neoliberal doxa, *European Societies*, 1, 319–352.

Wannop, U. and Cherry, G. (1994) The development of regional planning in the United Kingdom, *Planning Perspectives*, 9, 29–60.

Wilks-Heeg, S. (1996) Urban experiments limited revisited: Urban policy comes full circle? *Urban Studies*, 33, 1263–1279.

Yelling, J. (2000) The incidence of slum clearance in England and Wales, 1955–1985, *Urban History*, 27, 234–254.

Young, T. (2002) *How to Lose Friends and Alienate People*, London: Abacus.

Part IV

Embedding environmental concerns in regional governance and policy

9 From ecotopia to heterotopia

Alternative pathways to territorialising the environment

Andrew Karvonen

Introduction

In 1975, the American environmentalist and author Ernest Callenbach published a novel titled *Ecotopia: The Notebooks and Reports of William Weston.* Callenbach's ecological utopia involved the secession of the Pacific Northwest – Northern California, Oregon and Washington – from the United States to become a self-sufficient bioregion. The new eco-state was founded on principles of human survival, quality of life, ecosystem protection, self-sufficiency, and a balanced relationship between humans and nature. Ecotopians rejected the dominant mantra of economic growth and progress that proliferated in the twentieth century and, instead, placed the environment at the centre of governance, economy and culture. In effect, the Ecotopian concept provided a route for developed economies to reinvent the human relationship with nature to be co-productive rather than extractive (Callenbach, 1975; Karvonen, 2011). Callenbach's novel rapidly became a touchstone for visionary environmental thought in the 1970s, alongside influential books such as Stewart Brand's *Whole Earth Catalog: Access to Tools,* Ernest Schumacher's *Small is Beautiful: Economics as if People Mattered* and Amory Lovins's *Soft Energy Paths: Towards a Durable Peace. Ecotopia* provided a multitude of radical ideas to counter the environmental impacts due to the spread of capitalism and consumerism in the second half of the twentieth century (for a contemporary perspective on the influence of Callenbach's book, see Timberg, 2008).

At the heart of the Ecotopian vision was a geographical container that harmonised human and non-human flows by drawing on bioregionalism, the dominant perspective of influential planning advocates in the late nineteenth and early twentieth centuries including Patrick Geddes, Lewis Mumford and Benton MacKaye (McKennis, 1999; Thayer, 2003). It suggested that humans could work in harmony with nature rather than try to conquer it. Bioregionalists recognised an indelible connection between ecosystem flows and human settlement. As Dryzek (2000, p. 157) notes:

> Bioregionalism is not just a matter of redrawing political boundaries: it is also a matter of living in place. Redesigned political units should promote, and in

turn be promoted by, awareness on the part of their human inhabitants of the biological surroundings that sustain them.

Four decades on from Callenbach's Ecotopian vision, the ethos of bioregionalism has been joined by a multitude of strategies to territorialise the environment. The region as a container for the 'environment' can still be found in debates about resource extraction (e.g. fracking, deforestation), renewable energy (solar, wind, hydro) and natural disasters (droughts, hurricanes), but it has been joined by other conceptions of territory that encompass more modest scales of neighbourhoods, districts, streets and even individual sites. This proliferation of ideas about environmental territories can be attributed to the mainstreaming of ideas related to sustainable development and sustainability. The environment is no longer a radical or marginal concept confined to ecologically minded activists, but is embedded in mainstream agendas and is considered alongside economic development, quality of life and social equity (see Gibbs *et al.*, Chapter 10, this volume). And cognitively, there is a growing recognition that humans are not separate from nature but are part and parcel of it; the environment is not something that is 'out there' but comprises both inhabited and uninhabited places. This is particularly true in cities where nature is increasingly recognised as being co-constitutive of the urban condition (see Keil and Graham, 1998; Gandy, 2006; Karvonen, 2015).

So how is the environment territorialised today? If bioregionalism is not the dominant way of conceptualising spaces of the environment, then what is? Who defines the spatial extents of these territories and for what reasons? Looking across the various discourses and debates about nature and society, environmental protection, sustainable development, climate change and environmental justice, it is apparent that the territorialisation of the environment has mirrored the proliferation of environmental governance beyond the traditional activities of the state to include a variety of actors. Callenbach's idealised alignment of government jurisdiction and ecosystem flows has given way to a twenty-first century condition of multiple territories shaped by a wide range of agendas. This creates a messy picture of environmental governance but opens up environmental issues to a wider array of perspectives.

To understand the multiple ways that the environment is territorialised in the twenty-first century, I adopt a pathways approach to unpack some of the emerging territories of environment that are being envisioned, designed and realised today. The pathways approach embraces a pluralist understanding of the world and is useful as a comparative tool for uncovering the motivations and logics that underpin the conceptualisation, construction and maintenance of various territories. The multiple territories of the environment provide insights on the different ways that human-nature relations are being reworked while also suggesting different desired futures and alternatives for governance. They embody what Michel Foucault refers to as 'heterotopias', those alternative or other spaces that reflect the diversity of the world (Foucault, 1984).

In this chapter, I focus specifically on urban locales due to the multitude of ways that environmental territories are being realised in cities around the world. Cities are not the only place where environmental territories are being reconstituted and reimagined, but they provide a vivid and prominent example of these processes. I begin by defining the pathways approach and how it is useful for interpreting and making sense of the multiple ways that the environment is territorialised today. I then describe four alternative pathways of environmental territorialisation that serve as a counter to the dominant understanding of the environment as being defined and managed by either ecological flows or by the geographical extent of governmental jurisdiction. I conclude by arguing that the various ways that the environment is being spatialised today have implicit normative assumptions about desirable futures and the governance of human/nature relations.

Making sense of multiple environments

Today, the environment is conceptualised, interpreted and framed in a multitude of ways. National, regional and local governments continue to serve as the principal arbiters of resource extraction and environmental protection. However, they are increasingly being joined by a variety of organisations and actors promoting ideas and agendas about human-nature relations that can be confusing and at times contradictory. Alternatively, we can see this diversity of ideas and actions as a positive development. The environment is no longer a social movement or a moral crusade restricted to a vocal minority; instead, it is tied in with everything that we say and do because it is inextricably bound up in notions of economy, culture and society.

Over the past two decades, a number of academics have adopted a pathways approach to address or manage the diversity of ideas about the environment, nature, sustainability and sustainable development (see Table 9.1). Rejecting positivist tendencies towards a single definition of the world (Law, 2004), these scholars are informed by post-colonial, feminist and post-structural critiques of modernity and recognise that there is no single approach to understanding the relationship between humans and their surroundings. Instead, they embrace the multiple, discursive and contested notions of the environment as a productive development. Hess (2007, p. 4) argues that pathways 'make it possible to avoid drawing premature boundaries when confronted with the fluidity of goals and repertoires of action'. And reflecting on urban-sustainability agendas, Guy and Marvin (2001, p. 31) contend that pathways are helpful in 'the recognition that a wide diversity of sustainable urban futures are likely to coexist within a single city'.

The notion of pathways rejects the predefined norms and universal assumptions that have historically underpinned theoretical and empirical work on the environment and instead recognises the environment as discursive, contested and multiple. As Leach and colleagues (2010, p. 168) argue, 'a pathway approach aims to uncover diversity, broaden out the debate and open up possibilities for ways forward.' This suggests that the pathways approach is an analytic tool for identifying how the environment configures particular actors and trajectories

Table 9.1 Examples of pathways scholarship on environment, nature, sustainability and sustainable development

Topic	Author(s)
Urban development and planning	Haughton, 1997; Guy and Marvin, 1999, 2000; Finco and Nijkamp, 2001; Pinderhughes, 2004, 2008
Sustainable architecture	Guy and Farmer, 2000, 2001; Farmer and Guy, 2002; Guy and Moore, 2005, 2007
Energy systems	Marvin *et al.*, 1999; Guy 2004; Rydin *et al.*, 2013
Food systems	Allen *et al.*, 2003
Transport systems	Evans *et al.*, 2001
Social movements	Gottlieb, 2001; Hess, 2007
Environmental politics/governance	Jamison, 2001; Moore, 2007, Leach *et al.*, 2010
Urban nature	Karvonen, 2015
Sustainable consumption	Davies *et al.*, 2014

of change. It is a heuristic device to organise the complexity of environmental visions and agendas. The pathways approach acknowledges that there are different perspectives and visions, and encourages us to contemplate why a particular vision of the environment was adopted and by whom. It shifts the emphasis away from the environment as a container (see Graham and Healey, 1999) and more towards the processes that produce the environment, how interests are negotiated, how actions are formulated and undertaken, and how outcomes are assessed (Karvonen, 2015).

The pathways approach does not provide 'the answer' or the 'proper solution' to questions about the environment. Instead, it serves as a framework for assessing, considering, comparing and weighing different options and configurations. It encourages a comparative sensibility amongst different visions (Jamison, 2001) rather than a judgment; it is not so much a model as an attitude or mode of inquiry. Furthermore, the pathways identified are not static or independent, but instead they overlap, compete and coalesce with other pathways. Leach *et al.* (2010, p. 168) conclude that 'a pathways approach thus offers a way to overcome the kinds of simplifications that have limited options and stultified debate about sustainable development'. Ultimately, the pathways approach is not about identifying the best or most effective route to improved futures but recognising that there are many different ways that the future could be realised.

This embrace of multiplicity of spaces resonates with Foucault's notion of heterotopias (Foucault and Miskowiec, 1986). The term 'heterotopias' refers to 'other places' and provides an antidote to commonplace interpretations of space (Dehaene and De Cauter, 2008; Chatzidakis *et al.*, 2012). It provides a lens for studying alternative spaces that are often overlooked or neglected. Dehaene and De Cauter (2008, p. 4) argue that heterotopias serve as 'a strategy to reclaim places of otherness inside an economized public life'. In this way, heterotopias resonate with the work of Henri Lefebvre and Michel de Certeau in opening up contemporary notions of space to alternative voices and conceptions. The pathways approach described here is a useful way to reveal the heterotopic character of contemporary environmental territories. It suggests that there are multiple ways that the environment is conceived, spatialised and governed by a wide range of actors and agendas.

In the following sections, I describe four alternative pathways of environmental territorialisation that are dominant today: design, empirical, innovation and community. These pathways embody distinct conceptions of the environment, producing particular spatial configurations and social arrangements of the world. The identified pathways are not independent or exclusive but draw on overlapping stakeholders, resources and conceptions. They serve as interpretive lenses to understand the multiple ways that the environment is territorialised in the twenty-first century and the varying consequences and implications.

The design pathway

One of the most feted environments in the first two decades of the twenty-first century is The High Line in New York City. The High Line, constructed in three phases between 2006 and 2014, is an urban park built on 2.33 km of abandoned elevated rail line in southwest Manhattan. It includes a wide variety of plantings, numerous opportunities for walking and sitting, unique views of the city and temporary and permanent art installations, all two stories above the busy streets below (Friends of the High Line, 2008, 2015; Sternfeld, 2009; David and Hammond, 2011). Even before the project opened in June 2009, it captured the imagination of New York residents, tourists, policymakers, designers and academics because of its imaginative approach to 'ecologising' an existing built-up landscape (on the notion of 'ecologising', see Latour, 1998, 2004; Murdoch, 2001; Hinchliffe *et al.*, 2005). The park challenges conventional dichotomies of natural/industrial, aesthetic/functional and wild/tamed, and has rapidly emerged as an exemplar of the transformative power of urban greening.

The widespread popular and critical acclaim for The High Line since the first section opened in 2009 has spawned a plethora of new initiatives aimed at adopting this model of urban development in other cities around the globe. Similar projects have been proposed or developed on abandoned elevated train lines in Chicago, Philadelphia, Jersey City, St. Louis, Atlanta, Seattle, Morristown (Tennessee), Pittsburgh, Rotterdam, Manchester and elsewhere. As a journalist notes, 'The High Line has become, like bagels and CompStat, another kind of New York export' (Taylor, 2010, A1). At first glance, this is a welcome development because it suggests that the 'ecologising' of cities is no longer a fringe activity of ecocentric, tree-hugging activists but a desirable goal for a wide swath of urban actors.

However, the embrace of The High Line as a 'best practice' tends to perpetuate an instrumental approach to urban development. It assumes that successful projects can be replicated unproblematically in another locale without making a concerted effort to consider the different contexts (Farmer and Guy, 2002; Bulkeley, 2006). As Rybczynski (2011, WK9) notes, 'The High Line may be a landscaping project, but a good part of its success is due to its architectural setting' between 'interesting old and new buildings.' The unique physical context, rather than the innovative design, is central to the project's success. And in addition to the surrounding buildings, the High Line is a product of particular historical, political and social contingencies. To attempt to re-create the project in another locale without considering the contested processes that went into its making is to reduce The High Line to a set of building blocks, individual pieces that are simply dropped into place. In other words, all abandoned elevated rail lines are not equal and some (perhaps many) should not automatically be envisioned as future parks or public spaces. As The High Line's chief designer, James Corner, readily admits, 'The High Line is not easily replicable in other cities' (quoted in Shevory, 2011, B6).

Focusing less on The High Line as a *product* of the urban landscape and instead as a geographically constituted *process* of territorialisation, we can recognise a pathway that embodies a particular framing of the environment. The historical development of The High Line involved an intriguing synergy of community and economic forces that came together in the late 1990s to appropriate an abandoned urban space. The space of the railway is defined by previous business activity as well as its subsequent abandonment due to changes in resource flows and transportation infrastructure. This resonates with other projects that have relied on a compelling narrative of redemption and reform to repurpose an existing industrial site such as the Eden Project in southwest England (Smit, 2011), Gasworks Park in Seattle (Olin, 1988) and Zeche Zollverein in Essen, Germany (Dorstewitz, 2014). The aim here is to reinvent industrial landscapes for a post-industrial age and, in the process, challenge the boundaries between what is understood to be 'nature' and what is understood to be 'human'.

At the heart of The High Line's character is a design response that focuses on a particular piece of infrastructure. The environment is defined through the imagination and the creative repurposing of the built environment to reflect twenty-first century values. It is a micro approach, inventing environment in an interstitial space of a built-up city using clever and strategic design gestures (see Franck and Stevens, 2007; Sim, 2009; Karvonen and Yocom, 2011). Seen in this way, we can start to connect The High Line with other design responses that reconfigure underused spaces through the introduction of green roofs and walls, small plots of urban agriculture, pocket parks and so on. These one-off interventions diverge significantly from Callenbach's bioregional vision of harmonising ecology and humans because they lack a totalising and holistic understanding of territory. Instead, the environment is produced through piecemeal and opportunistic interventions that serve as pinpricks of change, an 'urban acupuncture' approach that targets particular conditions (Sim, 2009; Villagomez, 2010; Lerner, 2014). The territory is thus comprised of a patchwork quilt of discrete interventions.

On the other hand, these projects share with Callenbach's Ecotopia an understanding of the indelible connections between humans and nature and between society and space, and forward a relational approach to environmental territorialisation. They are an indicator of the resurgence of landscape architecture as an influential design discipline in mediating the relationships between humans and nature (Steiner, 2011) through contemporary notions of ecological urbanism (Mostafavi, 2010), landscape urbanism (Waldheim, 2006) and biophilic cities (Beatley, 2010). The *design pathway* produces a particular environmental territory, one that is informed by creative intervention to rework human/nature relations.

The empirical pathway

A parallel pathway of environmental territories exists in the natural sciences through a wide range of laboratories and field sites. Contemporary examples of empiricising the environment abound with the rise of climate science and climatology research (see Webb, Chapter 11, this volume). A precursor to this work is the Long Term Ecological Research (LTER) programme initiated by the US National Science Foundation. The programme began in 1980 with six projects in the United States designated as field sites for monitoring and testing of different ecological conditions over an extended period of time. In subsequent years, the programme has expanded to include 26 projects across North America, the South Pacific and Antarctica (see Table 9.2). The LTER projects range from a few thousand to several million hectares and cover multiple biomes. These sites function as field sites where experiments are conducted and data are collected and analysed to characterise the long-term dynamics of ecological systems. As Hobbie (2003, p. 18) puts it, 'The central, organizing intellectual aim of the LTER program is to understand long-term patterns and processes of ecological systems at multiple spatial scales.' Unlike more traditional ecological field sites, the LTER project is also designed to assess human-induced changes due to land use, resource extraction and pollution (Redman *et al.*, 2004, LTER Network, 2015). The majority of the sites are rural with small to moderate levels of human disturbance. However, in 1997, two cities were designated as LTER projects, Baltimore and Phoenix, providing closer links between the production of ecological knowledge and the built environment (Evans, 2011; Steiner, 2011).

While the LTER projects have less cachet with the general public than urban green-design projects, they are celebrated by natural scientists because of the opportunities they afford to gather a wide array of real-world data from field sites over extended periods of time. The LTER network facilitates the sharing of data and research methodologies, and comparison between different empirical findings. The sites also represent a significant commitment by the US government to 'big science' projects that go beyond space exploration and fundamental research in the natural sciences, engineering and medicine. The LTER sites can be understood as heterotopias because they do not attempt to mimic the traditional laboratory or field site; they embrace place rather than attempt to obliterate it (Henke, 2000; Henke and Gieryn, 2008) by destabilising the cognitive boundary between lab and field (Kohler, 2002; Evans, 2011). This is particularly evident in the urban LTER sites in Baltimore and Phoenix where the intermingling of humans and nature is highly visible. Experiments are more difficult to control due to influence by 'outside' forces, but the embrace of the messiness and unpredictability of the

Table 9.2 The National Science Foundation's long-term ecological research projects

Site	Location
Andrews Forest	Oregon
Arctic	Alaska
Baltimore	Maryland
Bonanza Creek	Alaska
California Current Ecosystem	California
Cedar Creek Ecosystem Science Reserve	Minnesota
Central Arizona – Phoenix	Arizona
Coweeta	Georgia
Florida Coastal Everglades	Florida
Georgia Coastal Ecosystems	Georgia
Harvard Forest	Maine
Hubbard Brook	New Hampshire
Jornada Basin	New Mexico
Kellogg Biological Station	Michigan
Konza Prairie	Kansas
Luquillo	Puerto Rico
McMurdo Dry Valleys	Antarctica
Moorea Coral Reef	Tahiti
Niwot Ridge	Colorado
North Temperate Lakes	Wisconsin
Palmer Antarctica	Antarctica
Plum Island Ecosystems	Maine
Santa Barbara Coastal	California
Sevilleta	New Mexico
Shortgrass Steppe	Colorado
Virginia Coast Reserve	Virginia

Source: LTER Network (2015).

real world provides unique insights on how ecological systems work in the real world. As Evans (2011, p. 232) summarises, 'place is critical as the visible arbiter of truth.'

The LTER sites are closely related to the proliferation of 'urban laboratories' and 'living laboratories' to stage environmental interventions in recent years (Evans, 2011; Evans and Karvonen, 2011, 2014; Bulkeley and Castán Broto, 2012; Castán Broto and Bulkeley, 2013; Nevens *et al.*, 2013; Karvonen *et al.*, 2014). There is an understanding that climate change and other wicked problems require disruptive strategies to promote radical change. Laboratories and field sites involve the creation of specific territories where innovative experiments can be conducted on energy, food, water, transport and other resource flows. These spaces resonate with the design pathway described in the previous section because of their bespoke creation. However, they have a distinct emphasis on empirical data collection that can then be used to influence evidence-based policies about environmental protection, economic development and social learning (Evans and Karvonen, 2011).

Like Callenbach's Ecotopia, the territory of the environment is defined by ecological flows. However, ecological flows are not understood as a means to define a new locus of governance but to feed into scientific knowledge production. The environment is defined through the activities undertaken to perform experiments to bolster the scientific knowledge base and to be applied to established circuits of policymaking. This represents an *empirical pathway* where data gathering and analysis activities are used to understand human-nature relationships more comprehensively. The empirical pathway recognises that we live in the age of the 'anthropocene' where human actions are dominant and cannot be separated from scientific knowledge production. At the same time, the non-human aspect of these territories is the primary determinant for establishing these environments, similar to Callenbach's bioregional vision. The focus of these environmental territories is to characterise ecosystem processes to understand how they change over time while taking into account the influence of humans.

The innovation pathway

Another alternative pathway of environmental territorialisation leverages cutting-edge technologies to realise resource efficient cities. A prominent example of this approach is Masdar City in the United Arab Emirates. Located 17 km outside of Abu Dhabi, Masdar City was launched in 2006 as an ambitious project that is simultaneously an experimental setup, a holistically designed city and a model for a new mode of twenty-first century urban economic development. Masdar City comprises six km^2 of a new city that will have zero waste and zero carbon emissions through the application of a suite of technologies and design strategies. Green architecture and urban design features are woven into the mixed-use development with innovative infrastructure networks to realise a futuristic and holistic twenty-first century city (Cugurullo, 2013a, 2013b; Rapoport, 2014).

At Masdar City, technological innovation is understood as the key to realising improved urban futures. This resonates with the scientific and experimental approach of urban laboratories and living laboratories described in the previous section. However, the testing and gathering of data from the technologies is not an end in itself, as in the empirical pathway, but rather as a means to realise economic gains by selling the proven technologies to the world. Innovation is at the heart of economic development and there is a significant market opportunity in developing and selling environmentally friendly technologies. As Cugurullo (2013b, p. 13) summarises, 'the core of the Masdar City project is made of production and diffusion of green technology.' Adhering to an ecological modernisation ethos, there is an understanding that economic development and environmental protection are complementary rather than contradictory (Hajer, 1995; Dryzek, 2005). Rapoport (2014, pp. 141–142) argues that 'such projects seek to work within, rather than challenge, growth-oriented models of urban development'. This is in direct opposition to Callenbach's Ecotopian vision because it embraces rather than rejects economic growth.

Masdar is one of many high-profile eco-cities around the world that are attempting to reinvent cities through technological development. Dongtan, Tianjin,

Chongming and Caofeidian International Eco-City are examples of the hundreds of eco-city projects that have been launched in the past decade to promote a techno-centric form of urban development (Joss, 2009, 2011; Chang and Sheppard, 2013; Caprotti, 2014; de Jong *et al.*, 2015). A related agenda can be found in smaller-scale eco-districts such as Hammarby Sjöstad in Stockholm, Sweden and Quartier Vauban in Freiburg, Germany (Iverot and Brandt, 2011; Kasioumi, 2011), as well as the emerging smart cities agenda exemplified by projects such as the Amsterdam Smart City, Kalundborg Smart City (Denmark) and the IBM Operations Centre in Rio de Janeiro (Luque *et al.*, 2014; Vanolo, 2014; Viitanen and Kingston, 2014). These projects vary in their emphasis on design and empirics but share a common agenda of applying the latest technologies to optimise environmental performance.

The environment here is shaped by capital accumulation strategies rather than the creation of distinctive spaces (as in the design pathway) or through the production of ecological knowledge (as in the empirical pathway). Scale is a salient feature of these projects because it serves to demonstrate the efficacy of the technology being deployed, whether it be renewable energy technologies, sensors for detecting air pollution, driverless vehicles, or otherwise, in an actual place. Moreover, these projects tend to be outward facing and showy; they are showrooms that materialise innovation and are designed and built 'to advertise their "eco-ness"' (Rapoport, 2014, p. 138). By serving as real-world, at-scale and highly visible projects, the aim is to replicate these activities in other locales and create a global network of ecological modernisation underpinned by the fruits of corporate research and development. The territories inscribed by eco-cities, eco-districts and smart cities are not valued for the places they create but for the ideas that can be transferred elsewhere. Advocates of eco-cities, eco-districts and smart cities are focused on diffusing a singular blueprint of sustainable urban development. The territory produced in the *innovation pathway* is driven by an enterprising developer who is leveraging the global circuits of capitalism.

The community pathway

A fourth alternative pathway of environmental territorialisation is centred on social transformation rather than technological innovation. A well-known example of this is the Transition Towns model initiated in the United Kingdom by environmental and community activist Rob Hopkins. Hopkins spearheaded the first transition town in 2005 in the village town of Totnes in South West England by creating a suite of bespoke, locally based programmes around green building, community energy provision, local food production and self-sufficient economic development to address issues of peak oil and climate change (Hopkins, 2008, 2011). The underpinning logic of Transition Towns is permaculture, which has roots in bioregionalism and the back-to-the-land movements of the 1970s (Pursell, 1993; Smith, 2005, 2011a, 2011b). The ideas introduced by Hopkins in Transition Town Totnes have rapidly spread around the globe and, today, the Transition Network website lists some 477 initiatives that are connected to the transition movement, as well as 16 national hubs (mostly in Europe) (Transition Network, 2014).

Transition Towns serve as an example of 'grassroots innovation' that aims to realise alternatives futures through place-based social transformation (Smith, 2011a; Seyfang and Haxeltine, 2012; Seyfang and Longhurst, 2013; Feola and Nunes, 2014). Building on a history of alternative social movements stretching back to the Levellers and the Luddites, community-based social movements are gaining increasing public recognition as an antidote to the dominant agendas of globalisation and neoliberal capitalism (Pickerill and Maxey, 2009; Pickerill, 2011; Chatterton, 2013, 2015; Rapoport, 2014; Diggers and Dreamers, 2015). They build on radical configurations of green living strategies that first emerged in the 1970s – communal living, co-housing, eco-villages, intentional communities and low-impact lifestyles – and have gradually moved into the mainstream consciousness. While (2014, p. 45) summarises this agenda as 'transformative green restructuring around low-growth, alternative growth and localisation strategies'.

The community pathway takes on the tenor of a social movement with a strong localist agenda based on self-sufficiency and place-based identity (Walker, 2011). The territory of environment lies somewhere between the individual/family and the state, and is an attempt to find the sweet spot between individual values and state responsibility (Shutkin, 2000; Aiken, 2012). It is a return to more self-sufficient, contained and locally empowered society that has control over its environmental resources (North, 2010; While, 2014). There is a shared frustration with the slow and inadequate responses to date to environmental problems (Bulkeley and Newell, 2010). Rather than relying on an expert designer, a diligent scientist or a creative urban developer, the community pathway leverages 'a collective, progressive mobilising force' (Aiken, 2014, p. 4).

In many ways, the *community pathway* serves as a contemporary vision of Callenbach's ecotopian vision. It provides a route for making environmentalism more than a slogan or political campaign and more a way of life. However, the territories defined by social transformation diverge from Ecotopia in important ways. Rather than embrace a bioregional understanding of the environment that aligns government jurisdiction with ecological flows, this pathway targets the shared values and ambitions of a particular group of people in a particular place. The result is a 'place-bound' territory (see Moore and Karvonen, 2008), where the scale can range from a handful of houses to a block, a neighbourhood, a village or an entire city. The embrace of local identity is strikingly different from the innovation pathway because of its celebration of physical context and the people who reside there. The territory creates a common goal for a particular set of actors and a network of sharing and learning, similar to the empirical pathway. But the territory here serves as a platform for action to realise an alternate future; it is a site where ideas and values can be enacted (Cannavò, 2007; Aiken, 2014). And unlike the other pathways, the community pathway is unequivocally antagonistic towards capitalism and globalisation. There is an explicit desire to fundamentally rearrange the current configurations of human-nature relations by leveraging the notion of community. The result is a territory that is localised and specific to a particular human population.

Alternative pathways of environmental territorialisation

Territories of the environment continue to be dominated by state-led environmental regulations and management located within jurisdictional containers that define local, national and pan-national boundaries. Jones and MacLeod (2004, p. 437) attribute this to the *realpolitik* of *doing* regulation and administration that relies on 'a pre-existing or aspirant spatial scale or territorially articulated space of dependence through which to conduct their actually existing politics of engagement'. However, the pathways identified in the previous sections offer multiple alternative framings of the environment that reveal the different motivations and activities of a wide range of stakeholders that go beyond conventional political jurisdictions (city, region, nation, world). The pathways approach developed by a wide range of environmental scholars over the past few decades serves as a useful heuristic tool for making sense of these multiple territories. They reveal different understandings of how the world is understood, different modes of knowledge creation and circulation and different agendas for action. Ultimately, the alternative pathways reveal a range of different relationships between humans, technology and nature to reflect a heterotopian worldview.

The alternative pathways identified in this chapter are summarised in Table 9.3. The design pathway is informed by the tenets of landscape architecture, urban ecology and sustainable urban design. The aim is to reveal human/nature interactions through creative interventions. The empirical pathway takes its cue from ecology and resilience with an overarching agenda of scientific discovery and robust data gathering. The territory of environment is produced through monitoring activities by natural scientists that can then inform the scientific knowledge base and environmental policymaking. The innovation pathway focuses on technological development as a means to reduce environmental impacts while simultaneously bolstering neoliberal political agendas. Here, it is the entrepreneurial developer who enacts territories to tap into the global flows of finance. And finally, the community pathway is inspired by identity-based politics and localism. Local activists define the environmental territory through the development of social bonds and the realisation of self-sufficiency through a suite of place-based activities.

It is important to emphasise that these pathways should not be considered as exclusive or discrete; this is not a menu of choices to consider and select (either individually or collectively). Instead, they overlap and intermingle, producing a messy picture of environmental territories. For example, designers can be found working on urban laboratories, eco-cities and Transition Town programmes. Likewise, capitalism is not the sole domain of the innovation pathway but influences the others in significant ways. And the four pathways identified here are not the only ones. Protest activities around fracking, planning visions for mega-regions of renewable-energy provision, natural disasters such as hurricanes and flooding and innovations in regulatory frameworks all represent other distinct ways that the environment is being territorialised. However, the pathways outlined

Table 9.3 A comparison of alternative pathways of environmental territorialisation

	Design	*Empirical*	*Innovation*	*Community*
Examples	The High Line, green roofs and walls, pocket parks	LTER Programme, urban laboratories and living laboratories	Eco-cities, eco-districts, smart cities	Transition Towns, eco-villages, intentional communities
Theoretical frameworks	Landscape urbanism, urban ecology	Ecological science, socio-ecological systems, resilience	Technological change, ecological modernisation	Ecological democracy, civic environmental-ism, social movements
Principal objective	Bespoke expression through creative intervention	Scientific discovery through data collection	Economic development through technological innovation	Self-governance through social transformation
Key actor	Opportunistic designer	Progressive scientist	Enterprising developer	Constructive activist

here provide insights on four ways that the environment is being reconfigured in urban contexts.

The identified pathways reveal the alternative territories that are defined by different actors and agendas. Whereas the design and community pathways place a priority on particular locales, the empirical and innovation pathways see place more generically as a means to collect ecological data and to demonstrate the efficacy of cutting-edge technologies. In all cases, the territories are not bounded but rather bridge local and global circuits of knowledge through professional networking, flows of capital, grassroots networking and so on. Even the most isolationist pathway – community – has connections and knowledge flows that extend beyond its physical boundaries. This suggests that territories should be interpreted not as containers or fixed locations but 'as bundles of interconnected relationships' (Whitehead, 2007, p. 6). Each of the identified pathways attempts to bundle the relations in different ways with varying outcomes. Territories then emerge as relational achievements of the agendas and activities of the involved stakeholders (Karvonen, 2011). The pathways identified are useful for revealing how these relations are configured, by whom and for what ends. There is less of an emphasis on the scale of territorialisation (local, regional, national or global) and more on the ways that the relations that comprise these territories are defined and sustained over time.

Furthermore, the emphasis on the relational configuration of pathways suggests different visions of environmental governance. Each of the pathways extends or challenges the existing role of the state as the primary arbiter of socio-environmental regulation and represents a form of 'eco-state restructuring' (While, 2014; Gibbs *et al.,* Chapter 10, this volume). Whereas the empirical and innovation pathways rely on existing modes of governance, the design and community pathways have the potential to recast the governance of the environment in novel ways. The design pathway suggests the need for creativity in place-based interventions to reconfigure the twentieth-century fixation on separating nature from humans. The empirical pathway sees data collection as the most important way of understanding the relations between humans and their surroundings. The findings can be fed into policies, reinforcing existing control by the state over environmental flows. In the innovation pathway, the emphasis on profit-driven, low-carbon technological development reinforces global capitalism and the long-standing notion of technology-driven economic growth. And the community pathway enacts an anti-capitalist protest politics and re-centres the emphasis of human-nature relations on everyday, familiar surroundings. Governance here is a local affair, as in notions of ecological democracy and civic environmentalism. It is important to recognise that each pathway includes particular assumptions about politics, whether the pathway proponents acknowledge this or not.

Overall, the proliferation of alternative environmental territories provides multiple opportunities for deliberation and debate about the contemporary and future relationships between humans, nature and technology. By revealing the heterotopic character of these territories, the pathways approach encourages a critical engagement with the multitude of actions and agendas that are coalescing and intertwining to realise widespread transitions towards low-carbon, resilient and (it is hoped) more desirable futures. It is unlikely that any of the identified pathways will be sufficient on their own to address the significant challenges ahead with respect to climate change, inequality, eroding infrastructure networks and so on. Instead, these pathways suggest a multi-pronged approach to human-nature relations with a range of implications and outcomes. By subjecting these activities to critical inquiry and engagement, we can better understand how they interact and how they produce alternative future conditions.

References

Aiken, G. (2012) Community transitions to low carbon futures in the Transition Towns Network (TTN), *Geography Compass*, 6, 89–99.

Aiken, G. (2014) (Local-) community for global challenges: carbon conversations, transition towns and governmental elisions, *Local Environment*, 20, 1–18.

Allen, P., Fitzsimmons, M., Goodman, M. and Warner, K. (2003) Shifting plates in the agrifood landscape: the tectonics of alternative food initiatives in California, *Journal of Rural Studies*, 19, 61–75.

Beatley, T. (2010) *Biophilic Cities: Integrating Nature into Urban Design and Planning*, Washington, DC: Island Press.

Bulkeley, H. (2006) Urban sustainability: learning from best practice? *Environment and Planning A*, 38, 1029–1044.

Bulkeley, H. and Newell, P. (2010) *Governing Climate Change*, London: Routledge.

Bulkeley, H. and Castán Broto, V. (2012) Urban experiments and climate change: securing zero carbon development in Bangalore, *Contemporary Social Science*, 9, 393–414.

Callenbach, E. (1975) *Ecotopia: The Notebooks and Reports of William Weston*, Berkeley, CA: Banyan Tree Books.

Cannavò, P. (2007) *The Working Landscape: Founding, Preservation, and the Politics of Place*, London: The MIT Press.

Caprotti, F. (2014) Critical research on eco-cities? A walk through the Sino-Singapore Tianjin eco-city, China, *Cities*, 36, 10–17.

Castán Broto, V. and Bulkeley, H. (2013) A survey of urban climate change experiments in 100 cities, *Global Environmental Change*, 23, 92–102.

Chang, I. and Sheppard, E. (2013) China's eco-cities as variegated urban sustainability: Dongtan eco-city and Chongming eco-island, *Journal of Urban Technology*, 20, 57–75.

Chatterton, P. (2013) Towards an agenda for post-carbon cities: lessons from Lilac, the UK's first ecological, Affordable Cohousing Community, *International Journal of Urban and Regional Research*, 37, 1654–1674.

Chatterton, P. (2015) *Low Impact Living: A Field Guide to Ecological, Affordable Community Building*, London: Routledge.

Chatzidakis, A., Maclaran, P. and Bradshaw, A. (2012) Heterotopian space and the utopics of ethical and green consumption, *Journal of Marketing Management*, 28, 494–515.

Cugurullo, F. (2013a) The business of Utopia, *Utopian Studies*, 24, 66–88.

Cugurullo, F. (2013b) How to build a sandcastle: an analysis of the genesis and development of Masdar City, *Journal of Urban Technology*, 20, 22–37.

David, J. and Hammond, R. (2011) *High Line: The Inside Story of New York City's Park in the Sky*, New York: Farrar, Straus and Giroux.

Davies, A., Fahy, F. and Rau, H. (eds.) (2014) *Challenging Consumption Pathways to a More Sustainable Future*, London: Routledge.

Dehaene, M. and De Cauter, L. (2008) Heterotopia in a postcivil society, in: Dehaene, M. and De Cauter, L. (eds.) *Heterotopia and the City: Public Space in a Postcivil Society*, pp. 3–9, London: Routledge.

de Jong, M., Joss, S. Schraven, D. Zhan, C. and Weijnen, M. (2015) Sustainable—smart—resilient—low carbon—eco—knowledge cities; making sense of a multitude of concepts promoting sustainable urbanization, *Journal of Cleaner Production*, 109, 25–38.

Diggers and Dreamers (2015) Diggers and Dreamers website. Available: www.diggersanddreamers.org.uk (accessed 31 March 2015).

Dorstewitz, P. (2014) Planning and experimental knowledge production: Zeche Zollverein as an urban laboratory, *International Journal of Urban and Regional Research*, 38, 431–449.

Dryzek, J. (2000) *Deliberative Democracy and Beyond: Liberals, Critics, Contestations*, New York: Oxford University Press.

Dryzek, J. (2005) *The Politics of the Earth: Environmental Discourses*, Oxford: Oxford University Press.

Evans, J. (2011) Resilience, ecology and adaptation in the experimental city, *Transactions of the Institute of British Geographers*, 36, 223–237.

Evans, J. and Karvonen, A. (2011) Living laboratories for sustainability: exploring the politics and epistemology of urban transition, in: Bulkeley, H. Castán Broto, V. Hodson, M. and Marvin, S. (eds.) *Cities and Low Carbon Transitions*, pp. 126–141, London: Routledge.

Evans, J. and Karvonen, A. (2014) 'Give me a laboratory and I will lower your carbon footprint!' Urban laboratories and the governance of low-carbon futures, *International Journal of Urban and Regional Research*, 38, 413–430.

Evans, R., Guy, S. and Marvin, S. (2001) Views of the city: multiple pathways to sustainable transport futures, *Local Environment*, 6, 121–133.

Farmer, G. and Guy, S. (2002) Conditional constructions: environmental discourses on natural ventilation, *International Journal of Environmental Technology and Management*, 2, 187–199.

Feola, G. and Nunes, R. (2014) Success and failure of grassroots innovations for addressing climate change: the case of the Transition Movement, *Global Environmental Change*, 24, 232–250.

Finco, A. and Nijkamp, P. (2001) Pathways to urban sustainability, *Journal of Environmental Policy and Planning*, 3, 289–302.

Foucault, M. (1984) Des Espace Autres, *Architecture, Mouvement, Continuité*, 5, 46–49.

Foucault, M. and Miskowiec, J. (1986) Of other spaces, *Diacritics*, 16, 22–27.

Franck, K. and Stevens, Q. (eds.) (2007) *Loose Space: Possibility and Diversity in Urban Life*, London: Routledge.

Friends of the High Line (2008) *Designing the High Line: Gansevoort Street to 30th Street*, New York: Friends of the High Line.

Friends of the High Line (2015) Friends of the High Line website. Available: www.the-highline.org (accessed 31 March 2015).

Gandy, M. (2006) Urban nature and the ecological imaginary, in: Heynen, N., Kaika, M. and Swyngedouw, E. (eds.) *In the Nature of Cities: Urban Political Ecology and the Politics of Urban Metabolism*, pp. 63–74, London: Routledge.

Gottlieb, R. (2001) *Environmentalism Unbound: Exploring New Pathways for Change*, Cambridge, MA: The MIT Press.

Graham, S. and Healey, P. (1999) Relational concepts of space and place: issues for planning theory and practice, *European Planning Studies*, 7, 623–646.

Guy, S. (2004) Consumption, energy, and the environment, *Encyclopedia of Energy*, 1, 687–696.

Guy, S. and Marvin, S. (1999) Understanding sustainable cities: competing urban futures, *European Urban and Regional Studies*, 6, 268–275.

Guy, S. and Farmer, G. (2000) Contested constructions: the competing logics of green building and ethics, in: Fox, W. (ed.) *Ethics and the Built Environment*, pp. 73–87, London: Routledge.

Guy, S. and Marvin, S. (2000) Models and pathways: the diversity of sustainable urban futures, in: Williams, K., Burton, E. and Jenks, M. (eds.) *Achieving Sustainable Urban Form*, pp. 9–18, London: E & FN Spon.

Guy, S. and Farmer, G. (2001) Reinterpreting sustainable architecture: the place of technology, *Journal of Architectural Education*, 54, 140–148.

Guy, S. and Marvin, S. (2001) Constructing sustainable urban futures: from models to competing pathways, *Impact Assessment and Project Appraisal*, 19, 131–139.

Guy, S. and Moore, S.A. (eds.) (2005) *Sustainable Architectures: Cultures and Natures in Europe and North America*, London: Routledge.

Guy, S. and Moore, S.A. (2007) Sustainable architecture and the pluralist imagination, *Journal of Architectural Education*, 60, 15–23.

Hajer, M. (1995) *The Politics of Environmental Discourse: Ecological Modernization and the Policy Process*, Oxford: Clarendon Press.

Haughton, G. (1997) Developing sustainable urban development models, *Cities*, 14, 189–195.

Henke, C. (2000) Making a place for science: the field trial, *Social Studies of Science*, 30, 483–511.

Henke, C. and Gieryn, T. (2008) Sites of scientific practice: the enduring importance of place, in: Hackett, E., Amsterdamska, O., Lynch, M. and Wajcman, J. (eds.), *The Handbook of Science and Technology Studies*, third edition, pp. 353–376, Cambridge, MA: The MIT Press.

Hess, D. (2007) *Alternative Pathways in Science and Industry: Activism, Innovation, and the Environment in an Era of Globalization*, Cambridge, MA: The MIT Press.

Hinchliffe, S., Kearnes, M., Degen, M. and Whatmore, S. (2005) Urban wild things: a cosmopolitical experiment, *Environment and Planning D*, 23, 643–658.

Hobbie, J. (2003) Scientific accomplishments of the Long Term Ecological Research Program: an introduction, *BioScience*, 53, 17–20.

Hopkins, R. (2008) *The Transition Handbook: From Oil Dependency to Local Resilience*, Totnes, UK: Green Books.

Hopkins, R. (2011) *The Transition Companion: Making Your Community More Resilient in Uncertain Times*, White River Junction, VT: Chelsea Green Publishing Company.

Iverot, S. and Brandt, N. (2011) The development of a sustainable urban district in Hammarby Sjöstad, Stockholm, Sweden? *Environment, Development and Sustainability*, 13, 1043–1064.

Jamison, A. (2001) *The Making of Green Knowledge: Environmental Politics and Cultural Transformation*, Cambridge: Cambridge University Press.

Jones, M. and MacLeod, G. (2004) Regional spaces, spaces of regionalism: territory, insurgent politics and the English question, *Transactions of the Institute of British Geographers*, 29, 433–452.

Joss, S. (2009) *Eco-cities: A preliminary survey and analysis of recent developments and initiatives*, Washington, DC, Eco-Cities Workshop, Lemelson Center.

Joss, S. (2011) Eco-cities: the mainstreaming of urban sustainability; key characteristics and driving factors, *International Journal of Sustainable Development and Planning*, 6, 268–285.

Karvonen, A. (2011) *Politics of Urban Runoff: Nature, Technology, and the Sustainable City*, Cambridge, MA: The MIT Press.

Karvonen, A. (2015) Pathways of urban nature: diversity in the greening of the twenty-first-century city, in: Hou, J. Spencer, B. Way, T. and Yocom, K. (eds.), *Now Urbanism: The Future City Is Here*, pp. 274–286, London: Routledge.

Karvonen, A. and Yocom, K. (2011) The civics of urban nature: enacting hybrid landscapes, *Environment and Planning A*, 43, 1305–1322.

Karvonen, A., Evans, J. and van Heur, B. (2014) The politics of urban experiments: realising radical change or reinforcing business as usual? in: Hodson, M. and Marvin, S. (eds.) *After Sustainable Cities?* pp. 104–115, London: Routledge.

Kasioumi, E. (2011) Sustainable urbanism: vision and planning process through an examination of two model neighborhood developments, *Berkeley Planning Journal*, 24, 91–114.

Keil, R. and Graham, J. (1998) Reasserting nature: constructing urban environments after Fordism, in: Braun, B. and Castree, N. (eds.), *Remaking Reality: Nature at the Millennium*, pp. 100–125, London: Routledge.

Kohler, R. (2002) *Landscapes and Labscapes: Exploring the Lab-Field Border in Biology*, Chicago, IL: Chicago University Press.

Latour, B. (1998) To modernise or ecologise? That is the question, in: Braun, B. and Castree, N. (eds.), *Remaking Reality: Nature at the Millennium*, pp. 221–242, London: Routledge.

Latour, B. (2004) *Politics of Nature: How to Bring the Sciences into Democracy*, Cambridge, MA: Harvard University Press.

Law, J. (2004) *After Method: Mess in the Social Sciences*, London: Routledge.

Leach, M., Scoones, I. and Stirling, A. (2010) *Dynamic Sustainabilities: Technology, Environment, Social Justice*, London: Earthscan.

Lerner, J. (2014) *Urban Acupuncture: Celebrating Pinpricks of Change that Enrich City Life*, Washington, DC: Island Press.

LTER (Long Term Ecological Research Network) (2015) The Long Term Ecological Research Network website. Available: www.lternet.edu (accessed 31 March 2015).

Luque, A., McFarlane, C. and Marvin, S. (2014) Smart urbanism: cities, grids and alternatives? in: Hodson, M. and Marvin, S. (eds.), *After Sustainable Cities?* pp. 74–90, London: Routledge.

McKennis, M. (ed.) (1999) *Bioregionalism*, London: Routledge.

Marvin, S., Chappells, H. and Guy, S. (1999) Pathways of smart metering development: shaping environmental innovation, *Computers, Environment and Urban Systems*, 23, 109–126.

Moore, S. (2007) *Alternative Routes to the Sustainable City: Austin, Curitiba, and Frankfurt*, Lanham, MD: Lexington Books.

Moore, S. and Karvonen, A. (2008) Sustainable architecture in context: STS and design thinking, *Science Studies*, 21, 29–46.

Mostafavi, M. (ed.) (2010) *Ecological Urbanism*, Baden: Lars Müller Publishers.

Murdoch, J. (2001) Ecologising sociology: Actor-Network Theory, co-construction and the problem of human exemptionalism, *Sociology*, 35, 111–133.

Nevens, F., Frantzeskaki, N., Gorissen, L. and Loorbach, D. (2013) Urban transition labs: co-creating transformative action for sustainable cities, *Journal of Cleaner Production*, 50, 111–122.

North, P. (2010) Eco-localisation as a progressive response to peak oil and climate change– a sympathetic critique, *Geoforum*, 41, 585–594.

Olin, L. (1988) Form, meaning, and expression in landscape architecture, *Landscape Journal*, 7, 149–168.

Pickerill, J. (2011) Building liveable cities: urban Low Impact Developments as low carbon solutions? in: Bulkeley, H., Castán Broto, V., Hodson, M. and Marvin, S. (eds.) *Cities and Low Carbon Transitions*, pp. 178–197, London: Routledge.

Pickerill, J. and Maxey, L. (2009) Geographies of sustainability: low impact developments and radical spaces of innovation, *Geography Compass*, 3, 1515–1539.

Pinderhughes, R. (2004) *Alternative Urban Futures: Planning for Sustainable Development in Cities Throughout the World*, Lanham, MD: Rowman and Littlefield Publishers.

Pinderhughes, R. (2008) Alternative urban futures: designing urban infrastructures that prioritize human needs, are less damaging to the natural resource base, and produce less waste, in: Heberle, L. and Opp, S. (eds.) *Local Sustainable Urban Development in a Globalized World*, pp. 9–18, Aldershot: Ashgate.

Pursell, C. (1993) The rise and fall of the Appropriate Technology Movement in the United States, 1965–1985, *Technology and Culture*, 34, 629–637.

Rapoport, E. (2014) Utopian visions and real estate dreams: the eco-city past, present and future, *Geography Compass*, 8, 137–149.

Redman, C., Grove, J. and Kuby, L. (2004) Integrating social science into the Long-Term Ecological Research (LTER) network: social dimensions of ecological change and ecological dimensions of social change, *Ecosystems*, 7, 161–171.

Rybczynski, W. (2011) Bringing The High Line back to Earth, *New York Times*, 14 May, p.WK9. Available: http://nyti.ms/1Gfvnw3 (accessed 31 March 2015).

Rydin, Y., Turcu, C., Guy, S. and Austin, P. (2013) Mapping the coevolution of urban energy systems: pathways of change, *Environment and Planning A*, 45, 634–649.

Seyfang, G. and Haxeltine, A. (2012) Growing grassroots innovations: exploring the role of community-based initiatives in governing sustainable energy transitions, *Environment and Planning C*, 30, 381–400.

Seyfang, G. and Longhurst, N. (2013) Desperately seeking niches, grassroots innovations and niche development in the community currency field, *Global Environmental Change*, 23, 881–891.

Shevory, K. (2011) Cities see the other side of the tracks, *New York Times*, 2 August, p. B6. Available: http://nyti.ms/1xWAfPM (accessed 31 March 2015).

Shutkin, W. (2000) *The Land That Could Be: Environmentalism and Democracy in the Twenty-First Century*, Cambridge, MA: The MIT Press.

Sim, D. (2009) The sustainable city as a fine-grained city, in: Radovic, D. (ed.) *Eco-Urbanity: Towards Well-Mannered Built Environments*, pp. 47–62, London: Routledge.

Smit, T. (2011) *Eden*, New York: Random House.

Smith, A. (2005) The alternative technology movement: an analysis of its framing and negotiation of technology development, *Human Ecology Review*, 12, 106–119.

Smith, A. (2011a) Community-led urban transitions and resilience: performing Transition Towns in a city, in: Bulkeley, H., Castán Broto, V., Hodson, M. and Marvin, S. (eds.) *Cities and Low Carbon Transitions*, pp. 159–177, London: Routledge.

Smith, A. (2011b) The Transition Town Network: a review of current evolutions and renaissance, *Social Movement Studies: A Journal of Social, Cultural and Political Protest*, 10, 99–105.

Steiner, F. (2011) Landscape ecological urbanism: origins and trajectories, *Landscape and Urban Planning*, 100, 333–337.

Sternfeld, J. (ed.) (2009) *Walking the High Line*, Göttingen, Germany: Steidl.

Taylor, K. (2010) After High Line's success, other cities look up, *New York Times*, 14 July, p. A1. Available: http://nyti.ms/1yyRFSZ (accessed 31 March 2015).

Thayer, R. (2003) *LifePlace: Bioregional Thought and Practice*, Berkeley, CA: University of California Press.

Timberg, S. (2008) The novel that predicted Portland, *The New York Times*, 14 December, p. ST2. Available: www.nytimes.com/2008/12/14/fashion/14ecotopia.html (accessed 31 March 2015).

Transition Network. (2014) Transition Network website. Available: www.transitionnetwork.org (accessed 31 October 2014).

Vanolo, A. (2014) Smartmentality: the smart city as disciplinary strategy, *Urban Studies*, 51, 883–898.

Viitanen, J. and Kingston, R. (2014) Smart cities and green growth: outsourcing democratic and environmental resilience to the global technology sector, *Environment and Planning A*, 46, 803–819.

Villagomez, E. (2010) Claiming residual spaces in the heterogeneous city, in: Hou, J. (ed.) *Insurgent Public Space: Guerrilla Urbanism and the Remaking of Contemporary Cities*, pp. 81–95, London: Routledge.

Waldheim, C. (ed.) (2006) *The Landscape Urbanism Reader*, Princeton, New Jersey: Princeton Architectural Press.

Walker, G. (2011) The role for 'community' in carbon governance, *Wiley Interdisciplinary Reviews: Climate Change*, 2, 777–782.

While, A. (2014) Carbon regulation and low carbon urban restructuring, in: Hodson, M. and Marvin, S. (eds.) *After Sustainable Cities?* pp. 41–58, London: Routledge.

Whitehead, M. (2007) *Spaces of Sustainability: Geographical Perspectives on the Sustainable Society*, London: Routledge.

10 The implications of the low-carbon economy for the politics and practice of regional development

David Gibbs, Andrew E.G. Jonas and
Aidan While

Introduction

A concern with the adverse environmental impacts of economic development, including enhanced global warming, climate change and sea-level rise, has increasingly entered into the mainstream of economic policymaking and represents a key challenge for national, regional and local policymakers (Yohe and Schlesinger, 2002). While it is generally accepted that climate change cannot be reversed in the short term, mitigation measures, defined as 'actions aimed at reducing the sources or enhancing the sinks of greenhouse gases' (UKCIP, 2009, p. 4), can limit its impact. Mitigation in the form of the reduction of carbon emissions has become a key international and national-policy priority reflecting a new realism about climate change, as well as concerns about energy security, peak oil and rising fossil-fuel costs. At the international level, the Kyoto Protocol adopted in 1997 set legally binding limits and reductions in greenhouse gases for the period 2008–12. The Protocol was subsequently extended to 2020 and discussion for a successor treaty is ongoing. Similarly, concerns about climate change, energy security and low-carbon competitiveness have led national and sub-national governments to push forward on emissions-reduction initiatives. The European Union's (EU) Emissions Trading Scheme (ETS) sets out a low-carbon policy framework and a long-term reduction trajectory for EU countries (Deloitte, 2008). Similar cap and trade schemes have been introduced on a voluntary basis in the USA (e.g. in Chicago, in California and, through the Regional Greenhouse Gas Initiative (RGGI), in nine Northeast states) and their wider rollout is proposed by the Obama administration (City of Chicago, 2008). In the United Kingdom, the Climate Change Act (2008) established five-year carbon budgets, set targets for a reduction in CO_2 emissions and introduced both new carbon-trading schemes and a Carbon Reduction Commitment to encourage large organisations in the public and private sector to reduce their emissions. In January 2012, China, the world's largest national source of emissions, implemented the 12th Five Year Plan on Emission Control which aimed to reduce the amount of carbon emitted per unit of Gross Domestic Product (GDP) by 17% by 2015, compared with 2010 levels. This includes specific regional and municipal carbon intensity and energy consumption intensity targets, as well as pilot carbon-trading schemes in a number of municipalities (Ni, 2012).

Our focus in this chapter is on the consequences of addressing these environmental concerns for economic development at the local and regional scale. Since environmental changes are likely to have uneven impacts on cities and regions in different countries, they are an increasingly important part of the context in which urban and regional development theorists and policymakers are thinking about the economic impacts of different responses to climate change. At one level, it could be argued that there is nothing new about policymakers' concerns over the environmental consequences of economic development – these date back (at least) to the Rio de Janeiro Earth Summit in 1992. However, despite the widespread adoption of sustainable development following Rio, and the potential opportunity to combine economic, environmental and social aims within policy, relatively little progress has been made in most nation states in the Global North. For the most part, economic-development strategies and policies remain wedded to a high-growth, carbon-based, consumer-led economy where success is measured by increasing Gross Value Added (GVA) and higher levels of personal consumption (Jackson, 2009). However, in contrast to the sustainable development agenda, the emergence of carbon-control policies has led to much greater debate around the potential for change to existing socio-economic-development pathways. Much attention has focused on low-carbon initiatives and the development of a low-carbon economy (see for example, Smith *et al.*, 2010; Davies and Mullin, 2010). While sustainable development frequently appeared to be a vague and nebulous concept, open to a wide range of interpretation, decarbonising the global economy appears to be more straightforward – the aim is to reduce the amount of greenhouse gases being emitted and so mitigate climate change.

While climate change may have been the initial driver for carbon-reduction measures, policymakers have increasingly come to recognise that the shift to a low-carbon future can be conceived in ways that move beyond seeing the environment as a barrier to economic development. This new conceptualisation sees a low-carbon economy offering the prospect of a more resilient and sustainable economy and/or an alternative mode of economic development. Low-carbon regulation has, therefore, emerged as a key competitive factor between nation states, as well as a potential source of competitive advantage at the urban and regional scale. This chapter examines the emergence of carbon control or carbon regulation as an increasingly dominant feature of national economic-policy discourse, and explores its potential ramifications for the regulation of economy-environment relations at the urban and regional scales. In the chapter it is proposed that the added weight given to low-carbon governance and regulation introduces a new set of principles centring around cost efficiency and environmental regulation with the potential to challenge mainstream modes of urban and regional development. Moreover, in contrast to those academics (e.g. Tomaney and Pike, 2009) who have argued that the rise of 'green collar jobs' may offer opportunities for the reindustrialisation of peripheral areas, we propose that the move towards a low-carbon economy may simply exacerbate and intensify urban and regional differences and disparities.

The organisation of the chapter is as follows. In the next section, we examine how the low-carbon economy can be conceptualised in the context of urban and regional development. Subsequent sections address the main features of the low-carbon economy and outline the consequences of the new era of carbon regulation for urban and regional economic development. A concluding section pulls the arguments of the chapter together and critiques existing low-carbon policy solutions. Although reference is made to other national contexts, our main focus here is on developments in the United Kingdom.

Conceptualising the low-carbon economy

An increasingly dominant way in which the current state of environmental regulation is conceptualised (at least by policymakers) is through ecological modernisation (EM) approaches, at the heart of which is a belief in technology, innovation and progress to solve environmental problems (Roberts and Colwell, 2001; Mol, 2002). As they have gained greater salience, 'EM theories have helped to describe the ways in which environmental problems come to be framed as issues that are politically, economically and technologically solvable within the context of existing institutions and power structures and continued economic growth' (Bailey *et al.*, 2011, p. 683). Adopting an EM approach would involve both a structural change at the macro-economic level, such as broad sectoral shifts in the economy towards carbon reduction, and at the micro-economic level, e.g. through the adoption of low-carbon technologies by firms. For its proponents, EM indicates the possibility of overcoming environmental crises without leaving the path of modernisation. Rather, the assumption is made that it is possible to restructure processes of production and consumption on ecological terms through the institutionalisation and internalisation of ecological aims.

The concept of EM has been developed as both a theory and a guide to more pragmatic policy action. As a theoretical concept, it has been used to analyse those changes to the central institutions in modern society deemed necessary to solve the ecological crisis. In this use of the concept, EM represents a major transformation, or 'ecological switchover', of the process of industrialisation onto a different basis which takes account of the need to maintain the sustenance base (Huber, 1985). EM has certainly gained purchase as a pragmatic political programme to combine environmental policymaking with economic development, even if many of its proponents do not use the term itself (Huber, 1985). This is certainly increasingly reflected in the low-carbon policy agenda (see, for example, OECD, 2011). However, as a concept it lacks any real sense of the power relations at work and under-theorises both the role of politics and the state, even though these factors are central to its implementation as a societal project. In order to address these shortcomings, the concept of eco-state restructuring (ESR) can be invoked as a way of conceptualising the ongoing restructuring of the state in relation to environmental regulation (While *et al.*, 2010). More specifically, ESR as a concept reflects

> the reorganisation of state powers, capacities, regulations and territorial structures around institutional pathways and strategic projects, which are (at least

from the vantage of state interests at a given moment in time) viewed as less environmentally damaging than previous trajectories. In this process, the state takes a more active and directed role in regulating the environmental inputs and outputs of mainstream economic and social activities (resource extraction, production and consumption). This includes organising and mobilising strategic interests and actors to undertake specific projects and activities that the state (or certain actors operating in and around the state apparatus) understands to be consistent with strategic environmental goals and outcomes set at international and national levels.

(While *et al.*, 2010, p. 80)

The recent shift towards a low-carbon polity has given rise to a distinctive political economy associated with climate mitigation which necessitates (and legitimises) an extension of state intervention into both production and consumption. One of its main differences from sustainable development as a mode of socio-environmental governance is that it moves away from an *either* economy *or* environment approach. Despite the supposed ability of sustainable development to consider economy, environment and society in an holistic manner and to establish trade-offs between these three elements, sustainability was frequently seen as a threat to economic activity and remained secondary to economic competitiveness in many localities (Jonas *et al.*, 2011). Reframing climate change as an economic opportunity through the specific form of a low-carbon economy has allowed governments to set demanding targets for decarbonisation yet, at the same time, to present these as measures designed to increase economic competitiveness (Bailey *et al.*, 2011). In this manner, 'although presented as a response to socio-ecological crisis, low-carbon restructuring is perhaps more accurately read as a political-economic fix enacted through the domain of state environmental regulation' (While *et al.*, 2010, p. 83). This form of 'ecological fix' has been strongly influenced and shaped by the larger context of neoliberal environmental governance, which has constrained what it is politically possible to implement. Thus, a low-carbon economy 'exhibits a strong privileging of neoliberal and technocentric values that creates serious obstacles for the contemplation of alternatives, particularly more ecocentric ways of curbing greenhouse-gas emissions' (Bailey and Wilson, 2009, p. 2325). As Bailey and Wilson (2009, p. 2335) go on to argue

carbon commodification can, thus, be seen as a partial assimilation of a new idea (the need to curb human interference with the climate system) into the prevailing paradigm, with framing of the problem and its solutions in the context of pre-existing discourses (the promise of economic efficiency and environmental effectiveness), rather than the adoption of less 'conventional' strategies that focus, for example, on economic relocalisation or direct behavioural constraints to reduce fossil-fuel consumption and greenhouse-gas emissions.

Thus, the specific forms and definitions of the low-carbon economy adopted to date create decision-making pathways that tie future low-carbon developments into particular bounded formats through path dependency or lock-in effects (Unruh, 2000).

Furthermore, it can be argued that the low-carbon economy is a distinctively new mode of socio-environmental governance that differs from previous modes in its implications for urban and regional development. To put this differently, discourses of carbon reduction and control have rapidly become the guiding rationality underpinning new national modes of societal regulation as well as informing urban and regional development discourses and politics (Jonas *et al.*, 2011). All of this does not imply some inevitable normative progression towards an ideal environmental or 'eco-state' (Meadowcroft, 2005), but rather is intended to reflect the contested and often conflicting demands on the state as it seeks to reconcile and manage economic and environmental interests over time. The shift towards low-carbon politics can be seen as a new wave of ESR, albeit layered onto existing state forms and functions, but with a particular emphasis on cost-effective strategies to achieve a transition to a low-carbon economic future (While *et al.*, 2010). In this way, ESR can give rise to a variety of strategic state-environmental relations, with the possibility of distinctive national modes of regulation and different pathways for translating national-level regulations into concrete institutional mechanisms at the urban and regional scale.

The particular form in which such climate and low-carbon policies are rolled out across cities and regions will, therefore, be constrained by the political economy of both national and regional politics, and only certain forms of policy and strategy are possible in specific nation states and regions (Bulkeley, 2010). For example, we have seen the emergence of distinctive national climate-control regimes, with climate policy mediated by different modes of socio-environmental regulation and different contexts for carbon reduction. As the chapter will indicate, some regional governments and actors have also proved to be at the forefront of promoting low-carbon activities within their areas. Thus, decarbonisation strategies may be empowering new strategic alliances at the urban and regional scale and impacting inter-territorial competition and place promotion (Jonas *et al.*, 2011).

The low-carbon economy

The low-carbon economy, with its promised combination of new technologies and changing institutions, is increasingly becoming a mainstream source of policy responses and initiatives in the Global North (Barry and Paterson, 2003; Barry and Doran, 2006). A key moment in the shift to a focus on the economic-development *opportunities* that arise from the requirement to reduce greenhouse-gas emissions and carbon usage was the response of a number of international and national agencies and institutions to the 'credit crunch' of 2008. This response proposed national stimulus measures or 'green new deals' to transform and re-regulate the international financial sector; to provide an opportunity for state intervention to redirect, or at least encourage, restructuring towards new economic forms – i.e. a low-carbon economy; and to address issues of 'peak oil' or the 'energy crunch' associated with dependence on oil. All of these measures, it was envisaged, would not only mitigate climate change through a reduction in carbon emissions but also provide economic benefits. As Bowen *et al.* (2009, p. 4) comment

> If the appropriate mix of policies is adopted, action to tackle climate change could form a central part of a fiscal package designed to moderate the economic slowdown. The development of a low-carbon economy can provide new jobs and new opportunities for innovative businesses. A 'green' fiscal stimulus can be a more effective fiscal stimulus, building the foundations for sustainable, strong growth in the future, rather than unsustainable bubbles.

A number of influential reports in the late 2000s identified sectors that should be targeted for investment by national government stimulation packages as a way out of financial, as well as environmental, crisis (see UNEP, 2008a; Deutsche Bank, 2008; HSBC Bank, 2009; New Economics Foundation, 2009; SDC, 2009). Table 10.1 provides a summary of these different reports' priority sectors indicating broad agreement on future targets for policy. Some nation states subsequently included a substantial green element in their economic stimulus packages to address the credit crunch, notably South Korea, China and the USA (HSBC Bank, 2009; SDC, 2009). Increasingly, many commentators and governments have become convinced not only that developing a low-carbon economy is an environmental imperative but also that it can form the basis of a new accumulation strategy and provide a competitive advantage (Climate Institute and E3G, 2009). For example, in Germany ecological industrial policy is seen not just as a means to deliver better environmental protection and improvement but also to engender economic growth and innovation (BMU, 2009a, 2009b):

> the new green markets hold promise of vast opportunities for the German economy: energy generation, energy efficiency, sustainable water management, materials efficiency, recycling technology and sustainable mobility. Anyone who becomes established or gains a reputation as technological leader on these important lead markets of the future can be sure of growth, added value and employment
>
> (BMU, 2008, p. 8)

These policies link 'an economic and ecological modernisation strategy for more sustainability with an ecological and economic specialisation strategy for Germany' (BMU, 2008, p. 8). Government policy and intervention is seen as important in any shift to a low-carbon economy, and market mechanisms by themselves are not adequate to engender the changes needed. This is not just a national perspective but also occurs at the level of the Länder, where all state environment ministries support and promote environmental technology, for example, through industrial subsidies and overseas promotional support (BMU, 2009b). One of the most advanced of these initiatives is in Bavaria, where the Bavarian Environment

Table 10.1 Target sectors for 'green new deal' policies

UNEP	Deutsche Bank	HSBC	Green New Deal Group	Sustainable Development Commission
Clean technologies	Energy-efficient buildings	Low-carbon energy production	Renewable energy	Upgrading existing housing stock
Renewable energy	Electric power grid	Energy efficiency/energy management	Energy conservation	Renewable-energy supplies
Waste management	Renewable power	Water, waste and pollution control	Carbon finance	National grid
Sustainable agriculture	Public transport	Carbon finance	Re-regulating financial system	Sustainable mobility
Green cities			Changing taxation systems	Low-carbon public sector
Ecosystems management				Employment and skills

Source: Deutsche Bank (2008); Green New Deal Group (2008); HSBC Bank (2009); SDC (2009); UNEP (2008a).

Cluster links support for environmental industry to state carbon-reduction targets (Umweltcluster Bayern, 2016).

In the United Kingdom, the Stern Review on the Economics of Climate Change (2006) was followed by the Commission on Environmental Markets and Economic Performance (CEMEP), established to make recommendations that would help exploit the economic opportunities from a transition to a low-carbon economy. As in Germany, the UK government asserts that 'as well as being an environmental and economic imperative, the shift to a low carbon economy is also an economic opportunity' (HM Government, 2009a, p. 2). Energy efficiency, a new energy infrastructure, the development of low-carbon vehicles and placement of a good infrastructure for investment, R&D and skills are all seen as priority actions. The rationale for this strategy is that

> Greater energy efficiency improves economic productivity. The demand for environmental goods and services creates new jobs and new business opportunities. The development of new green technologies will create export markets throughout the world. Such technologies indeed offer the prospect of providing new drivers for economic growth in the 21st century as previous technologies did in the last. And the nations that seize this opportunity – which can show the rest of the world how a modern economy can grow sustainably – will reap the largest rewards.
>
> (HM Government, 2008, p. 2)

In 2009, the UK Labour government published its Low Carbon Transition Plan (HM Government, 2009b), which outlined plans to meet the carbon-emissions targets in the Climate Change Act (2008) through a transformation to a low-carbon economy, outlined in a companion document on the UK Low Carbon Industrial Strategy (HM Government, 2009c). The plan envisaged major shifts in energy production to low-carbon sources (including not just a target of 30% of electricity from renewable energy sources by 2020, but also carbon capture and storage for coal power and new nuclear power stations), greater home and workplace energy efficiency, changes to agriculture and land use, changes to travel modes and patterns and the future development of a 'smart grid'[1] for electricity. The plan further envisaged the United Kingdom becoming 'a world centre of the green economy', assisted by government investment in R&D for new low-carbon technologies (HM Government, 2009c) and the creation of substantial numbers of 'green jobs'. The Government's 2010 budget announced the establishment of a Green Investment Bank to invest in the low-carbon sector, using £1 billion of public money from asset sell-offs and £1 billion of private-sector finance (HM Treasury, 2010). The subsequent Conservative-Liberal Democrat Coalition government continued with the rhetoric of the low-carbon economy, with Prime Minister David Cameron promising soon after his election in 2010 that he would lead 'the greenest government ever'. However, despite the apparent enthusiasm by successive UK governments for a transition to a low-carbon economy, there has been criticism that the pace of change and actual implementation of policy has been slow in the United Kingdom (Aldersgate Group, 2009). Moreover, the UK government policies, such as the Coalition government's *Transition to a Green Economy* policy document, rely on market mechanisms (in contrast to German policies) and some business lobby groups have argued for much greater intervention including measures such as firm prices for carbon, tax breaks and improved capital allowances for investment in green technologies (Davis, 2009; HM Government, 2011). Of particular interest in the context of this chapter, however, is growing evidence to suggest that policymakers regard the city-region as an appropriate scale for convening and assembling new institutional arrangements for delivering cost-effective carbon-reduction strategies.

Urban and regional economic development in an era of carbon regulation

The policy shift towards low-carbon mitigation measures will differentially impact localities, cities and regions – 'the opportunities for practical action to develop a low-carbon economy are likely to vary between functional economic areas" (LGA, 2009, p. 7). Indeed, the UK's Low Carbon Industrial Strategy was initially seen as having a strong regional component with ministers arguing that 'we need to make sure that we drive the green industrial revolution from the regions as well as nationally, building on distinct regional and local advantages across the UK' (HM Government, 2009a, p. 2). As at the national scale, the emphasis was on the economic-development opportunities for some regions – 'globally, there will be advantages for those economies that lead the way in developing a economy – there will be new markets, new jobs and new export opportunities. There will be advantages for local economies that are well placed to make the most of the economic opportunities' (LGA, 2009, p. 11). In part, this was to be encouraged through policy measures to encourage the development of specific sectors in particular regions. The earlier CEMEP report had recommended the establishment of 'environmental innovation zones' where local area partnerships could experiment with innovative policy measures to encourage environmental innovations (HM Government, 2008). In the Low Carbon Industrial Strategy, this was translated into a less adventurous policy to designate eight Low Carbon Economic Areas (LCEAs) involving cross-agency working and partnership to develop the area's low-carbon economic strength, increase learning rates and build effective supply chains' (HM Government, 2009c, p. 53, see Table 10.2). Exactly how these were to operate, other than through rather vague exhortations to use existing policy levers to incentivise low-carbon development, support skills training and encourage inward investment, was unclear. Moreover, how the claims of different regions in the United Kingdom to pre-eminence for particular sectors can be reconciled remains to be addressed – for example, the North East, the Humber region and the Lowestoft/Great Yarmouth area of East Anglia all claim to be leading centres for the offshore wind industry (BIS, 2015).

Low-carbon regulation will impact on the politics of urban and regional development in various ways. The rising financial and regulatory costs of carbon

Table 10.2 LCEAs in the United Kingdom

Region	LCEA focus
South West England	Wave and tidal energy
North East England	Ultra low-carbon vehicles
North West England and Yorkshire	Civil nuclear energy
Greater Manchester	Built environment
Midlands	Advanced automotive engineering
South Wales	Hydrogen energy
London	Energy efficient buildings
Yorkshire and the Humber	Carbon capture and storage

Source: BIS (Department for Business, Innovation and Skills) (2010) London is designated a Low Carbon Economic Area for energy efficient buildings, press release, 31 March, London: BIS.

legislation will certainly put pressure on growth regimes to invest in low-carbon infrastructure, and this is likely to become an increasingly important aspect of spatial competition to attract and retain firms and skilled workers. Areas with a first-mover advantage may benefit, but those with a high concentration of carbon-intensive sectors or carbon-intensive infrastructure may face a more difficult task. In the United Kingdom, consultation on the role of local authorities in meeting these national targets initially considered whether this could 'combine an increased ambition on reducing carbon with possible new powers and flexibilities' (HM Government, 2009b, p. 94), although the then-Coalition government offered little of substance in this direction (HM Government, 2011).

At the same time, the major UK urban authorities are acutely aware of the potential future impacts of carbon legislation on economic competitiveness. In consequence, some have commissioned and completed 'Mini-Stern' reports to complement the original Stern review in the United Kingdom, some of which outline different scenarios towards low-carbon futures for the country's major city-regions, such as Manchester and Leeds (Deloitte, 2008; Gouldson *et al.*, 2012). For example, Manchester City Council's 'mini-Stern' report highlighted the costs of inaction on the low-carbon economy and the opportunities that 'first-mover' advantage might bring (Deloitte, 2008). The report argues: 'early action is therefore needed to respond to legislative drivers by cutting emissions, improving resilience and adapting economic priorities to take account of Climate Change legislation. In doing so the Manchester City region has the potential to enhance its competitive advantage over those Cities that are slower to adapt' (Deloitte, 2008, p. 7). Similarly in London, the London Climate Change Agency planned to reduce CO_2 emissions by 60% by 2050 (on 1990 levels) mainly through the implementation of a Low Emissions Zone. Other localities and regions have already begun to explore the consequences of climate change for their own area's economy. For example, the area around Blyth, in North East England, has attempted to make a shift into renewable energy, based on using existing skills developed in carbon-based energy production (Pike, 2008). Conversely, the Yorkshire and the Humber region has sought to exploit its carbon dependence and natural resources by becoming a hub for experimentation with carbon capture and storage (BIS, 2015).

In the future, then, we can expect to see many more local and regional authorities engaging with climate change as they seek to reconcile their aspirations for economic growth with mitigation measures for carbon emissions – there are likely to be different economic pathways in the low- carbon transition. Certainly, cities and regions look set to use carbon mitigation measures as yet another strategy to display competitive advantage in a global market for investment with the same kinds of inter-territorial competition that other place promotion strategies have involved (Jonas *et al.*, 2010). As a consequence, we are seeing moves towards 'eco-competitive relations' between places (Hodson and Marvin, 2009), echoing earlier competitive strategies designed to attract other types of inward investment. For example, in the United Kingdom the potential economic-development benefits to be gained following the government's announcement of three large offshore wind-farm zones (Hornsea, Dogger Bank and Humber Gateway) led to fierce competition from a variety of economically depressed cities (for example, Hull, Dundee, Glasgow), each claiming to be the United Kingdom's leading centre for offshore wind and its associated supply chain.

Some localities, cities and regions will face bigger challenges than others in the low-carbon transition – emissions levels vary over space with the United Kingdom's major urban areas facing a bigger challenge to reduce emissions than other areas (AEA, 2008). The impact will also vary spatially depending on the mix of economic activity within the area as well as the prevailing energy infrastructure (Carbon Trust, 2008). Natural resources such as access to wind or the right sort of geologic conditions for carbon capture and storage might also make a difference, and here it should be emphasised that future urban and regional economic futures will be shaped by the intersection between climate impacts and new carbon economies. It could be argued those UK regions with a high presence of energy-intensive sectors such as power generation and chemicals (such as Yorkshire and the Humber) or plastics and metal processing (such as North East and North West England), for example, are likely to find it harder to make the low-carbon transition (White *et al.*, 2008; BIS, 2009). The 16 UK sectors where electricity accounts for more than 10% of GVA are disproportionately located in Wales (1.9% of employment in these sectors), the North East (1.7%) and Yorkshire and the Humber (1.5%) (HM Government, 2009c). Alternatively, these regions might be better placed to make the transition as they have more incentive to invest in low-carbon infrastructure. The argument might be that their economic future depends on investment in certain kinds of low-carbon infrastructure relative to what is on offer in other locations.

While urban and regional policymakers are concerned with the potential employment benefits, these impacts fall into short-, medium- and long-term categories. In the short-term, jobs will be lost in carbon-intensive sectors (e.g. coal-fired power plants) and gained in low-carbon sectors (e.g. renewable energy). The medium-term impacts come about as jobs are created and lost along the value chains of affected industries, while in the long-term innovative behaviour will create job opportunities – Schumpeter's 'creative destruction' (Fankhauser *et al.*, 2008). These changes will lead to a demand for particular skill sets, with a need for both generic skills, such as leadership and management skills, and more specialist environmental skills, such as energy-efficiency experts and technicians to install low-carbon technologies. However, while one in three UK environmental firms report skills shortages, evidence suggests that a lack of certainty and the absence of a clear regulatory framework by government has discouraged investment in low-carbon skills by employers (ProEnviro, 2008). Moreover, as ever with industrial restructuring, job creation may not be in the same locations as job losses (UNEP, 2008b). For example, some UK regions have some clusters relevant to low-carbon activities, and it has been argued that their manufacturing legacy may be beneficial in providing skills and knowledge relevant to the low-carbon transition. These include advanced engineering and materials in South Yorkshire, clean technologies in the area from Huddersfield to Sheffield, carbon capture and storage in Yorkshire and the Humber and in Teesside and low-carbon vehicles in North East England (Innovas, 2009). However, it is important to keep this perceived potential for the rejuvenation of the UK's more peripheral regions in perspective. A report by Innovas (2009) on low-carbon environmental goods and services (LCEGS) clearly illustrated the combined dominance of London, the South East and Eastern England – these three regions contained 40% of the total UK turnover in LCEGS, compared, for example, to 21% in the three English Northern regions (see Table 10.3). More recent figures for employment (for the English regions only) also show the continued dominance of these three regions, with 38.4% of low-carbon industry employment (BIS, 2015). Thus a shift towards a low-carbon economy may not necessarily represent an opportunity for the reindustrialisation of parts of the United Kingdom through 'green collar jobs' as claimed by Tomaney and Pike (2009). By contrast, the outcome could be the exacerbation of existing regional differences. Of course, the impacts may depend on the type of policy framework and measures adopted. For example, a market-based approach may simply lead to the creation of jobs outside the United Kingdom in the absence of any capacity-building activity.

Conclusion

In the future, regions, cities and localities will have to address climate change as one of their major challenges (Lerch, 2008). In doing so, policymakers will come up against all kinds of difficult problems and decisions over both climate-change adaptation and carbon mitigation in relation to urban and regional development. Low-carbon legislation and the adoption of specific carbon-mitigation measures have begun to have an important impact at the urban and regional scales. As this chapter has outlined, a growing response at a variety of these spatial scales has been to suggest that a low-carbon strategy can not only mitigate climate change but also provide a new or alternative source of economic development. What is new about the low-carbon agenda is the extent to which the environmental challenge of climate change is seen as an economic opportunity rather than a barrier to capital accumulation. Thus, climate change becomes 'both a threat to

Table 10.3 Low-carbon and environmental goods and services in the United Kingdom by region

	Market values for LCEGS by region, 2007/08					
	Environmental sectors £bn	Renewable energy sectors £bn	Emerging low-carbon sectors £bn	Total, all sectors £bn	% UK total	Total GVA% of UK
London	3.78	6.43	10.71	20.93	19.50	19.27
South East	2.67	3.61	6.70	12.98	12.09	14.83
North West	1.99	2.81	5.54	10.34	9.63	9.86
East of England	2.31	2.49	5.35	10.16	9.46	8.77
South West	2.12	2.10	4.47	8.69	8.10	7.93
West Midlands	1.71	2.70	4.14	8.55	7.96	7.88
Scotland	2.14	2.60	3.76	8.49	7.91	8.06
Yorkshire and Humber	2.11	2.21	3.61	7.93	7.39	7.28
East Midlands	1.14	2.47	3.45	7.06	6.58	6.57
Wales	1.06	1.62	1.98	4.66	4.34	3.78
North East	0.62	1.05	2.58	4.25	3.96	3.44
N Ireland	0.77	1.20	1.33	3.30	3.08	2.34
Total	22.41	31.29	53.63	107.33	100.00	100.00
Sector as % total	20.88	29.15	49.97	100.00		

Source: Innovas (2009, p. 43).
Notes: Percentages may not add up to 100% due to the effects of rounding.

the accumulation of capital (from climate risks and expensive mitigation) and a new opportunity for profit' – accumulation by decarbonisation (Bumpus and Liverman, 2008, p. 131). This not only focuses on cost savings and efficiencies for firms and consumers (e.g. energy efficiencies) but also demonstrates ways in which the low-carbon transition can stimulate policy innovation and entrepreneurialism at the city-regional scale. Nations, regions and cities have begun to try and position themselves as leaders in this low-carbon economy and as destinations for new forms of investment (Gibbs and O'Neill, 2014). There will be many different potential pathways to carbon control, with very different social, economic, ecological and spatial consequences. For example, contestation over different low-carbon transition pathways is already evident in debates about nuclear power.

The primary focus here has been on examining how the shift to a low-carbon approach has begun to affect the ways in which governments and policymakers conceptualise particular forms of urban and regional development, and the ways in which governance structures are affected. In addition to new urban and regional development strategies, these low-carbon strategies are giving rise to new forms of urban and regional advantage and disadvantage. It has been suggested that '[r]egimes of carbon control will be layered onto those of existing inter-place competition, with already economically successful places being best equipped to retrofit their economic, social and physical infrastructures for the low carbon transition' (While *et al.*, 2010, p. 88). Certainly, the example of the UK's LCEGS indicates that the already successful Southern and Eastern English regions have a current advantage in these sectors. Unlike sustainable development and Local Agenda 21, which were amenable to well meaning, but bland, policy rhetoric in the past, carbon-control measures require action on the part of urban and regional actors and institutions. Moreover, given the increased salience of carbon pricing, a failure to act will cost firms and residents money and will thus impact on economic competitiveness as well as wellbeing. This was not the case with the earlier phase of ESR focused on sustainable development.

However, much of this activity has largely been geared towards reconstituting the status quo ante i.e. restoring the basis for growth and consumption,[2] albeit what we are consuming may be less environmentally damaging than before. Many of these strategies effectively envisage future economies and societies as being different from current forms (e.g. energy will come from renewable sources; vehicles will use different fuels; new sectors and types of jobs will be created while older ones disappear etc.), but the basis of our capitalist, consumer-led economies will remain much the same. While low-carbon strategies are welcome at one level – to mitigate the effects of climate change – current UK policy glosses over the contradictions involved in positioning these as a source of renewed economic growth at the urban and regional scale. As Jackson (2009, p. 8) comments, 'most analyses assume that the ultimate aim is to re-stimulate the kind of consumption-driven growth that has dominated the last few decade … this goal is in the long-term entirely unsustainable without significant changes in both macro-economic structure and the social dynamics of consumerism'. Although there are arguments that 'by altering the basis of strategic calculation, carbon control would appear to open up alternative socio-economic possibilities for localities and regions locked into the narrow growth pathways of the neo-liberal competition state' (While *et al.*, 2010, p. 87), in reality it would appear that both national and regional policy-makers are interpreting the opportunities offered by the low-carbon economy in a particular form and in ways which are familiar to them. As Bailey and Wilson (2009, p. 2338) comment, 'perhaps the most worrisome aspect of the carbon economy is the extent to which the logics and system memory of neoliberal ecological modernisation appear to be depoliticising and de-democratising climate policy through scientific and econocentric discourses that exclude consideration of alternative strategies from the political and social mainstream.' Much current government low-carbon thinking is based around the continuation of past 'top-down' economic-development policies, with little scope for more radical community-led initiatives on energy, housing or economic activities (North, 2010).

Some authors have seen opportunities in the carbon-reduction agenda as creating space for 'subaltern and competing discourses' (Slocum, 2004, p. 777) that are not easily co-opted by more mainstream neoliberal market solutions. These alternative perspectives suggest that current low-carbon economy policies are inadequate to deal with the scale of climate change and that, moreover, they will simply reinforce the consumer-led, profit-seeking forms of economic development that have led to the problem in the first place (North, 2010). Instead, we need to shift towards a different model of economic development, one that is locally based and more democratic, and which measures success in terms of well-being and happiness, not material possessions (Jackson, 2009). Moreover, there are issues with how carbon-control policy relates to mainstream global development where there is a continuing rhetorical emphasis on growth rather than sustainability. As Barry and Doran (2006, p. 257) comment

> the notion that orthodox economic growth, employment investment patterns and the cross-sectoral goals of sustainable development might be in serious tension is excluded from the government's rhetoric on the environment and the 'greening of the economy'; it is certainly not presented as a possibly problematic issue for industrial production processes or for global capitalism or the new orthodoxy of export-led growth. Instead, environmental protection and economic growth are portrayed as a positive-sum game, a 'business opportunity'.

In this fashion, low-carbon policies have 'offered reassurance, disempowered radical ecologist movements and helped to pacify eco-political conflicts whilst bolstering the argument that radical system change is not actually required as environmental goals can be realised through the modification of existing structures' (Blühdorn and Welsh, 2007, p. 194). In taking this specific form, other, more radical and ecocentric, approaches to carbon reduction and climate-change policy have effectively been foreclosed. Indeed, a counter argument to optimistic visions of economic and social transformation is that the transition to the low-carbon economy could necessitate policies which reinforce existing social and spatial inequalities, acting to extend the reach of the market into environmental decisions and strengthening the power of the state and capital at the expense of social and spatial equity (Bailey, 2007a, 2007b; Lohmann, 2001, 2008).

While it is unrealistic to expect urban and regional policy on its own to solve these problems, there is scope for a greater mix of policies. Developing new technologies and encouraging sectoral shifts is one component of a low-carbon transition, but more locally based and 'bottom-up' initiatives could be encouraged as well. To take just three examples, the Soil Association and National Trust's local food production initiative, proposals for 'low impact development zones' in urban areas (Pickerill and Maxey, 2009) and the Transition Town movement (Transition Towns, 2006) all offer examples of local, community-led initiatives that could be encouraged and supported by urban and regional policy. Finally, while some kind of policy stimulus makes sense in terms of protecting jobs and making the transition to a low-carbon economy, the ultimate goal for many involved is to restore economic growth (albeit of a different, 'greener' kind) and materialistic consumerism, which negate the potential for people to develop sustainable and fulfilling lives (Jackson, 2009; New Economics Foundation, 2009). In particular, much more needs to be done to address the issue of consumption in UK low-carbon policy rather than simply making it a matter of individual choice. It is this tension between a view that consumer capitalism is non-negotiable and that radical change is required to tackle climate change which is one of the most important issues yet to be addressed, both by policymakers and academics (Blühdorn and Welsh, 2007; Milanez and Bührs, 2007).

Notes

1   Smart grids involve using digital technology to manage power generation, distribution, transmission and consumer demand. It is anticipated they will lead to reduced costs and more efficient energy use (Nidumolu *et al.*, 2009).
2   As the financial crisis progressed and mutated into a more specific 'Eurocrisis', some of the 'green stimulus' arguments were weakened. In particular, the linkage between these initiatives and the call for a fundamental restructuring of the international financial sector was not followed through into action.

References

Aldersgate Group (2009) *Commission Statement: Driving Investment and Enterprise in Green Markets.* Available: www.aldersgategroup.org.uk (accessed 22 July 2016).

AEA (Atomic Energy Authority) (2008) *Local and Regional CO$_2$ Emissions Estimates for 2005–2006 for the UK*, Report to DEFRA, ED 05452101, Didcot, UK: AEA.

Bailey, I. (2007a) Neoliberalism, climate governance and the scalar politics of EU emissions trading, *Area* 39, 431–442.

Bailey, I. (2007b) Climate policy implementation: geographical perspectives, *Area* 39, 415–417.

Bailey, I. and Wilson, G. (2009) Theorising transitional pathways in response to climate change: technocentrism, ecocentrism and the carbon economy, *Environment and Planning A*, 41, 2324–2341.

Bailey, I., Gouldson, A. and Newell, P. (2011) Ecological modernisation and the governance of carbon: a critical analysis, *Antipode*, 43, 682–703.

Barry, J. and Paterson, M. (2003) The British state and the environment: New Labour's ecological modernisation strategy, *International Journal of Environment and Sustainable Development*, 2, 237–49.

Barry, J. and Doran, P. (2006) Refining green political economy: from ecological modernisation to economic security and sufficiency, *Analyse & Kritik*, 28, 250–275.

BIS (Department for Business, Innovation and Skills) (2009) Towards a low carbon economy - economic analysis and evidence for a low carbon industrial strategy, *BIS Economics Paper 1*, London: BIS.

BIS (Department for Business, Innovation and Skills) (2010) London is designated a Low Carbon Economic Area for energy efficient buildings, press release, 31 March, London: BIS.

BIS (Department for Business, Innovation and Skills) (2015) *The Size and Performance of the UK Low Carbon Economy*, London: BIS.

Blühdorn, I. and Welsh, I. (2007) Eco-politics beyond the paradigm of sustainability: a conceptual framework and research agenda, *Environmental Politics*, 16, 185–205.

BMU (Federal Ministry for the Environment, Nature Conservation and Nuclear Safety) (2008) *Ecological Industrial Policy: Sustainable Policy for Innovation, Growth and Employment*, Berlin: BMU.

BMU (2009a) *Executive Summary Report on the Environmental Economy 2009*, Berlin: BMU.

BMU (2009b) *GreenTech Made in Germany 2.0*, Munich: Verlag Vahlen.

Bowen, A., Fankhauser, S., Stern, N. and Zenghelis, D. (2009) *An Outline of the Case for a Green Stimulus*, Policy Brief, Grantham Research Institute on Climate Change and the Environment/Centre for Climate Change Economics and Policy.

Bulkeley, H. (2010) Cities and the governing of climate change, *Annual Review of Environment and Resources*, 35, 229–253.

Bumpus, A. and Liverman, D. (2008) Accumulation by decarbonisation and the governance of carbon offsets, *Economic Geography*, 84, 127–155.

Carbon Trust (2008) *Climate Change: A Business Revolution?* London: Carbon Trust.

City of Chicago (2008) *Chicago Climate Action Plan*, Chicago, IL. Available: www.chicagoclimateaction.org (accessed 26 March 2009).

Climate Institute and E3G (2009) *G20 Low Carbon Competitiveness*, London: Vivid Economics.

Davies, A. and Mullin, S. (2010) Greening the economy: interrogating sustainability innovations beyond the mainstream, *Journal of Economic Geography*, 11, 793–816.

Davis, T. (2009) Firms demand incentives to go low carbon, *TimesOnline*. Available: business.timesonline.co.uk/tol/business/economics/article6727582 (accessed 5 August 2009).

Deloitte (2008) '*Mini-Stern' for Manchester: Assessing the Economic Impact of EU and UK Climate Change Legislation on Manchester City Region and the North West*, London: Deloitte.

Deutsche Bank (2008) *Economic Stimulus: The Case for 'Green' Infrastructure, Energy Security and 'Green' Jobs*, Chicago, IL: Deutsche Bank.

Fankhauser, S., Schlleier, F. and Stern, N. (2008) Climate change, innovation and jobs, *Climate Policy*, 8, 421–429.

Gibbs, D. and O'Neill, K. (2014) The green economy, sustainability transitions and transition regions: a case study of Boston, *Geografiska Annaler, Series B, Human Geography*, 96, 201–216.

Gouldson, A., Kerr., N, Topi, C., Dawkins, E., Kuylenstierna, J. and Pearce, R. (2012) *The Economics of Low Carbon Cities: A Mini Stern for the Leeds City Region*, Centre for Low Carbon Futures.

Green New Deal Group (2008) *A Green New Deal: Joined-up Policies to Solve the Triple Crunch of the Credit Crisis, Climate Change and High Oil Prices*, London: New Economics Foundation.

HM Government (2008) *Building A Low Carbon Economy: Unlocking Innovation and Skills*, London: DEFRA.

HM Government (2009a) *Low Carbon Industrial Strategy: A Vision*, London: DBERR/DECC.

HM Government (2009b) *The UK Low Carbon Transition Plan: National Strategy for Climate and Energy*, London: The Stationery Office.

HM Government (2009c) *The UK Low Carbon Industrial Strategy*, London: DBIS/DECC.

HM Government (2011) *Enabling the Transition to a Green Economy: Government and Business Working Together*, London: The Stationery Office.

HM Treasury (2007) Stern Review on the Economics of Climate Change. Available: http://webarchive.nationalarchives.gov.uk/+/http:/www.hm-treasury.gov.uk/sternreview_index.htm (accessed 16 November 2016).

HM Treasury (2010) Budget March 2010 – the environment and green issues, press release, 25 June, London: HM Treasury. Available: http://webarchive.nationalarchives.gov.uk/20121015000000/http://www.direct.gov.uk/en/Nl1/Newsroom/Budget/Budget2010/DG_186643 (accessed 20 October 2016).

Hodson, M. and Marvin, S. (2009) 'Urban ecological security': a new urban paradigm? *International Journal of Urban and Regional Research*, 33, 193–215.

HSBC Bank (2009) *A Climate for Recovery: The Colour of Stimulus Goes Green*, London: HSBC Global Research.

Huber, J. (1985) *Die Regenbogengesellschaft: Ökologie und Sozialpolitik*, Frankfurt am Main: Fisher Verlag.

Innovas (2009) *Low Carbon and Environmental Goods and Services: An Industry Analysis*, Report to the Department of Business Enterprise and Regulatory Reform. Available: www.gov.uk/government/uploads/system/uploads/attachment_data/file/224068/ bis-13-p143-low-carbon-and-environmental-goods-and-services-report-2011-12.pdf (accessed 16 November 2016).

Jackson, T. (2009) *Prosperity Without Growth?* London: Sustainable Development Commission.

Jonas, A., While, A. and Gibbs, D. (2010) Carbon control regimes, eco-state restructuring and the politics of local and regional development, in: Pike, A., Rodriguez-Posé, A. and Tomaney, J. (eds.) *Handbook of Local and Regional Development*, pp. 283–294, London: Routledge.

Jonas, A., Gibbs, D. and While, A. (2011) The new urban politics as a politics of carbon control, *Urban Studies*, 48, 2537–2554.

Lerch, D. (2008) *Post Carbon Cities: Planning for Energy and Climate Uncertainty*, Sebastopol, CA: Post Carbon Press.

LGA (Local Government Association) (2009) *Creating Green Jobs: Developing Local Low-Carbon Economies*, London: LGA.

Lohmann, L. (2001) *Democracy or Carbocracy? Climate Trading and the Future of the Climate Debate*, Dorset, UK: The Corner House, Sturminster Newton.

Lohmann, L. (2008) Carbon trading, climate justice and the production of ignorance: ten examples, *Development*, 27, 1–7.

Meadowcroft, J. (2005) From welfare state to ecostate, in: Barry, J. and Eckersley, R. (eds.), *The State and the Global Ecological Crisis*, pp. 3–24, Boston, MA: MIT Press.

Milanez, B. and Bührs, T. (2007) Marrying strands of ecological modernisation: a proposed framework, *Environmental Politics*, 16, 565–583.

Mol, A. (2002) Ecological modernisation and the global economy, *Global Environmental Politics*, 2, 92–115.

New Economics Foundation (2009) *Green Stimulus or Simulus?* London: New Economics Foundation.

Ni, V. (2012) China sets new greenhouse gas emission reduction goals, 18 January, *China Briefing*. Available: www.china-briefing.com/news/2012/01/18/china-sets-new-greenhouse-gas-emission-reduction-goals.html (accessed 20 October 2016).

Nidumolu, R., Prahalad, C. and Rangaswami, M. (2009) Why sustainability is now the key driver of innovation, *Harvard Business Review*, 87, 56–64.

North, P. (2010) Eco-localisation as a progressive response to peak oil and climate change: a sympathetic critique, *Geoforum*, 41, 585–594.

OECD (The Organisation for Economic Co-operation and Development) (2011) *Towards Green Growth*, Paris: OECD.

Pickerell, J. and Maxey, L. (2009) *Low Impact Development: The Future in our Hands*. Available: www.lowimpactdevelopment.wordpress.com (accessed 19 June 2009).

Pike, D. (2008) From doom to de-carb, *Green Futures*. Available: www.forumforthefuture. org/greenfutures/articles/doom-de-carb (accessed 16 November 2016).

ProEnviro (2008) *Skills for a Low Carbon and Resource Efficient Economy: A Review of Evidence*, Report to DEFRA, Rugby: ProEnviro. Available: http://www.swslim.org.uk/documents/themes/lt18-resource21.pdf (accessed 16 November 2016).

Roberts, P. and Colwell, A. (2001) Moving the environment to centre stage: a new approach to planning and development at European and regional levels, *Local Environment*, 6, 421–37.

Slocum, R. (2004) Consumer citizens and the Cities for Climate Protection campaign, *Environment and Planning A*, 36, 763–782.

Smith, A., Voß, J-P. and Grin, J. (2010) Innovation studies and sustainability transitions: the allure of the multi-level perspective and its challenges, *Research Policy*, 39, 435–448.

SDC (Sustainable Development Commission) (2009) *A Sustainable New Deal*, London: SDC.

Tomaney, J. and Pike, A. (2009) The 'triple crunch' and the future of the North East, in: Tomaney, J. (ed.) *The Future of the North East*, pp. 7–14, London: Smith Institute.

Transition Towns (2006) Transition Towns. Available: www.transitiontowns.org (accessed 11 August 2007).

UKCIP (2009) *Identifying Adaptation Options*, UKCIP. Available: www.ukcip.org.uk/index.php?id=23&option=com_content&task=view (accessed 22 September 2009).

Umweltcluster Bayern (2016) Umweltcluster Bayern website. Available: www.umwelt-cluster.net (accessed 20 October 2016).

UNEP (United Nations Environment Programme) (2008a) *Towards a Green Economy*, Geneva: UNEP.

UNEP (United Nations Environment Programme) (2008b) *Green Jobs: Towards Decent Work in a Sustainable Low-carbon World*, Nairobi: UNEP.

Unruh, G. (2000) Understanding carbon lock-in, *Energy Policy*, 28, 817–830.

While, A., Jonas, A. and Gibbs, D. (2010) From sustainable development to carbon control: eco state restructuring and the politics of urban and regional development, *Transactions of the Institute of British Geographers*, 35, 76–93.

White, G., Gardner, N. and Swift, J. (2008) Carbon reduction: obligation and opportunity at regional and local levels, *Local Economy*, 23, 235–241.

Yohe, G. and Schlesinger, M. (2002) The economic geography of the impacts of climate change, *Journal of Economic Geography*, 2, 311–341.

11 The production and consumption of urban-climatology science in New York City's PlaNYC

Brian Webb

Introduction

Most urban environments have not been conceived as a whole, but are assemblages created by myriads of actors over extended periods of time. Seen in ecological terms, the anthropogenic landscape is partly the outcome of a process of competition or struggle and partly a socio-political construct, insofar as urban construction involves some degree of collaborative behaviour between a range of actors and acceptance of rules imposed by the state. Whether in desert or tundra, coastline or valley, each human settlement has a distinctive climate, modified by the form and mass of its buildings and by the configuration of its streets and open spaces. Its design markedly affects its temperature, humidity, air movement and even precipitation at the block level, and such local scale microclimates are the scientific object of urban climatology (Erell *et al.*, 2011).

Yet for the study of the relationship between the built environment and local weather patterns to have any impact on the development of the urban landscape, there is a need for the scientist studying urban climatology to engage with the regulatory power of the state and the myriad of non-state actors that are collectively involved in the governance of urban spaces (Eliasson, 2000). For such an approach to be successful, scientists must recognise that the knowledge they produce 'upstream' of the urban-policy process is not in itself objective and free of bias, as so often is claimed, but rather is imbued with a range of subjectivities that influence the ways in which the scientist conducts, generates and discusses the science (Demeritt, 2001).

At the other end of the spectrum, how that science is interpreted and used by state and non-state actors 'downstream' to influence the development of urban policy and regulation of the built and natural environment must also be understood as a socio-cultural and political process with a range of embedded interests and norms that must be negotiated. Despite, for example, the recent mainstreaming of environmental ideas and imperatives in political discourse, it is generally accepted that any category of environmentalism starts from a handicap, the tragedy of the commons, but the claims of urban climatology are doubly disadvantaged by the common-sense perception of the invisible atmosphere as a free outlet for any orifice, vent, chimney, exhaust pipe and smokestack. Matthew Crenson's (1973) concepts of 'unpolitics' and 'nondecisionmaking' apply not just to the politics of air pollution but to all aspects of the urban environment that have unintended climate consequences. Therefore, whatever the scientific claims related to urban climatology, scientists of the subject often have to wait in the lobby among all other calls on policy, within an issue-attention cycle that offers only intermittent opportunity to act 'downstream' (Eliasson, 2000). Even when policy windows arise for action, difficulties in translating scientific knowledge into a form that is understandable to those empowered to influence urban policy or those with an interest in specific territorial governance processes is difficult due to a lack of technical expertise (Corburn, 2009; Lövbrand, 2011).

The application of urban climatology into urban policy, therefore, potentially faces a range of issues. 'Upstream' concerns exist around the role of the scientist in knowledge generation, 'downstream' they rest in the use and translation of that knowledge by state and non-state actors into regulations or other actions that influence the built and natural environment. In order to understand these issues, this chapter explores the ways in which urban-climatology science and urban policy interact. The use of urban-climatology science, how it is represented in policy and the ways in which current and future problems are framed are examined through a case study of New York City and its urban sustainability strategy PlaNYC. The details of the co-production of urban-climate knowledge, the actors and relationships involved and the translation of knowledge into policy are then discussed, followed by a particular focus on the localisation of urban-climate science into territorial governance practices. How urban-climatology data are produced and consumed and the politics of urban future proofing are then discussed.

The science-urban policy interface

Concern has been raised on how scientific knowledge is developed within local context, communicated and then used to inform environmental policy debates at a range of spatial scales (Bulkeley and Betsill, 2005). A significant amount of work has focused on the global or national scale in relation to climate change, where too often 'science has been imagined as independent of the political process and feeding information into it' (Demeritt, 2001, p. 308). At the neighbourhood scale, the focus has largely been on how locally generated scientific knowledge is used to inform national and global policy debates, rather than the impact of that knowledge on territorial policy discussions at the urban scale. For urban climatology, however, the 'local' is a key focal point of study. It is not a field that admits generalisation, as both the 'upstream' process of generating the science and the 'downstream' translation and application to policy need to be specific to both local territorial particularities and the political dynamics present to ensure implementation.

The interaction between the science of urban climatology and the politics of cities has been widely debated (see Jasanoff and Martello, 2004; Miller, 2004; Whitehead, 2009; Lövbrand, 2011), with commentators seeking to explore the relationship between knowledge making and wider socio-political decisions, specifically in relation to environmental science and policy. More recently, there has been an increasing focus on the localisation of environmental policy, given the accepted role that urban areas now play in mitigating and adapting to climate change. Corburn (2009) has explored knowledge exchange with a particular emphasis on the interaction between urban-climatic knowledge and local public policy through a local co-production of environmental science framework. For him, the application of scientific knowledge cannot be separated from the social processes that are inevitably linked to the implementation of local climate-change policies. In his view, science and social factors must not be understood as mutually exclusive, but rather dynamic and interconnected, with each influencing the other. The interface, then, between scientific knowledge and social processes requires that a level of negotiation and collaboration occurs, both in relation to the identity of practices – the science and the policy – and the actors – the scientists and the policymakers (Tuinstra *et al.*, 2006). This interaction means that co-production 'not only aims to bring the social back into science policy-making, but also to explore how this knowledge is applied, stabilised and institutionalised over time' (Corburn, 2009, p. 415).

The origins of co-production lay in the fields of political economy and public administration with a focus on citizen involvement in government decision making, whereby Ostrom (1996, p. 1073) defined co-production as 'the process through which inputs used to produce a good or service are contributed by individuals who are not "in" the same organization'. The concept refers to a symbiotic relationship so that 'coproduction plans and delivers in mutually beneficial ways and acknowledges and rewards local "lay" experience while continuing to value professional expertise' (Boyle and Harris, 2009, p. 15). Over time, ideas of co-production have been modified and used to explain the difficulties and opportunities of translating 'expert' scientific knowledge into policy, as too often scientific knowledge is presented and viewed as inaccessible to policymakers and politicians, as well as used as a tool to limit accountability and public debate (Jasanoff, 2003).

In order for co-production of scientific knowledge to be successful, there is a need for a more dynamic interaction between scientist and policymaker so that scientific results are not merely discussed with policymakers but rather integrated into policy development in a sustained and iterative manner. Doing so is useful as it blurs the lines between 'upstream' production and 'downstream' consumption and allows for the creation of effective science-informed policy that is linked to defined territorial scales (Lemos and Morehouse, 2005). Urban climatology is no stranger to this science versus policy disconnect as cities – as well as other territorial configurations - often lack the institutional structure, political will and external non-state support necessary to translate urban-climatology science into policy, as well as challenge and influence the way in which that science is produced (Demeritt, 2001; Hebbert and MacKillop, 2013). Confronted with the twenty-first century challenge of climate change, however, cities are beginning to re-discover the need to link urban climatology to urban policy to develop climatically sensitive mitigation and adaptation strategies.

Faced with a geographic context and built environment that makes it particularly vulnerable to climate change, New York City stands as a recent example of an attempt to re-establish, at the metropolitan scale, a lost institutional structure for connecting scientific climatic considerations to urban policy. The following is based on an ESRC-funded project on climate science and urban design, which explored the historical and contemporary dimensions of the application of urban climatology to the design of the built environment. The research draws on desk studies based on historical and contemporary documentary analysis, 21 interviews with practitioners, city officials, politicians and academics, as well as a detailed analysis of the city's major sustainability plan, PlaNYC, and associated documents to understand the socio-political process of how urban climatology is being applied at the metropolitan scale in New York City.

PlaNYC and urban climatology

Dating back to the mid-twentieth century, the New York City administration was highly involved in a flurry of investigations into the impact of the built environment on the urban climate, initially stemming from toxic smog caused by street traffic, industrial emissions and domestic oil burning. Urban climate quality became a headline issue during the mayoralty of John Lindsay (1966–73), whose leadership was put to the test by snowstorms in 1969 and summer smog the following year (Bach, 1972). Lindsay employed meteorologists in City Hall, set up a New York City weather station network in 1967 and encouraged research on urban form and breeze systems through a partnership with scientists at Columbia, NYU Bronx and Cooper Union. For a time, New York City led the world in the investigation of urban wind flow and the thermal dynamics of street canyons (Bornstein, 1968; Bornstein and Thompson, 1981). But as air pollution eased through environmental controls and de-industrialisation, the issue slipped off the political agenda, weather stations were dismantled and urban-climate research was discontinued.

A waning interest in environmental issues followed in the early 1980s. As a result, New York City has been a relative latecomer to the contemporary urban environmental push compared to other US cities, such as Seattle, Portland or Chicago. Moreover, it has only recently started to develop the necessary environmental institutional capacity by making 'upstream' connections to scientists in an attempt to begin addressing existing gaps in knowledge related to the impact of built form on climate processes and effects. Federally, climate-change policy has been largely absent in the United States due to persistent legislative disagreements between the House of Representatives, Senate and the Office of the President (Goulder and Stavins, 2012). This void has opened up opportunities for individual states and municipalities to take on leadership roles in the development of climate-change strategies, particularly in the regulation of greenhouse-gas emissions and the development of clean energy.

In New York City, it was with the election of Michael Bloomberg as mayor in 2002 that the city began to pursue a coherent environmental agenda, epitomised by the administration's urban-sustainability strategy, PlaNYC. Published in 2007, PlaNYC was initiated to deal with the projected population growth of one million people by 2030 and the renewal of ageing infrastructure, and to develop a plan to reduce greenhouse-gas emissions (City of New York, 2007). In order to address the challenges facing the urban environment, PlaNYC implemented a partnership approach involving public, private and non-profit agencies throughout the city-region that required the production of new scientific knowledge and its implementation in practice.

PlaNYC seeks to address a wide range of climatic concerns through a multi-sectoral approach covering housing and neighbourhoods, parks and public space, brownfield land, waterways, water supply, transportation, energy, air quality, solid waste and climate change. These topics are complemented by a range of cross-cutting measures and initiatives. Within these initiatives, urban climatology is not explicitly mentioned as a means of achieving the goals of the plan; however, it is implicit in many of the mitigation and adaptation interventions that are proposed. For example, the plan includes strategies to improve air quality and reduce greenhouse-gas emissions, as well as to create vegetated ditches in parkways to store rainfall and improve the permeability of surfaces, helping to reduce the urban heat island effect (City of New York, 2007).

Despite the commitments to urban-climate management made in PlaNYC, the relationships among lay and expert understandings of climate science are complex, as are the relationships between climate politics and policies underpinning urban development. Too often, environmental science is applied naively in ways that assume scientific neutrality and the absence of politics (see Demeritt, 2001). Urban climatology is no different, with analysis often being undertaken without consideration being given to the multiple other factors that exist and interact within cities (Erell, 2008). As climate science is drawn-down by built environment professionals to inform the design and development of climate mitigation and adaptation strategies, so the science of climatology is understandably politicised. How is climate science to be integrated into existing policy frameworks? Whose science matters? How are the findings interpreted? Are there enough analysts and policymakers 'downstream' of the science qualified or able to understand often complex scientific principles and findings? Perhaps more importantly, are they able to understand the ramifications of their decisions when climate mitigation strategies are implemented alongside other policy interventions? These questions lie at the heart of current debates regarding the relationship between urban-climatology science and urban policy in New York City and elsewhere.

Co-producing PlaNYC

Although coordinated from the mayor's office, PlaNYC involves a wide range of stakeholders and is, therefore, heavily reliant on enabling forms of governance. Apart from city agencies, partnerships have been formed with the state and federal government, universities, the private sector and non-profit community groups to help deliver on the plan's initiatives. The goal is for the city government to be able to draw on its own in-house expertise across a wide variety of policy sectors while, at the same time, contracting out knowledge generation to external partners when necessary. These partnerships often take the form of advisory committees where internal city staff and external partners work to co-produce knowledge through an iterative process of negotiation. This process at times creates tensions, with both scientists and policymakers questioning the standard practices of each other, all the while under the influence of the political preferences of the mayor's office (Corburn, 2009).

Key actors in this process are the academics involved in a number of initiatives, who provide technical advice and data on trends and potential impacts of policy interventions. Their contributions vary, from calculating the carbon-dioxide equivalent of painting a square metre of white roof to providing practical advice on implementation. The mayor's office at the time of the plan's first publication was particularly keen on white roofs as they were seen as the most obvious 'low-hanging fruit' through which to achieve a reduction in the urban heat island quickly and economically. However, studies commissioned as part of PlaNYC demonstrated the potential problems of pursuing white roofs as a solution to the urban heat island due to their diminishing effectiveness as they turn grey over time. This created tensions between the scientific community, the results they were producing through their science and the pragmatic outlook that often underpins policy development. The need for more localised science has also forced academic climate modellers to explore the meso- and micro-scale environment, a scale with which many of them are not particularly familiar. Climate modellers at the Goddard Institute of Space Studies (GISS) in the Earth Institute of Columbia University, for instance, have been monitoring the effectiveness of various city initiatives and have contributed to climate modelling for the New York City Climate Change Panel. They utilised an MM5 regional model, which was then 'urbanised' for the conditions of New York City. However, there are concerns that these 'downscaled' predictions are not entirely accurate yet, and efforts are continuing to refine the model further so as to ensure more precise monitoring of PlaNYC and the impact of particular initiatives on the urban climate, specifically at the neighbourhood scale.

Citizen groups and not-for-profit organisations eager to engage in the debate around the urban climate have championed and campaigned for many of PlaNYC's environmental efforts (Rosan, 2012). In this context, the 'downstream' institutional capacity rests in neither government nor the private sector. Expert knowledge is not vested in a single department or institution, but rather is collectively harnessed in an attempt to achieve individual goals designed to improve the urban climate and meet the needs of a growing population in the hope that discrete solutions cumulatively scale up to the metropolitan level. The private sector contributes to the city's efforts also, providing services and leading task forces. This loosely coupled approach works for New York City in large part due to the sheer abundance and variety of expert knowledge and enthusiasm present within the city.

Yet while PlaNYC has been successful at engaging a range of expert actors across the public, private and non-profit sectors it has been heavily criticised for poor local-level public participation processes (Angotti, 2008a, 2008b; Jabareen, 2013; Marcuse, 2008; NY Metro APA, 2007). Critics argue that the plan was formulated from the top-down, with little local level input, that participation was seen more as an after thought and that there was a relative lack of focus in terms of identifying consultative outputs which would then feed back into the plan. So while the mayor's office was comprehensive in terms of identifying expert knowledge to contribute to the range of initiatives in the plan, there has been a disconnect between the incorporation of expert knowledge and that of local lay experience, thereby hindering effective co-production at the neighbourhood scale.

Many of the initiatives in the plan are focused heavily on the reduction of greenhouse-gas emissions, while less is made of adaptation mechanisms (Jabareen, 2013). The adaptation mechanisms that exist relate largely to infrastructure and flood protection. However, climate change will also bring about more frequent and intense heat waves and will also result in particular communities being affected more than others due to their geographic and built environment characteristics. Of particular concern are issues related to environmental equity and the ways in which policies may negatively impact already disadvantaged communities (Sze, 2007). PlaNYC attempted to address these concerns through the creation of the Sustainability Advisory Committee, which included two environmental-justice advocates, and an intense emphasis on issues of environmental equity in the development of initiatives. While lauded for these strategic efforts, local communities often felt ignored and marginalised from decision-making processes, while political and economic concerns eroded some of the positive gains, such as the even distribution of waste facilities across the urban area (Rosan, 2012).

Without the existence of a more locally focused governance mechanism to allow community-derived knowledge to be inserted into the policy-development process, there is a danger that the implementation agenda for PlaNYC will fail to recognise and address issues of environmental justice at the neighbourhood scale (Corburn, 2002). Responding to criticism of the consultation process and the lack of inclusion of environmental-justice components in the original plan, the 2011 update included a broad series of community meetings with greater emphasis afforded to environmental-justice initiatives and the value of embedding co-production activities in local communities as a way of improving the success of metropolitan-level climate initiatives (Rosan, 2012).

The localisation of climate science

For a city as large and complex as New York, the scale at which climate science is generated presents numerous challenges. Precision based on small-scale observations is time consuming and costly, while macro-level models produce generalisations that are not necessarily an accurate representation of local characteristics. The science that is produced, therefore, is always dependent on the level of resource provided for its generation. The emphasis in PlaNYC has been to move away from specificity and towards the implementation of solutions that are largely generalisable, including the creation of a Green Codes Task Force dedicated to reviewing city-wide regulations, an initiative to plant a million trees throughout the city and new management approaches to storm water run-off. A particular focus was placed on translating climate measures into regulations and codes that can be routinised in design practice and are capable of regular enforcement by city staff, rather than one-off retrofits of buildings through the provision of incentives. Many of the building regulations studied by the Green Codes Task Force were decades old and, therefore, required updating to promote sustainable building design. However, the particularities and impacts of those broad changes on specific urban spaces were inadequately addressed. In this way, the 'downstream' use of the science reflects the challenge to urban climatology to localise science in an affordable and comprehensive manner for a large and diverse territorial space.

For example, energy and ventilation codes were updated to oblige that every building has an energy audit and makes all reasonable renovations that will pay back investment in less than five years. In addition, all building retrofits must now be code compliant, a change from the previous situation that provided an exemption for minor renovation work. The impacts of these changes on particular neighbourhoods, with some building owners more capable of meeting costs, were not appropriately considered. Regulations to reduce pressure on the electricity grid were also included through the re-introduction of passive solar features such as awnings. In addition, the New York City Building Code was updated to require the use of more reflective and emissive materials on rooftops (City of New York, 2011). Design codes were also used to incorporate sustainable-source controls and other forms of storm-water management within the built environment. Standard designs for bioswales, consisting of trees, plants, soils and rocks along city streets were introduced to allow the collection of rain and storm-water runoff, while also contributing to improvements in the public realm. However, there was no acknowledgement that certain solutions will have different impacts depending on the precise local context. More positively for local contextualisation, storm-water performance standards were introduced in July 2012 for developments as well as redevelopments, in an attempt to ensure that sustainable measures are incorporated early in the design process (City of New York, 2013).

Volunteers drawn from across the city, meanwhile, have proved a useful and cost-effective means of achieving the goals of the plan, and a way of localising the science 'downstream' through community engagement. The MillionTrees NYC initiative to plant a million new trees in the city was aimed at building resident capacity to plant and care for the city's trees through workshops and community events. By hosting more than 170 events, the city developed a network of 2,700 volunteers who took responsibility for the care of over 3,700 trees – features of the green infrastructure that are needed to ensure a healthy urban climate. Additionally, through the °Cool It Yourself programme, volunteers are also used to implement the NYC °CoolRoofs initiative, which encourages building owners to paint their rooftops with a white reflective coating to reduce energy consumption, carbon emissions and cooling costs. Since the programme's introduction, 374,524 square feet of roofs have been voluntarily painted, out of the total 1.2 million square feet reported as complete in the city. However, questions about the long-term effectiveness for urban heat island reductions discussed earlier remain.

These incremental regulatory and voluntary initiatives have important impacts on the urban climate of the city at a macro level. Together, they work to regulate the urban heat island effect and improve air quality (Akbari *et al.*, 2001). PlaNYC relies heavily on this subsidiarity approach, as it provides two key advantages to achieving the goals of the plan. The first is that rather than one-off retrofits or new capital development, this approach regularises particular practices within the governance structure of the metropolitan area. Over the long term, it is designed to ensure continuity of policy. The second is that the range of initiatives being undertaken across the various city departments and agencies means that the success of the plan does not rest on the achievements of a single initiative. If several of the proposed initiatives fail, others can help achieve a successful outcome. In a metropolis as large and fragmented as New York City, this may be the most prudent approach for long-term success. But in doing so, the context-specific generation of the science may be lost, along with the benefits of more precise localisation of knowledge. From a political perspective, a diffuse approach may also allow civic leaders to divest themselves of responsibility for failed implementation of individual objectives, yet allow them the scope to take credit for specific successful accomplishments and the advancement of the plan as a whole.

The production and consumption of climate-science data

Unlike cities such as Stuttgart, Germany, where urban climatologists are employed as city staff with a mandate to provide guidance to the planning department on the alignment of climatic considerations with development agendas (Hebbert and Webb, 2011), the New York City administration lacks an embedded institutional connection between urban climatologists and city planners. This lack of institutional interaction potentially means that the generation of the science and the development of the policy occur in isolation of one another. This complicates implementation of the science 'downstream', as the generated 'upstream' knowledge may fail to be appropriately localised due to the emphasis on generalisability, a lack of coordination among key individuals and institutions, and the absence of an established process of local citizen engagement (Corburn, 2009). Climate science is, instead, largely generated in isolation by scientists or consultants and then presented to and discussed with policymakers at advisory meetings. These meetings can often lend themselves to conflict as the methodological assumptions used in the production of the data are questioned on the basis of the local knowledge of policymakers, leading policymakers to question the utility of the data and the 'fit' of the science to local circumstances (Corburn, 2009). More positively, these interactions allow for opportunities to advance the science in innovative ways, such as in the case of the New York City Climate Change Adaptation Task Force, launched in 2008 with 40 members drawn from the public (city, state, federal) and private sectors. The report of its technical panel was prepared interactively, with all drafts reviewed by the Task Force, leading to constructive policy development that was applicable to local circumstances.

The incorporation of a wide range of stakeholders, hundreds of individual initiatives and multiple task forces and advisory committees for PlaNYC allows the generation of an extensive range of information and recommendations. A key concern, however, is the lack of a comprehensive approach to problem solving necessary to apply urban climatology to urban policy, resulting in a poor appreciation of the overall impact of policies on the urban climate. Urban density, street orientation, street aspect ratio, neighbourhood and building typology, size, type and location of urban parks and building and paving materials all impact upon the urban climate. Their cumulative effect needs to be understood to ensure certain activities are not having a detrimental impact on others (Erell, 2008). While the role of urban parks and building and paving materials is more generally understood due to a broad awareness of the urban heat island effect, there is the danger of a disconnect existing between the creation of policies that individually impact urban density, street orientation, street aspect ratio, neighbourhood and building typology and the urban climate, unless these elements are made spatially explicit.

While some of the plan's initiatives are linked to spatially focused studies, such as air quality data derived from the New York City Community Air Survey – this prompted changes to laws and regulations that require the phasing out of particular types of fuel oil use in buildings – there is no overarching understanding of how targets and multiple initiatives spatially and collectively manifest themselves within PlaNYC. Examples of how urban-climate considerations can be spatially visualised abound, such as through the creation of a climate atlas which specifies areas for development or non-development based on climatic factors (Ren *et al.*, 2011), but the 'spatial gaps' in PlaNYC means that the complexities of the urban microclimate may not be fully understood by the wide range of stakeholders involved in the governance of particular geographically defined neighbourhoods (Parlow *et al.*, 2001; Ward, 2003; Hsie and Ward, 2006; Gal and Unger, 2009).

A key goal of PlaNYC is to create a million more homes. This initiative has largely been undertaken through the rezoning of neighbourhoods to direct growth and increase density near transit corridors in areas such as Bedford-Stuyvesant in Brooklyn and West Harlem in Manhattan, as well as the full-scale redevelopment of areas such as Steward Park and Hunters Point South. A review of the development plans highlighted in the PlaNYC progress report (City of New York, 2013) shows a deep understanding of the role played by natural systems in the development of climate-resilient cities. This includes the challenges of improving flood protection through the management of green infrastructure and the role that green buildings can play in reducing energy consumption. Yet from a climatological perspective, there is a general lack of consideration of the cumulative impact of dense buildings on the exterior environment, the impact of building orientation on the solar exposure of streets, the aspect ratio of streets to air flow and the impact of varying building forms and materials on the urban climate. This may stem from a lack of climatological knowledge by the planners and developers involved in these developments, the high cost of modelling and the lack of incentive provided.

The production of urban climatology 'upstream' is undeniably aligned to its consumption 'downstream'. Not only can the 'upstream' generation of knowledge be bias laden, but the process by which that knowledge is consumed 'downstream' is also heavily influenced by the ways in which scientific arguments are framed. The amount of value attributed to the science is dependent on factors such as the level of localisation to context, how the science is communicated and visualised, the connection of that knowledge to other external concerns and an appreciation by producers and consumers of the need for the science to be sensitive to scalar effects as the level of analysis moves from the micro to the macro scale and vice versa.

The politics of urban future proofing

Developed by the Bloomberg administration, PlaNYC is, unsurprisingly, a political document. It relies on the generation of science as much as it does corporate buy-in and citizen placation to develop, support and implement policies (Jabareen, 2013). Much of PlaNYC is structured around the importance of infrastructure development, couched in the language of sustainability, to secure the economic future of the city (Angotti, 2008a). Improvements to public transit are projected to reduce congestion and negate $13 billion in lost productivity. Energy costs are projected to fall as a result of proposed energy-efficiency improvements, resulting in savings estimated at some $2–4 billion.

Additionally, the plan proposes the development of natural flood-protection systems. To identify these areas, PlaNYC used current meteorological data to update the existing flood insurance risk maps produced by the Federal Emergency Management Agency, and analyse the distribution of hazards. Outer boroughs were required to install detention ponds or cisterns to manage surges and were encouraged to promote permeable paving and swales for water retention. For Manhattan, which has the steepest run-off and fewest available sites for sewage ponds, effort was focused on green roofs to retain rainwater and mitigate the peak flow of storm water. These measures were all designed to remove the need for billions of dollars of investment in traditional water-filtration systems. In this way, climate-change mitigation is largely framed as an economic imperative rather than a social or even environmental one.

Specifically within the field of urban climatology, there remains a distinct lack of understanding of the financial costs and benefits of interventions, as the focus of most academic effort is on improving the science. The reality is that urban-climatology policy interventions may conflict with the economic demands and financial realities of cities. Erell (2008) argues that for the science to be taken seriously at the political level, the economic benefits and drawbacks of improved urban climates need to be understood, quantified and communicated to provide a counterbalance to economic arguments against interventions. As highlighted earlier, it has been demonstrated that painting a rooftop white can lessen the urban heat island effect, as the reflective nature of the white surface reduces the external radiant load on a building, lowering the surface temperature during the daytime.

The measure is often seen as a very low-cost solution compared to the installation of a green roof. The effect of white roofs, however, declines over time, in some cases rather dramatically after as little as two months, due to natural weathering and soil build-up (Bretz and Pon, 1994). While cleaning the roof can restore the effects of whitewashing, this is resource intensive in terms of both time and money. A requirement for white roofs was included as a new component of the building code as part of PlaNYC, but no mention was made of cost versus benefits of this measure over time.

Commentators have also noted how the 59 community boards of the city were dictated to rather than consulted on the development of the plan. This left those on the boards largely unable to vocalise concerns around the plan and unaware of the financial implications of the initiatives (Angotti, 2008a). While a myriad of economic benefits are highlighted throughout the plan, there is a lack of systematic analysis of costs and benefits, particularly in relation to the trade-offs between 'traditional' solutions to issues such as flooding, sewage or energy management, and more 'sustainable' solutions, with economic impact spoken of in generalities rather than specificities. A key reason for this is the context-dependent nature of urban climatology that makes the generalisation of environmental and financial costs and benefits substantially more difficult. Each microclimate is a geographical particularity, requiring local mapping and analysis (Geiger, 1965). Studies on the impact of urban parks, known as 'park cool islands', for example , have demonstrated a wide range of potential benefits depending on the size of the park (Upmanis *et al.*, 1998; Saito *et al.*, 1990), as well as park siting and local wind speed (Ca *et al.*, 1998; Shashua-Bar and Hoffman, 2000; Upmanis and Chen, 1999). Most studies have noted the complexity of urban environments as a key reason for variability in the benefits of urban parks, thereby requiring that the science generated be at a highly localised level. This resource-intensive localisation leads to higher costs that are often politically unpalatable.

The generation of localised urban-climate knowledge is also hindered by the lack of predictive development in the science (Erell, 2008). Integrating urban climatology into urban policy is disadvantaged by this inability to demonstrate clear and immediate benefits derived from adopting urban-climatology recommendations. Without an understanding of the predictive impacts of urban-climatology interventions, 'decision-makers, in general, tend to downgrade the importance of climatic considerations' (Erell, 2008, p. 100). While some urban climatologists are starting to develop such methods (Santamouris *et al.*, 2001; Kolokotroni *et al.*, 2006; Rosenzweig *et al.*, 2009), there is a need for further methodological development which will help to quantify the impacts of urban-climatology interventions rather than provide static lays of the land, as often occurs at the moment, or predictions based on business-as-usual scenarios. This would allow politicians and decision makers, who are increasingly concerned with economic costs, to have a greater evidence base to draw on, while also providing more local communities with the science necessary to understand the financial implications of policy interventions.

Conclusion

The interface when urban policy is aggregated to the metropolitan level and climatology science disaggregated to the urban scale is a complicated one, with a range of implications for policy and governance. Central to this is the tension stemming from the translation of the 'upstream' production of science and the 'downstream' consumption of that science by policymakers (Demeritt, 2001; Corburn, 2009). Problem definition itself will vary depending on the perspective taken, and mediating the two often becomes a dynamic process as a solution for a common problem is sought. This co-production activity is fraught with problems as the multitudes of actors involved drive their own interests and biases into the process.

The 'upstream' production of scientific climate-change knowledge has shifted in recent decades, away from the global scale and increasingly towards understanding the impacts on lower territorial scales as policy responses are sought. For urban climatology, the problem has been the opposite, as there has been a need to scale up from the highly localised 'block' scale, which scientists are used to studying, towards wider neighbourhoods, cities and even metropolitan regions. With this comes a challenge for scientists as they attempt to generalise methods and approaches that have been developed for small-scale environments, often in isolation from the range of external factors that regularly impact upon urban territories. As the case of New York City demonstrated, this can, at times, result in misunderstandings of the accuracy of the science produced, as well as the desire by scientists continually to refine the process during the policy development. As admirable as the improvement of the science may be, it comes with a cost that local governments are often unable to afford. The challenge, then, is to find ways to produce scaled up urban-climate science that is comprehensive and rigorous, at a price that is affordable for local government. At the same time, there is also a need to ensure that the expertise is present to interpret scientific data and construct knowledge that can then inform policy intervention.

Of perhaps greater concern for the production of urban-climate science is that the lack of predictive development, as well as demonstrable clear and immediate (often economic) benefits, also hinders the consumption and translation of urban climatology into urban policy. While small-scale interventions can be monitored, larger scale metropolitan initiatives are difficult to evaluate given the complexity of the built environment and climate of urban areas. The lack of a comprehensive evidence base for urban-climatology interventions, therefore, means that it is difficult for policymakers to argue for the inclusion of such approaches – particularly at the metropolitan scale. The contextually dependent nature of urban microclimates also means that it is difficult to understand the differential impact of interventions on neighbourhoods when monitored through a metropolitan lens, leading to concerns around environmental equity and the distribution of financial costs to different parts of an urban area.

The challenge for the consumption of urban-climate science 'downstream', meanwhile, is a struggle between a range of embedded interests and norms, as actors seek to advance their own concerns across a range of governance scales.

At the neighbourhood level, poor public consultation combined with top-heavy decision making and a lack of inclusion of lay experience in honing the science to the local context threatens the successful co-production of climate-science knowledge as part of urban policy. Connected to this is the danger that the science itself is used as a means to stifle genuine discussion and exclude those unable to comprehend occasionally complex scientific results as policy is scaled up. In New York City, the inclusion of the stakeholders, experts and professionals generated healthy, though at times contentious, debate around the science of climate change, although it ultimately aided in the refinement of urban-policy approaches. However, those not included in these committees of experts were often marginalised. There is also the potential for scientific knowledge to clash with political demands, as top-down policy implementation meets the precise and measured realities of scientific outcomes. In these cases, the consumption of science can become less about the knowledge generated and more about how it is used and manipulated to advance a particular cause. Taken together, New York City stands as a useful illustration of how the 'upstream' production of urban-climate science and its 'downstream' consumption is constantly being contested by a range of actors through an iterative co-production process that has meaningful impacts on the development of policy at different territorial scales.

References

Akbari, H., Pomerantz, M. and Taha, H. (2001) Cool surfaces and shade trees to reduce energy use and improve air quality in urban areas, *Solar Energy*, 70, 295–310.

Angotti, T. (2008a) *New York for Sale: Community Planning Confronts Global Real Estate*, Cambridge, MA: The MIT Press.

Angotti, T. (2008b) Is New York's Sustainability Plan sustainable?, paper presented to the Association of Collegiate Schools of Planning and Association of European Schools of Planning conference, 6–11 July, Chicago, IL.

Bach, W. (1972) Urban climate, air pollution and planning, in: Detwyler, T. and Marcus, M. (eds.) *Urbanization and Environment*, pp. 69–96, Belmont, CA: Duxbury.

Bornstein, R. (1968) Observations of the urban heat island effect in New York City, *Journal of Applied Meteorology*, 7, 575–582.

Bornstein, R. and Thompson, W. (1981) Effects of frictionally retarded sea breeze and synoptic frontal passages on sulfur dioxide concentrations in New York City, *Journal of Applied Meteorology*, 20, 843–858.

Boyle, D. and Harris, M. (2009) *The Challenge of Co-production*, London: NESTA.

Bretz, S. and Pon, B. (1994) Durability of High Albedo Coatings, *Recent Research in the Building Energy Analysis Group at Lawrence Berkeley Laboratory*, No. 5., Building Energy Analysis Group, p. 1.

Bulkeley, H. and Betsill, M. (2005) Rethinking sustainable cities: multilevel governance and the 'urban' politics of climate change, *Environmental Politics*, 14, 42–63.

Ca, V., Asaeda, T. and Abu, E. (1998) Reductions in air conditioning energy caused by a nearby park, *Energy and Buildings*, 29, 83–92.

City of New York (2007) *PlaNYC: A Greener, Greater New York*, New York, NY: City of New York. Available: www.nyc.gov/html/planyc/downloads/pdf/publications/full_report_2007.pdf (accessed 16 November 2016).

City of New York (2011) Local Laws 21 of 2011, New York, NY: City of New York. Available: www1.nyc.gov/assets/buildings/local_laws/ll21of2011.pdf (accessed 16 November 2016).

City of New York (2013) *PlaNYC Progress Report 2013*, New York, NY: City of New York. Available: www.nyc.gov/html/planyc/downloads/pdf/publications/planyc_progress_report_2013.pdf (accessed 16 November 2016).

Corburn, J. (2002) Combining community-based research and local knowledge to confront asthma and subsistence-fishing hazards in Greenpoint/Williamsburg, Brooklyn, New York, *Environmental Health Perspectives*, 110, 241–248.

Corburn, J. (2009) Cities, climate change and urban heat island mitigation: localising global environmental science, *Urban Studies*, 46, 413–427.

Crenson, M. (1973) The un-politics of air pollution: a study of non-decision making in the cities, *American Journal of Sociology*, 79, 233–235.

Demeritt, D. (2001) The construction of global warming and the politics of science, *Annals of the Association of American Geographers*, 91, 307–337.

Eliasson, I. (2000) The use of climate knowledge in urban planning, *Landscape and Urban Planning*, 48, 31–44.

Erell, E. (2008) The application of urban climate research in the design of cities, *Advances in Building Energy Research*, 2, 95–121.

Erell, E., Pearlmutter, D. and Williamson, T. (2011) *Urban Microclimate: Designing the Spaces Between Buildings*, London: Earthscan.

Gal, T. and Unger, J. (2009) Detection of ventilation paths using high resolution roughness parameter mapping in a large urban area, *Building and Environment*, 44, 198–206.

Geiger, R. (1965) *The Climate Near the Ground*, Cambridge, MA: Harvard University Press.

Goulder, L. and Stavins, R. (2012) Interactions between state and federal climate change policies, in: Fullerton, D. and Wolfram, C. (eds.) *The Design and Implementation of US Climate Policy*, pp. 109–126, Chicago, IL: University of Chicago Press.

Hebbert, M. and Webb, B. (2011) Towards a liveable urban climate: lessons from Stuttgart, in: Gossop, C. and Nan, S. (eds.) *Liveable Cities: Urbanising World*, pp. 132–149, The Hague: ISOCARP.

Hebbert, M. and MacKillop, F. (2013) Urban climatology applied to urban planning: a postwar knowledge circulation failure, *International Journal of Urban and Regional Research*, 37, 1542–1558.

Hsie, T. and Ward, I. (2006) A GIS-based method for determining natural ventilation potentials and urban morphology, paper presented to the 23rd Conference on Passive and Low Energy Architecture, Geneva, Switzerland.

Jabareen, Y. (2013) Planning for countering climate change: lessons from the recent plan of New York City – PlaNYC 2030, *International Planning Studies*, 18, 221–242.

Jasanoff, S. (2003) (No?) accounting for expertise, *Science and Public Policy*, 30, 157–162.

Jasanoff, S. and Martello, M. (eds.) (2004) *Earthly Politics: Local and Global in Environmental Governance*, Cambridge, MA: The MIT Press.

Kolokotroni, M., Giannitsaris, I. and Watkins, R. (2006) The effect of the London urban heat island on building summer cooling demand and night ventilation strategies, *Solar Energy*, 80, 383–392.

Lemos M. and Morehouse, B. (2005) The coproduction of science and policy in integrated climate assessments, *Global Environmental Change*, 15, 57–68.

Lövbrand, E. (2011) Co-producing European climate science and policy: a cautionary note on the making of useful knowledge, *Science and Public Policy*, 38, 225–236.

Marcuse, P. (2008) *PlaNYC Is Not a Plan and It Is Not for NYC*, New York, NY: Hunter College. Available: www.hunter.cuny.edu/ccpd/sustainability-watch (accessed 2 January 2014).

Miller, C. (2004) Resisting empire: globalism, relocalization, and the politics of knowledge, in: Jasanoff, S. and Martello, M. (eds.) *Earthly Politics: Local and Global in Environmental Governance*, pp. 81–102, Cambridge, MA: MIT Press.

NY Metro APA (2007) *Response to the Bloomberg Administration's PlaNYC 2030 Long Term Sustainability Planning Process and Proposed Goals*, New York, NY: City of New York. Available: http://www.nyplanning.org/docs/PlaNYC_2030_response_final_3-14-07.pdf (accessed 18 February 2014).

Ostrom, E. (1996) Crossing the great divide: coproduction, synergy and development, *World Development*, 24, 1073–1087.

Parlow, E., Scherer, D. and Fehrenbach, U. (2001) *Climatic analyse map for grenchen und umgebung. CAMPAS, Klimaanalyse- und Planungshinweiskarten für den Kanton Solothurn*, Basel: University of Basel.

Ren C., Ng, E. and Katzschner, L. (2011) Urban climatic map studies: a review, *International Journal of Climatology*, 31, 2213–2233.

Rosan, C. (2012) Can PlaNYC make New York City 'greener and greater' for everyone? Sustainability planning and the promise of environmental justice, *Local Environment*, 17, 959–976.

Rosenzweig, C., Solecki, W. Hammer, S. and Mehrotra, S. (eds.) (2009) *Climate Change and Cities: First Assessment Report of the Urban Climate Change Research Network*, Cambridge: Cambridge University Press.

Saito, I., Ishihara, O. and Katayama, T. (1990) Study of the effect of green areas on the thermal environment in an urban area, *Energy and Buildings*, 15–16, 493–498.

Santamouris, M., Papanikolaou, N., Livada, I., Koronakis, I., Georgakis, C., Argiriou, A. and Assimakopoulos, W. (2001) On the impact of urban climate on the energy consumption of buildings, *Solar Energy*, 70, 201–216.

Shashua-Bar, L. and Hoffman, M. (2000) Vegetation as a climatic component in the design of an urban street: an empirical model for predicting the cooling effect of urban green areas with trees, *Energy and Buildings*, 31, 221–235.

Sze, J. (2007) *Noxious New York: The Racial Politics of Urban Health and Environmental Justice*, Cambridge, MA: MIT Press.

Tuinstra, W., Hordijk, L. and Kroeze, C. (2006) Moving boundaries in transboundary air pollution: co-production of science and policy under the convention of long-range transboundary air pollution, *Global Environmental Change*, 16, 349–363.

Upmanis, H. and Chen, D. (1999) Influence of geographical factors and meteorological influences on nocturnal urban-park temperature differences: a case study of summer 1995 in Goteborg, Sweden, *Climate Research*, 13, 125–139.

Upmanis, H., Eliasson, I. and Lindqvist, S. (1998) The influence of green areas on nocturnal temperatures in a high latitude city (Goteborg, Sweden), *International Journal of Climatology*, 18, 681–700.

Ward, I. (2003) The usefulness of climatic maps of built-up areas in determining drivers for the energy and environmental efficiency of buildings and external areas, *International Journal of Ventilation*, 2, 277–286.

Whitehead, M. (2009) *State, Science and the Skies: Governmentalities of the British Atmosphere*, Chichester, UK: Wiley.

12 Conclusion

Iain Deas and Stephen Hincks

> Something funny happened in the 1980s. The region, long considered an interesting topic to historians and geographers, but not considered to have any interest for mainstream western social science, was rediscovered by a group of political economists, sociologists, political scientists and geographers.
>
> (Storper, 1997, p. 3)

The resurgence of regionalism in many countries from the late-1980s reflected the increasingly visible ascendency of regions and city-regions as key nodes in a globalising world (Agnew, 2000). With this came a growing focus by policymakers on bolstering the economic competitiveness of regions and, latterly, city-regions. This involved efforts to promote more cohesive regional governance arrangements and focus policy support more directly on harnessing the opportunities afforded by the internationalisation of economic activity. Advocates of what was termed the 'new regionalism' articulated the contentious view that by modernising institutional infrastructure and tailoring policy to reposition regions in the context of a global economy, all regions ultimately would benefit.

In reality, evidence suggested that regional policy in different countries often involved concentrating support on areas of existing or potential dynamism, sometimes exacerbating long-standing inter-regional disparity (Jonas and Ward, 2002; Harrison, 2008; Muštra and Škrabić, 2014; Martin, 2015). Nevertheless, the suggestion that all places could benefit from globalisation came to constitute a powerful and pervasive narrative that was to inform policymaking in subsequent years (see Bristow, 2005, for a critical review). It is perhaps unsurprising, then, that over successive decades there have been periodic bursts of region building. What has distinguished much of this from earlier eras is the increasingly complex, loose and network-based character of regional policy and governance, and its more fluid geography (see Amin and Thrift, 1994; Allen *et al.*, 1998; Blatter, 2004; Deas and Lord, 2006; Allen and Cochrane, 2007; Cox, 2010; Harrison, 2013).

In retrospect, the period from the late 1980s until the aftermath of the global financial crises of 2007–08 represented the apogee of this form of 'new' regional governance and policy. As we outlined in Chapter 1, regionalist projects have been under attack across the world in recent years (Fioramonti, 2012).

In the United Kingdom, for instance, the era of ordered and systematic regional governance and policy associated with the Labour governments of the 1990s and 2000s proved less durable than originally anticipated, seemingly reaching a decisive end with the British General Election of 2010 (Bentley *et al.*, 2010; Herrschel, 2012). Yet, it is our contention that regional governance and policy endures, even in places like the United Kingdom where it is thought to be in decline. As chapters documenting experience in Britain, continental Europe and North America demonstrate, regional governance territories of different types have proved more adaptable than is sometimes anticipated. Regions, the ideas that underpin them and the collective identities that sustain them, have often shown a resilience in the face of efforts to dismantle institutional structures or curtail the powers and resources available to regional policymakers. Reflecting the relational basis on which regions are at least in part founded, regional thinking and regional consciousness are durable entities that can outlast structures and policies.

It was recognition of the persistence of regionalism and the malleability of regional governance structures and policy initiatives that prompted us to collate this volume. The aim was twofold. First, we set out to identify the lineaments of the new forms of sub-national policy and governance beginning to emerge in what some commentators speculated might be a post-regional era of state territoriality, characterised by an ever more complex, variable and localised array of relational spaces (see, for example, Herrschel, 2012). In what ways were these spaces – and the structures, policies, people and perceptions that defined them – constructed, deconstructed and reconstructed? And how might their empirical experiences, in different contexts, be interpreted in conceptual terms?

Alongside this, the second aim, as detailed in Chapter 1, was to explore some of the wider debates and dilemmas about regional (or post-regional) governance and policy and consider the repercussions of reform for policymakers striving to respond to the geographically uneven effects of the economic crises of the early twenty-first century. In the remainder of this concluding chapter, we try to address these aims by synthesising findings across the earlier chapters and, in doing so, highlight remaining priorities for future research. We draw conclusions under four principal headings.

Shadow regions and the persistence of regionalism

The recurring message throughout this book is that regions, not only in terms of the structures through which they are articulated but also – and to an even greater degree – the thinking that underpins them, are more resilient than might be expected. Regionalism, despite recurring prophecies of its demise, continues to exert a powerful lure on policy actors (Harrison, 2008). This durability applies to regional ideas, to identity (especially among policy elites) and to processes and structures, the legacy of which can remain in evidence over long periods of time (Martin *et al.*, 2015a). Even where regional structures have been abolished, and where national governments explicitly reject the idea of regional spaces as a basis for organising some aspects of public policy, there is evidence of much in the way of continued energy and innovation in respect of sub-national territories of governance (Harrison, 2012; Bellini *et al.*, 2014).

The result, as detailed in earlier chapters, is several examples of what might be termed 'shadow regions', where regionalist consciousness continues among policy actors and infuses institutional structures and policy initiatives in a way that is more than merely vestigial. The geography of shadow regions in some cases matches now defunct formal governance territories, providing a sometimes obscure but subversive alternative to state-authored public policy. In other instances, regionalism endures in the form of regions configured with new and different boundaries, both soft and hard. As Haughton and Allmendinger (Chapter 5) note, new policy initiatives based on soft spaces have emerged to occupy the void left behind by the abolition of formal regional institutions and policies. In some cases, such as the city-regions in England's Northern Powerhouse discussed by Harrison (Chapter 4), emergent regional bodies, both soft and hard, may seek to work in tandem with central government but, nevertheless, provide an important way of continuing regional thinking at odds with the notion of a post-regional world.

In some respects, the continuation of regional thinking, or the existence of shadow regions, is not a new phenomenon. It would be unrealistic to expect the abolition of policies or structures to extinguish the ideas that underpinned them in a clear-cut way. Historical experience of regional policy in countries such as the United Kingdom supports such a contention. The Thatcher governments of 1979–90 were in most senses resolutely opposed to regional governance and policy, viewed as an obsolete relic of earlier statist experiments in economic planning and land-use strategy (see, for example, Baker *et al.*, 1999). Yet even at the zenith of Thatcherism, regionalism continued in a variety of forms, from grant funding for 'enterprise' in assisted areas to support for inward investment promotion by regionally based organisations (see Martin, 1993). Even regional strategic land-use planning – later derided by a Conservative minister as 'Soviet tractor style top-down planning' (DCLG, 2010, n.p.; Lord, Chapter 8) – came to be championed by some within the Thatcher administrations as a necessary means of reconciling inter-governmental conflict and managing land release in areas where housing shortages were impeding economic growth. It is often forgotten that the initial impetus for the system of statutory regional planning in England, which was subsequently to provoke the ire of later generations of free-marketeers derived from the Conservatives' tentative experiments with light-touch regional land-use strategy, and the publication in 1988 of *Regional Planning Guidance for the South East of England* (DoE, 1988).

The continuing resonance of regionalism is a function of more than just the unavoidable circularity of policy. It demonstrates the striking extent to which the ideas and innovations of the past influence those of the present (Larner and Walters, 2002; Fawcett, 2004). This may appear a pat conclusion, but it is important not to let the apparently repetitive rhythm of policy evolution conceal the continuing influence of earlier rounds of region building or the persisting relevance of regionalist ideas. As Lord (Chapter 8) notes, apparent innovation and experimentation in respect of governance and policy models often conceal more important threads of continuity. Urban and regional initiatives that purport to be pioneering, Lord argues, often constitute a re-packaging of earlier policy endeavours, in doing so reinforcing dominant policy goals and reproducing established modes of working.

Sometimes, earlier policy preoccupations may accord with those of their contemporary successors. But they can also jar against the policy *zeitgeist*. Case-study evidence in England (Harrison, Chapter 4) demonstrates how stability and continuity in terms of the actors steering spatial policy reform mean that the legacy of now largely forgotten experiments in regional policy occasionally injects a discordant note into present-day debate. For example, it is tempting to view the Northern Powerhouse as an expression of a set of deep-rooted neoliberal orthodoxies about agglomerative growth (Lee, 2016), but the continuing involvement of policy opinion formers with experience of policy initiatives some decades in the past means that goals linked to social justice or environmental improvement feature to some extent (albeit a subordinate one) in contemporary policymaker deliberation (Deas *et al.*, 2015).

There is a collective memory here about past waves of institutional and policy reform that can be missed if the focus of research is too exclusively on contemporary aspects of region building (see Fawcett, 2004; Geppert, 2015). As Harrison (Chapter 4) also demonstrates, many of the regional policy elites who provided support for the formal regional spaces of old continue to play a prominent role in the more complex arrangements that now exist. This reiterates the conclusion that regions, as relational entities as well as formal bounded structures, cannot simply be expunged; the story of regional policy is often one in which territories, linked to particular constellations of actors, morph in sometimes subtle, complex and hidden ways that are at odds with crude periodised accounts of the birth and death of hard, formal regional initiatives over time.

The polymorphous nature of regions

A second and related set of conclusions concerns the shape and form of regional institutions and policy initiatives (see also Rodríguez-Pose, 2013; Tomaney, 2014). The increasingly polymorphous nature of regional governance and policy provides a substantial part of the explanation for its resilience. Earlier chapters documented territorial governance and policy in its multifarious forms, from the mega-regional spaces of the European Union (EU) chronicled by O'Brien, Sykes and Shaw (Chapter 3) to the tightly bounded Business Improvement Districts (BIDs) discussed by Ward and Cook (Chapter 7). It is this polymorphous character, and the ability of territorial governance and policy solutions to adapt to changing circumstances, which explains what might otherwise be its surprising longevity. For Jones (Chapter 2), localities – including regions – are by definition multi-faceted, dynamic and contingent entities that can be shaped in different ways, whether according to the specificities of local socio-economic circumstances or the objectives of political elites.

Earlier chapters exploring the evolution of the EU's regional policy illustrate something of the pliable nature of regionalism. Redistributive regional policy might have been expected to be dismissed as a waning feature of spatial Keynesianism, yet as O'Brien *et al.* (Chapter 3) demonstrate, multiple regionalisms have come to coexist with the continuing spatial policy of targeted compensatory support for lagging or declining regions. The notion of multi-level governance, long at the heart of Europe's regional project, means there is scope for multiple types of regional policy organised around a variety of territories and with different substantive emphases (Marks, 1993; Hooghe, 1996; Benz and Eberlein, 1999; see Jessop, 2016, for a critical repositioning of EU multi-level governance through the lens of multi-spatial meta-governance). Whereas at least part of the rationale for the EU's regional policy in the past was about narrowing inter-regional inequality, subsequent forms of regional intervention have sought to advance the competitiveness of the continental economy and promote its functional integrity, and more recent forays into regional policy have been tied to efforts to promote what O'Brien and colleagues refer to as 'place-based' agglomerative growth (see also Gardiner *et al.*, 2010; Avdikos and Chardas, 2016).

This repurposing of regional policy is also evident in respect of many of the regional spaces established to facilitate cross-border cooperation (see, for example, Scott, 1999; Perkmann, 2003; Perkmann, 2007; García-Álvarez and Trillo-Santamaría, 2013). Many of these originally emerged as part of wider efforts to create and complete the single European market, but, as Colomb *et al.* (Chapter 6) demonstrate, their utility has sometimes been reinforced by an increased emphasis on their role in enabling labour mobility in a managed way that balances sometimes conflicting economic and political concerns.

Elsewhere, the continuing need for a regional economic policy is thrown into sharper focus by the economic crises in Greece and other member states, some part of which reflected the difficulty in applying continental monetary policy in a context of Europe's highly uneven economic geography (Muštra and Škrabić, 2014; Nicholls, 2015). Regional and inter-regional initiatives have a continuing resonance in light of longstanding patterns of uneven development which have recently begun to undermine the integrity of the single European market, provoking for a time what looked to be an existential crisis for the Eurozone (Lapavitsas *et al.*, 2012; Nicholls, 2015). Against a backdrop of Euroscepticism in several countries – most notably Britain, as evidenced by Brexit and the referendum vote in 2016 to secede from the EU – continuing efforts to establish the Eurozone as an optimal currency area mean that regional policy remains an obvious complement or alternative to politically less palatable fiscal transfer.

Experience of the reorientation of European spatial policy over time, therefore, illustrates the multiple functions that regional initiatives can fulfil. At an EU level, regional policy has been deployed at different times in support of efforts to reduce inter-regional socio-economic disparity, promote economic convergence, facilitate labour mobility and stimulate economic growth in already dynamic local and regional economies. Some of these goals can conflict, but the point is that regions provide a convenient and tractable vehicle through which to pursue a variety of different policies – and it is this that explains a large part of the continuing attractiveness of regional policy and governance solutions. Rather than view changing forms of regional policy as a reflection of a continuing and as yet unrealised desire to agree the right spatial architecture for governance, it may be better to think of regions as expressions of restructuring in other areas of public policy, thereby explaining not only the persistence of regional approaches but also their continuing diversity.

Increased diversity in regional structures and initiatives: refining and extending theory

Much of the debate over recent decades on how best to conceptualise contemporary regions has centred on two issues. A large body of literature considers how the processes shaping the division of economic and political space, and their territorial outcomes, have changed in the context of the internationalisation of economic activity. A particularly fertile area of interest has been on the implications posed by new regional spaces for the geographical organisation of the state, and the associated scalar inter-relationships between institutions within a changing global-local hierarchy (e.g. MacLeod, 2001; Jessop, 2002; Brenner, 2004). Paralleling this, Jones and Harrison (Chapters 2 and 4) engage with a second area of sustained interest, around competing conceptions of regions as bounded territorial units or as relational entities characterised by their often complex and changing networked nature (Castells, 1996; Harrison, 2013; Jones and Paasi, 2013).

Within both sets of literature, there have been efforts to try to identify different types of territory associated with the upsurge of regions. Sometimes, these have drawn on debates about relationality and boundedness, with (as the chapters by Haughton and Allmendinger, Karvonen and Harrison note) particular focus on the 'unusual' and 'soft' spaces associated with relational conceptions of regionalism. Beyond these important attempts to distinguish between hard and soft institutional forms and policy initiatives, relatively little headway has been made in categorising the multiplicity of regional territories and types. Yet, the increasingly disparate nature of regional institutional and policy forms means that categorising regions becomes an ever more important priority. Crucially, it is one that needs not only to go beyond dichotomous conceptions of hard and soft but also to take into account time. As we have seen, snapshot categorisations are problematic because of the tendency of regional entities to adapt and change, and to endure even in seemingly unpropitious 'post-regional' circumstances (Martin, 2011; Harrison, 2012).

Regions, as is evident throughout this book, are often difficult to delimit in straightforward Cartesian terms. Their geometry can change; they can sometimes be bounded in overt ways but, at other times, exist in shadow form. Developing more nuanced categorisations of soft spaces, in particular, is an important conceptual priority, on which earlier chapters of the book began to shed some initial light (see Haughton and Allmendinger, Chapter 5). Whilst transience is one of the defining characteristics of soft spaces, we can draw further distinctions which incorporate something of a temporal dimension. What might be termed *elemental* regions are those in which ideas have yet to translate into any kind of concrete institutional expression, as with many of the soft spaces documented by

Haughton and Allmendinger in Chapter 5. For these types of regions, bottom-up pressures are of critical importance, but the degree to which they can formalise or institutionalise remains contingent on an array of internal and external factors. *Aspirational* regions (such as the Atlantic Gateway concept discussed by Harrison, Chapter 4) are those in which institutionalisation is still weak and the link to popular or political consciousness poorly developed, but initial territorialisation has begun to allow regions to move beyond the merely embryonic. *Developmental* regions (such as the UK's incipient combined authorities, based on city-regions) are those in which a longer-term process of institutionalisation has resulted in more formalised, solidified governance structures that have begun to acquire a greater degree of permanence.

Each of these prospective types exists along something of a continuum, sitting alongside existing spaces that benefit from governmental sanction in the form of statutory status. These fully *institutionalized regions* are formalised to a large extent, with greater legitimacy and political buy-in typically reflected in higher levels of resourcing and frequently greater degrees of popular visibility. However, here too there is a need to incorporate a temporal dimension in trying to develop a meaningful typology of regional spaces. There is a need to understand more fully the multiple paths along which regions travel in the process of becoming. Equally, it is critical here not to assume that there is a final, stable or ideal end point at which region building concludes. Regions may be characterised by differing levels of maturity, but even longer-established spaces continue to evolve and mutate.

In the context of the dynamic processes of region building, the decline or demise of a regional institution or initiative has often been viewed as a decisive endpoint (see Hebbert, 1982; Bentley *et al.*, 2010). Yet as we have argued, such finality is often difficult to discern in reality; hard structures may disappear and formal policy initiatives may end, but the people who populated and authored them continue to exert influence, and the ideas that accompanied past policies tend to live on to some degree (Danson and Lloyd, 2012; Rodríguez-Pose, 2013; Tomaney, 2014). Thinking about the multi-directional paths along which regions are made also ought to mean devoting more effort to understanding the variable trajectories of decline as well as growth for regional governance and policy.

Consideration of the evolution of regions also means understanding the variable adaptability of different spaces and the people, institutions and policies that define them. Karvonen (Chapter 9) charts the perennial search by stakeholders for a 'territorial fix' in environmental policy and governance in response to the emergence of different ideologies, logics and regulatory frameworks in different places and at different times. For Karvonen, this process of 'search' has seen the creation of multiple environmental pathways, each underpinned by flexible and malleable logics, which overlap and intermingle in ways that are both synergistic and conflictual. The chapter by Ward and Cook (Chapter 7) reveals how processes of mobility have seen the BID model, initially deployed in Canada, disseminate in uneven ways to different parts of the United States, Britain and elsewhere. The variable form and application of the model reflects the way in which ideas mutate and adapt as they encounter existing policy frameworks and cultures at their destination. In doing so, the imported idea provides a new frame of reference for policymakers as they look to experiment and innovate in new and exciting ways (see also Lord, Chapter 8).

As Harrison also demonstrates (Chapter 4), there is often an underlying policy argument that successful regions are those where the capacity to adapt is most thoroughly developed. Earlier chapters have highlighted inter-regional variability in the nature of responses to austerity, and unevenness in the effectiveness with which regions have responded. Unsurprisingly, less formalised regions have tended to be more successful in an era of retrenching resources because they can be presented as according to a wider narrative about the need for lighter-touch institutional arrangements attuned to the critical issue of inducing private sector-led economic growth. As Harrison reveals, England's Northern Powerhouse again stands out in this respect, as a quintessential relational region (its boundaries have never been defined) that has become steadily more prominent on the basis of few dedicated resources but with high levels of both local and national political commitment. At the same time, however, the variable adaptability of harder spaces is also evident in different responses to austerity politics. While some of the city-regional combined authorities in England have presented themselves to government as a means of generating cost savings via enhanced economies of scale in delivering public services across multiple local government jurisdictions, their larger polycentric regional predecessors – established in a context of relatively plentiful resourcing – were unable to avoid abolition driven by a desire to reduce public expenditure (Bentley *et al.*, 2010).

There is in this sense a kind of quasi-market in which particular types of regional structure and policy are able to compete more successfully, positioning themselves as most in tune with the broader thrust of spatial policy. Presentation and advocacy are, therefore, often critical in determining the ability of a regional initiative to embed, prosper and survive (Pike *et al.*, 2016). This explains why spatial imaginaries, as Haughton and Allmendinger (Chapter 5) note, have been important in allowing some soft spaces to move beyond the initial elemental stage and begin to formalise (see also Metzger and Schmitt, 2012). Representation is also important in relation to Lord's argument (Chapter 8) that some regions have shown an apparently enhanced capacity for mutability, superficially reinventing themselves to accommodate faddish policy preoccupations but without undermining their basic *raisons d'être*. As Webb illustrates in his chapter on metropolitan planning in New York (Chapter 11), case making has been important within regional bodies, in determining the substance of their approaches. Using case-study evidence from PlaNYC, Webb shows how competing interpretations of urban-climatology science translate via policy-actor contestation into specific metropolitan planning provisions. In this sense, quasi-markets apply not only to regional initiatives but also to the ideas that constitute them.

Regions, selectivity and inequality

Regional governance and policy historically have been associated in many instances with a series of progressive goals: increasing fiscal equity and delivering public services more effectively and efficiently by integrating urban cores and their suburban hinterland within metropolitan areas; enabling more effective policymaking for strategic issues across functional economic or environmental territories; addressing inter-regional social and economic disparities; and (more recently) promoting in some US cities the development of a social-movement regionalism in which larger territories provide a focal point around which to engage multiple (and sometimes marginalised) groups (Wannop 1995; Pastor *et al.*, 2009). More recently, however, it has been narratives of competitiveness and economic growth that have tended to provide much of the impetus for region building, particularly in relation to city-regions (While *et al.*, 2013; Deas, 2014; Haughton *et al.*, 2016).

Earlier chapters show that recent policy changes have accentuated this shift from regional policy as a progressive instrument of social and economic change to one geared towards growth irrespective of wider distributive consequences. At the continental scale, O'Brien and colleagues (Chapter 3) note the changing emphasis of European regional policy and, in particular, the acceptance of models of urban agglomerative growth. The result has been the increasing ascendancy of policy approaches intended to facilitate further economic development in already thriving areas, linked to the wider goal of ensuring that Europe possesses glob- ally significant powerhouse regional economies. At the national scale, Harrison (Chapter 4) highlights the role of the UK government in sanctioning only those combined authorities that are in tune with its ideals. The guiding philosophy in this context is again one that tolerates territorial inequality but views spatial policy as an instrument for creating and extending a selective number of rapidly growing local economies (see also While *et al.*, 2013).

These examples of spatial selectivity in regional policy have drawn inspiration from influential (but controversial) academic thinking on the importance of large, diverse and dense agglomerative economies in propelling national economic pros- perity (see, for example, Glaeser, 2011; Overman, 2012; and critiques by Haughton *et al.*, 2014, 2016; Peck, 2016, Martin *et al.*, 2015b). As Harrison observes, this has been important in underpinning a shift in the territorial basis of regional policy, with policy discourses emphasising more tightly bounded city-regions as opposed to more expansively delimited and often polycentric regions. Accompanying this shift in the geography of regional policy has also been important substantive and conceptual changes. In terms of the substance of policy, the emphasis on city- regions has helped to reinforce the shift away from progressive and redistributive concerns towards a narrower focus on instilling and extending economic growth, particularly in areas of existing or potential economic vibrancy. In conceptual terms, the increasing policymaker emphasis on city-regionalism has coincided with a shift in researcher interest, moving beyond the study of regions as part of an incipient multi-scalar, local-global hierarchy and engaging more with questions around the networked character of regions, their representational basis and their implications for state territoriality (Jonas, 2013; Harrison and Growe, 2014).

One of the consequences of the dominance of what Haughton *et al.* (2014) term 'agglomeration boosterism' is that spatial selectivity in territorial policy – picking winners – is accentuated. For critics, this perpetuates territorial inequality by con-centrating resources and marginalising areas beyond the selected urban economic cores deemed to have the necessary growth potential (Bristow, 2005). A conse-quence, as demonstrated throughout this book, is that relationships between (city-) regional spaces warrant more attention, extending the long tradition of research interest in central-local relations and the more recent interest in how scalar hierar-chies have shifted in a context of changing patterns of state territorialisation. Jones (Chapter 2), in rethinking the value of the localities concept, argues that there is a need to think about interactions between regional spaces, thereby avoiding the treatment of individual areas as discrete entities that exist somehow independent of inter-relationships between governance institutions, or policy initiatives.

Haughton and Allmendinger (Chapter 5) contend that a particular priority is to explore more fully how soft and hard spaces of regional governance interact. They note that there is sometimes a tendency to overemphasise conflict between soft and hard spaces, as each look to supplant the other. While inter-institutional competi-tion for resources and legitimacy is an obvious feature of a quasi-market in policy and governance, relationships between differently configured but overlapping ter-ritories of governance can be harmonious. Soft and hard spaces, as Haughton and Allmendinger note, can coexist in sometimes symbiotic fashion. Colomb and colleagues (Chapter 6) make a similar observation in respect of cross-border regions, where there is evidence of productive cooperation and mutual benefit. Equally, cross-border regions often exercise limited power in comparison with bounded territories of governance, and amicable coexistence in that light reflects the lack of threat posed by the latter to the former. Understanding how regions interact and how their interactions change over time is, therefore, an important future research priority, as we seek to explore in broader terms the ways in which regional governance and policy continue to evolve.

References

Agnew, J. (2000) From the political economy of regions to regional political economy, *Progress in Human Geography*, 24, 101–110.

Allen, J. and Cochrane, A. (2007) Beyond the territorial fix: regional assemblages, politics and power, *Regional Studies*, 41, 1161–1175.

Allen J., Massey, D. and Cochrane, A. (1998) *Rethinking the Region*, London: Routledge.

Amin, A. and Thrift, N. (eds.) (1994) *Globalization, Institutions and Regional Development in Europe*, Oxford: Oxford University Press.

Avdikos, V. and Chardas, A. (2016) European Union cohesion policy post-2014: more (place-based and conditional) growth – less redistribution and cohesion, *Territory, Politics, Governance*, 4, 97–117.

Baker, M., Deas, I. and Wong, C. (1999) Obscure ritual or administrative luxury? Integrating strategic planning and regional development, *Environment and Planning B*, 26, 763–782.

Bellini, N., Danson, M. and Halkier, H. (eds.) (2014) *Regional Development Agencies: The Next Generation? Networking, Knowledge and Regional Policies*, London: Routledge.

Bentley, G., Bailey, D. and Shutt, J. (2010) From RDAs to LEPs: a New Localism? Case examples of West Midlands and Yorkshire, *Local Economy*, 25, 535–557.

Benz, A. and Eberlein, B. (1999) The Europeanization of regional policies: patterns of multi-level governance, *Journal of European Public Policy*, 6, 329–348.

Blatter, J. (2004) From 'spaces of place' to 'spaces of flows'? Territorial and functional governance in cross-border regions in the Europe and North America, *International Journal of Urban and Regional Research*, 28, 530–548.

Brenner, N. (2004) *New State Spaces*, Oxford: Oxford University Press.

Bristow, G. (2005) Everyone's a 'winner': problematising the discourse of regional competitiveness, *Journal of Economic Geography*, 5, 285–304.

Castells, M. (1996) *The Rise of the Network Society*, Oxford: Blackwell.

Cox, K. (2010) The problem of metropolitan governance and the politics of scale, *Regional Studies*, 44, 215–227.

Danson, M. and Lloyd, G. (2012) Devolution, institutions and organisations: changing models of regional development agencies, *Environment and Planning C*, 30, 78–94.

DCLG (Department for Communities and Local Government) (2010) Eric Pickles puts stop to flawed regional strategies. Available: www.gov.uk/government/news/eric-pickles-puts-stop-to-flawed-regional-strategies-today (accessed27 July 2016).

Deas, I. (2014) The search for territorial fixes in subnational governance: city-regions and the disputed emergence of post-political consensus in Manchester, England, *Urban Studies*, 51, 2285–2314.

Deas, I. and Lord, A. (2006) From a new regionalism to an unusual regionalism? The emergence of non-standard regional spaces and lessons for the territorial reorganisation of the state, *Urban Studies*, 43, 1847–1877.

Deas, I., Haughton, G. and Hincks, S. (2015) 'A good geography is whatever it needs to be': evolving spatial imaginaries in North West England, in: Allmendinger, P., Haughton, G., Knieling, J. and Othengrafen, F. (eds.), *Soft spaces: Re-negotiating Governance, Boundaries and Borders*, pp. 25–45, London: Routledge.

DoE (Department of the Environment) (1988) *PPG9: Regional Planning Guidance for the South East*, London: HMSO.

Fawcett, L. (2004) Exploring regional domains: a comparative history of regionalism, *International Affairs*, 80, 429–466.

Fioramonti, L. (ed.) (2012) *Regions and Crises: New Challenges for Contemporary Regionalisms*, New York: Palgrave.

García-Álvarez, J. and Trillo-Santamaría, J. (2013) Between regional spaces and spaces of regionalism: cross-border region building in the Spanish 'state of the autonomies', *Regional Studies*, 47, 104–115.

Gardiner, B., Martin, R. and Tyler, P. (2010) Does spatial agglomeration increase national growth? Some evidence from Europe, *Journal of Economic Geography*, 11, 979–1006.

Geppert, A. (2015) The Sillon Lorrain (Nancy, Metz, Epinal, Thionville), in: Allmendinger, P., Haughton, G., Knieling, J. and Othengrafen, F. (eds.), *Soft spaces: Re-negotiating Governance, Boundaries and Borders*, pp. 77–94, London: Routledge.

Glaeser, E. (2011) *Triumph of the City*, New York: Penguin Press

Harrison, J. (2008) Stating the production of scales: centrally orchestrated regionalism, regionally orchestrated centralism, *International Journal of Urban and Regional Research*, 32, 922–941.

Harrison, J. (2012) Life after regions? The evolution of city-regionalism in England, *Regional Studies*, 46, 1243–1259.

Harrison, J. (2013) Configuring the new 'regional world': on being caught between territory and networks, *Regional Studies*, 47, 55–74.

Harrison, J. and Growe, A. (2014) When regions collide: in what sense a new 'regional problem'? *Environment and Planning A*, 46, 2332–2352.

Haughton, G., Deas, I. and Hincks, S. (2014) Making an impact: when agglomeration boosterism meets antiplanning rhetoric, *Environment and Planning A*, 46, 265–270.

Haughton, G., Deas, I., Hincks, S. and Ward, K. (2016) Mythic Manchester: Devo Manc, the Northern Powerhouse and rebalancing the English economy, *Cambridge Journal of Regions, Economy and Society*, 9, 355–370.

Hebbert, M. (1982) Births and deaths of regional planning agencies, *Environment and Planning B*, 9, 131–142.

Herrschel, T. (2012) Network regionalism, development agencies and peripheralisation through 'loss of voice': moving towards post-regionalism? in: Bellini, N., Danson, M. and Halkier, H. (eds.) *Regional Development Agencies: The Next Generation? Networking, Knowledge and Regional Policies*, pp. 172–186, London: Routledge.

Hooghe, L. (ed.) (1996) *Cohesion Policy and European Integration: Building Multi-Level Governance*, Oxford: Clarendon Press.

Jessop, B. (2002) *The Future of the Capitalist State*, Cambridge: Polity.

Jessop, B. (2016) Territory, politics, governance and multispatial metagovernance, *Territory, Politics, Governance*, 4, 8–32.

Jonas, A. (2013) Alternative regionalisms, *Progress in Human Geography*, 37, 822–828.

Jonas, A. and Ward, K. (2002) A world of regionalisms? Towards a US–UK urban and regional policy framework comparison, *Journal of Urban Affairs*, 24, 377–401.

Jones, M. and Paasi, A. (2013) Guest editorial: regional world(s): advancing the geography of regions, *Regional Studies*, 47, 1–5.

Lapavitsas, C., Kaltenbrunner, A., Labrinidis, D., Lindo, D., Meadway, J., Michell, J., Painceira, J., Pires, E., Powell, J., Stenfors, A., Teles, N. and Vatikiotis, L. (2012) *Crisis in the Eurozone*, London and New York: Verso.

Larner, W. and Walters, W. (2002) The political rationality of the 'new regionalism': towards a genealogy of the 'region', *Theory and Society*, 31, 391–432.

Lee, N. (2016) Powerhouse of cards? Understanding the 'Northern Powerhouse', *SERC Policy Paper 14*, London: London, School of Economics.

MacLeod, G. (2001) New regionalism reconsidered: globalization and the remaking of political economic space, *International Journal of Urban and Regional Research*, 25, 804–829.

Marks, G. (1993) Structural policy and multilevel governance in the EC, *The State of the European Community*, 2, 391–410.

Martin, L., Prokkola E., Saarinen J. and Zimmerbauer K. (2015a) Regions, borders and identity in a relational and territorial world, *Nordia*, 44, 1–4.

Martin, R. (1993) Remapping British regional policy: the end of the north-south divide? *Regional Studies*, 27, 797–805.

Martin, R. (2011) Regional economic resilience, hysteresis and recessionary shocks, *Journal of Economic Geography*, 12, 1–32.

Martin, R. (2015) Rebalancing the spatial economy: the challenge for regional theory, *Territory, Politics, Governance*, 3, 235–272.

Martin, R., Pike, A., Tyler, P. and Gardiner, B. (2015b) *Spatially Rebalancing the UK Economy: The Need For A New Policy Model*, Seaford: Regional Studies Association. Available: www.regionalstudies.org/uploads/documents/SRTUKE_v16_PRINT.pdf (accessed 27 July 2016).

Metzger, J. and P. Schmitt (2012) When soft spaces harden: the EU strategy for the Baltic Sea region, *Environment and Planning A*, 44, 263–280.

Muštra, V. and Škrabić, B. (2014) Regional inequalities in the European Union and the role of institutions, *Review of Urban and Regional Development Studies*, 26, 20–39.

Nicholls, W. (2015) Editorial: the politics of regional development, *Territory, Politics, Governance*, 3, 227–234.

Overman, H. (2012) *Investing in the UK's Most Successful Cities Is the Surest Recipe for National Growth*, London: Spatial Economics Research Centre, London School of Economics. Available: http://eprints.lse.ac.uk/44073/ (accessed 4 February 2016).

Pastor, M., Benner, C. and Matsuoka, M. (2009) *This Could be the Start of Something Big: How Social Movements for Regional Equity are Reshaping Metropolitan America*, Ithaca, NY: Cornell University Press.

Peck, J. (2016) Economic rationality meets celebrity urbanology: exploring Edward Glaeser's city, *International Journal of Urban and Regional Research*, DOI:10.1111/1468-2427.12321

Perkmann, M. (2003) Cross-border regions in Europe: significance and drivers of cross-border cooperation, *European Urban and Regional Studies*, 10, 153–171.

Perkmann, M. (2007) Policy entrepreneurship and multilevel governance: a comparative study of European cross-border regions, *Environment and Planning C*, 25, 861–879.

Pike, A., Rodríguez-Pose, A. and Tomaney, J. (2016) Shifting horizons in local and regional development, *Regional Studies*, DOI:10.1080/00343404.2016.1158802

Rodríguez-Pose, A. (2013) Do Institutions Matter for Regional Development? *Regional Studies*, 47, 1034–1047.

Scott, J. (1999) European and North American Contexts for cross-border regionalism, *Regional Studies*, 33, 605–617.

Storper, M. (1997) *The Regional World: Territorial Development in a Global Economy*, London: The Guilford Press.

Tomaney, J. (2014) Region and place I: institutions, *Progress in Human Geography*, 38, 131–140.

Wannop, U. (1995) *The Regional Imperative: Regional Planning and Governance in Britain, Europe and the United States*, London: Routledge.

While, A., Gibbs, D. and Jonas, A. (2013) The competition state, city-regions, and the territorial politics of growth facilitation, *Environment and Planning A*, 45, 2379–2398.

Index

For Product Safety Concerns and Information please contact our EU
representative GPSR@taylorandfrancis.com
Taylor & Francis Verlag GmbH, Kaufingerstraße 24, 80331 München, Germany